TO BE A JEWISH STATE

To Be a Jewish State

Zionism as the New Judaism

Yaacov Yadgar

NEW YORK UNIVERSITY PRESS

New York

NEW YORK UNIVERSITY PRESS
New York
www.nyupress.org

Library of Congress Cataloging-in-Publication Data
Names: Yadgar, Yaacov, author.
Title: To be a Jewish state : Zionism as the new Judaism / Yaacov Yadgar.
Description: New York : New York University Press, [2024] |
Includes bibliographical references and index.
Identifiers: LCCN 2023058752 (print) | LCCN 2023058753 (ebook)
| ISBN 9781479832408 (hardback) | ISBN 9781479832422 (ebook) |
ISBN 9781479832439 (ebook other)
Subjects: LCSH: Zionism and Judaism. | Jews—Israel—Identity. |
National characteristics, Israeli. | Jews—Attitudes toward Israel.
Classification: LCC DS149 .Y3174 2024 (print) | LCC DS149 (ebook) |
DDC 320.54095694—dc23/eng/20240325
LC record available at https://lccn.loc.gov/2023058752
LC ebook record available at https://lccn.loc.gov/2023058753

New York University Press books are printed on acid-free paper, and their binding materials are chosen for strength and durability. We strive to use environmentally responsible suppliers and materials to the greatest extent possible in publishing our books.

Manufactured in the United States of America

10 9 8 7 6 5 4 3 2 1

Also available as an ebook

CONTENTS

Introduction

Studying Israel to Interrogate Nation-Statism

What does it mean for Israel to be a Jewish state? What is Zionism's relation to Judaism? And what happens to Judaism when it is "nationalized"—that is, read, interpreted, and practiced in a manner that serves the interests of the modern sovereign nation-state? Considered in a global frame of reference, these questions have to do with what is proving to be the most resilient political ideology of our era: nationalism.

Centered around these "Jewish" and "Israeli" questions, this book is ultimately about nation-statism: the theopolitics of the modern sovereign nation-state, and the ways in which this theopolitics renders the nation-state—its interests and preferences, its hierarchies and prejudices, its injustices and misdeeds—a "natural" feature of our lives. As William T. Cavanaugh explains, the term "theopolitics" is aimed at stressing that, "far from being 'secular' institutions and processes," the state and other modern constructs (such as globalization and civil society) are "ways of imagining [that] organize bodies around stories of human nature and human destiny which have deep theological analogies. In other words, supposedly 'secular' political theory is really theology in disguise."[1] The encounter between this "theology in disguise" and the traditions that preceded it, built as they are on an explicit theology, is at the core of this book.

Our attention here is focused on nation-statism for reasons that are both global and local in kind. Globally, the early twenty-first century is proving to be an era of resurgent nationalism. "Long overshadowed or contained by Cold War bipolar geopolitics and the rise of commercial and NGO globalization," nationalism has "reasserted itself with Brexit, the 2016 US elections, attacks on transnational security alliances and multilateral trade pacts, and ethno-populist nationalist movements coming to power across Europe and Asia."[2] A reinvigorated nationalism, embodied in newly assertive nationalist leaders, movements, and geopolitical rivalry between nation-states, has upended what in the late 1990s and early 2000s seemed to be the hegemonic, postnationalist order of globalization. After decades of being prophesied as doomed, its reputation besmirched by World War II, nation-statism has been reasserting itself forcefully, violently, triumphantly. It builds and buttresses walls of separation, nurtures nativism, and promotes the politics of isolationism—all parts of a worldview based as much on the negation of others as it is on the assertion of the national self.[3]

On this level, this book is about interrogating the nation-statist order of things primarily through questioning, problematizing, and critiquing the underlying political theology or theopolitics of the nation-state. The nature of this theopolitics—"mixing," as it were, political, theological, historical, and legal concepts, arguments, and processes—demands a multidisciplinary approach, and this book is as much about religion, theology, and philosophy as it is about politics.[4]

But the engagement with nation-statism cannot be meaningfully conducted on this general, rather abstract level. Nationalism, that "thin-centered" political ideology, is indeed global in scope (it speaks of the organization of the world at large) but it is ever local and particular in application (it is always "our" nation that is spoken for).[5] While originating in a specific historical, geopolitical, and theological-philosophical context (namely, the Enlightenment's post-Reformation colonial Europe), nationalism has emerged as the most pervasive mode of sociopolitical organization across the globe. Encountering diverse traditions of thought, meaning, and identity, it has encouraged (and, in light of the historical legacy of colonialism, also compelled) communities around the world to reinterpret their traditions and reconstruct their identities and ways of life so as to fit within the dominant frame of nation-statehood. The modern European nation-state—the ultimate political form embodying nationalist ideology—has become the constitutive unit of world politics and the organizing principle of peoples, communities, identities, and traditions throughout the world. These communities, traditions, and identities have been remade and transformed to conform to the nation-state's imperatives. This has necessarily resulted in a kaleidoscopic collection of instances of the "nationalization" of these traditions, identities, and communities, in each case shaped by the idiosyncrasies of its histories and resources, the details of the relevant nationalist claim, the contingencies of the division of power, and many more conditions shaping this encounter.

The study of nationalism must, then, take a local or even particularistic form, focusing on specific case studies, which together can form a mosaic from which a more general image emerges. This must necessarily be a collective effort, and my aim here is to offer my humble contribution to this mosaic. I do so by exploring but one, fascinating, complicated, and challenging case: the State of Israel.

Specifically, this book focuses on the claim—made by both the state and the nationalist ideology upon which it is established, Zionism—to Jewish identity, Jewish history, and even Judaism itself. It is concerned with the encounter between the nation-statist theopolitics and the histories, traditions, practices, and ways of being-in-the-world that Jewish people and communities have carried. And, as I hope will become apparent early on, this encounter between Zionist nationalism or Israeli nation-statism, on the one hand, and Judaism or Jewish traditions, on the other, forms a fascinating case of the more general issues at hand, all having to do with the encounter between the nation-statist political theology and what we may term "traditional" theology.

In this regard, while focused on the Israeli case, this book (as, I would encourage the reader to see, are my previous works on Israeli nation-statehood and Zionism, with which the current book corresponds) is "not really" about Israel per se, but about nationalism and nation-statism generally.[6] As such, it is framed to be of interest, not only to those interested specifically in the politics of the Middle East, modern Judaism, and Israeli politics (though, of course, it does speak directly to these issues) but also to people who may not be immediately interested in the intricacies of debates over the meaning of "Jewish politics" in Israel. Here I find myself in agreement, embarrassing as this may be, with one of the more vocal contemporary ideologues of nationalism and nation-statism, who insists that Israel should be viewed as a role model of nationalist politics.[7] Israel should indeed be of interest to anyone interested in studying—and interrogating, as I aim to do here—nationalism generally. While uniquely, idiosyncratically, preoccupied with questions that are seen as matters of "Jewish politics," Israeli nation-statism can, and should, be seen as ultimately a local interpretation of a global script, the script of nationalism.

There is, then, an obvious tension underlying this book, between the need to dive deep, as it were, into the details and particularities of the case study at hand, and to locate these within the generalizations of the universal scripts they play out. This tension is an in-built feature of the human sciences. To give but one obvious and not irrelevant example: any attempt at formulating a "model" or a general overview of the universal matter of the interplay between what we commonly categorize as nationalism and religion is bound to keep on referring to specific case studies and their particularities to both formulate its generalizing argument and qualify it.[8] This tension also highlights the danger of offering simplistic comparative analyses, where little if any attention is given to the question of whether the allegedly universal but always context-bound concepts and categories (in this case, religion, the secular, ethnicity, and nationalism) are equally applicable to each of the cases at hand.

The temptation to highlight the similarities and affinities between what may seem, on the face of it, utterly different cases, is understandably strong. Done wrongly, such comparative analyses tend to ignore the specific historical, cultural, social, and political context from within which the local application of these concepts and categories emerges. Done rightly, these comparative views can prove to be most illuminating. Such is the case, for example, with Faisal Devji's study of Muslim nationalism in Pakistan in light of the Zionist "model."[9] Similarly, a long overdue discussion of Jewish and Hindu nationalisms side by side gives ample evidence of the merit of viewing the one against the background of the other.[10] In recent years, to give but one last example, references to the affinities between the assertive, manifestly anti-liberal renditions of nation-statism in Israel, Hungary, and Poland abound in the Israeli public sphere. Yet such insights must remain qualified. If anything, they call for a better understanding of each case on its own, before attempting to draw a universalizing picture.

This is a rather banal point to make, but it is one that seems to evade many of those social scientists who endeavor to render the study of humanity akin to the "hard" sciences and to formulate rules and generalizations that are universally applicable. In any event, without belaboring the point, let me clarify at this early stage that I am closely aware of the fact that while I do see the Israeli case to be playing out a general script, the focus here will remain primarily on understanding this specific case. I will, of course, offer throughout the book some reflections on the general matters at hand, and I hope the reader who is interested in other case studies and in the broader issues to which they speak will heed the invitation to see those other cases through the lens of the Israeli case.

The issues we are setting out to explore in this book all have to do with the encounter between nationalism and traditions that are carried by those whom the nation-state designates as the in-group, the nation in whose name the state claims sovereignty. In the Zionist and Israeli case, this takes the shape of Zionist nationalism's and the Israeli nation-state's encounter with Judaism and Jewish traditions more broadly. Both the ideology and the state that embodies it make a complicated, charged, and ultimately unresolved claim to Judaism, while "negating," dismissing, and even delegitimizing aspects of what would fall under the title of that same Judaism or Jewish traditions. This convoluted approach nourishes a set of tensions that in turn feed what Joyce Dalsheim has aptly called "Israel's Jewish problem" (I myself have resorted to the notion of "identity crisis" to address the same matter.)[11] Some of the more urgent manifestations of these tensions are discussed by what Dalsheim identifies as "a group of scholars [one may count among them, in addition to Dalsheim herself, Jonathan and Daniel Boyarin, Amnon Raz-Krakotzkin, Brian Klug, and Yakov Rabkin][12] who are primarily concerned with preserving Judaism and protecting Jewish identity from the dangers of Zionism."[13]

This book deals with what I find to be the foundations of these "Jewish problem" and "identity crisis." It interrogates, among other matters, the very meaning of "Jewish" politics and the derived understanding of Israel as a Jewish state; Zionism's relation to Judaism; the Zionist claim to messianic and redemptive politics; the nationalist and nation-statist approach to the past, and the ways in which it feeds the Israeli sense of history; the effects of the "nationalization" of Judaism; and the potential and limits of that same concern with preserving Judaism from the effects of this nationalization.

Chapter 1 studies Israel's claim to Jewish identity: the meaning of the state's identification as a Jewish state. The chapter approaches this issue by drawing a distinction between two contesting—conflicting, even— readings of the very meaning of Jewish identity and, derived from it, of Jewish politics more broadly and Jewish nation-statism specifically. As chapter 1 shows, the tensions surrounding Israel's Jewish identity are derived directly from Zionism's "complicated" (to use an understatement) relation to the Jewish past and to Judaism, which it nevertheless claims as parts of itself. Chapter 2 discusses this complicated Zionist relation to Judaism by exploring the viability of the framework of supersessionism to understand this relationship. Among the central points discussed in this context is Zionism's confrontational, negating approach to its Jewish past. Chapter 3 then moves on to discuss the shaping of the Israeli sense of history in light of this confrontational disposition. It does so by exploring two Israeli nostalgias, one prominent among the Ashkenazi ethnoclass and the other prevalent among Mizrahim, and contextualizing these against the background of the nationalist "restorative" nostalgia. Chapter 4 sets out to study what happens to the objects of the Zionist negation of its Jewish past, certain foundations of Jewish tradition that contradict the nation-statist sense of messianic and redemptive politics in the process of nationalizing this tradition. Chapter 5 considers alternative ways for reconsidering the relations among Zionism, Israel, and Jewish tradition through the analysis of an illuminating case of the concern for preserving Judaism from nation-statism. The chapter studies what may be termed (with apologies to Edward Said) a case of Zionism seen from the standpoint of its adherent Jewish victims.[14] The conclusion further explores options for "talking back" at nationalism. Drawing its lessons from the Jewish case at hand, it suggests that the preservation of traditional Jewish plurality in face of the homogenizing nation-statist political theology may hold some important keys for our ability to think beyond the nation-statist order of things.

The following is an interpretive intervention. It seeks to understand, by asking critical questions and exploring the paths their answers lead to. As the interpretive tradition teaches, there is no point in hiding behind a pretense of so-called neutrality: we each arrive at our interpretation, as we are already informed by the obviously subjective nature of the diverse backgrounds or horizons that we carry. We are also often motivated by conflicting concerns, which shape the nature of our engagement with the questions at hand. These are indeed the basic conditions that allow our interpretations and understandings in the first place. The interpretative stance also encourages us to abandon the pretense of proof, the holy grail of positivist research. Instead, it tells us that the most we can hope to achieve is to formulate an argument that our interlocutor would find convincing. This is my goal here.

1

The Jewish State versus the Jews' State

Introduction

As we have noted, it is not always clear what we mean when we refer to the State of Israel as the "Jewish state." What does the designation "Jewish" amount to in the context of this sovereign nation-state? What does it mean for the politics of the state to be identified as "Jewish"? And what does it mean for an academic and intellectual field to study Israel *as* a Jewish state?

These are some of the most fundamental questions of Israeli nation-statism. Yet they are often overlooked, as commentators assume a vague sense of the answers to these questions to be obvious "givens," a simple local application of some general (nation-statist) rule, hence not deserving of explication. What's more, these givens are often incompatible and contradictory.

To be more precise, I would like to suggest here that there are two distinct, contesting, and even contradictory political projects or horizons that are often entangled and confused in the discourse on Israeli politics, Jewish politics, and the interplay between these terms (i.e., Israeli politics as or versus Jewish politics). Many of us (e.g., students of the Middle East and specifically of the Israeli case; participants in Jewish and Israeli politics; people representing various groups and points of views in related debates) seem often to bear in mind—a usually amorphous, sometimes inconsistent—sense of a core meaning related to these terms that is quite strikingly different from that held by our interlocutors, without this difference being explicitly acknowledged. It is therefore useful to try to spell out some of the assumptions hidden behind our daily discourse and some of their implications.

This chapter thus explicates a tension that lies at the very root of our discourse on Israel as a Jewish state. It argues that the academic and

political fields tend to confuse and conflate two different, often contradictory understandings or constructions of the very meaning of Jewish
politics. These can be schematically labeled as Jewish politics versus the
politics of Jews. Derived from them, two contesting notions of Israeli
politics emerge: the outlook of Israel as a "Jewish state" versus the notion of it being solely a "Jews' state" or a "state of the Jews." This chapter argues that these conflicting political and ideological constructions
draw upon different readings of Jewish identity and authenticity, which
were first developed in Europe by leading (self-identified secular) Zionist ideologues and later shaped mainstream readings of Israeli politics. It
outlines the basic contours of this conceptual distinction, traces its roots
in Zionist ideology (as developed in Eastern and Central Europe), and
concludes with a consideration of the playing out of the tension at hand
in contemporary Israeli politics.

The Objective Jew and Jewish Normativity

We may begin this exercise by drawing a rather trivial terminologi-
cal distinction between two closely related but not indistinct English
words, both of which would usually be translated into Hebrew as *yehudit*
(female) or *yehudi* (male): Jew and Jewish. The two contesting political
outlooks or meanings are encapsulated in a certain distinction we sometimes employ when we use these English terms. I must clarify that the
following obviously does not presume to be an exhaustive genealogical,
philological, etymological, or historical exploration of the terms; nor is
it a genuine attempt at exhaustively studying the varying, often conflicting meanings associated with each of these terms.[1] Our concern here is
primarily (indeed, *only*) with a certain contemporaneous, common use
of the terms, in a most specific context of politics.

   "Jew" would be read in the context of the distinction I have in mind
as a noun, a name. It alludes to one's "being" (*a* Jew). This, quite obviously, would suggest that the matter at hand—one's "being a Jew"—is a
derivative of some so-called objective criteria, more often than not taken
as having to do with one's "natural" or "biological" ancestry or accident
of birth. (We may prefer to call it "ethnicity" if we find this term to be
clearer or less offensive.) This name tends to allude to some impartial
measure, an ought-to-be-simple definition that would mark one as ei-

ther a Jew or not a Jew. Crucially, for the purpose of the distinction I have in mind here, this measure may be only remotely (and sometimes not at all) dependent on the choice, preference or behavior, actions, ethics, or outlook of the individual: paradigmatically (again: *in the context of the narrow meaning on which we are focusing here*, and only in this context), one is "born a Jew." Needless to say, one can also "become" a Jew, but this, too, would suggest the workings-in-the-background of the above-mentioned objective criteria, a line of demarcation, that the non-Jew has to cross in order to become (i.e., to now come and "be") a Jew. Note that this "being" is by definition individual and personal, as in having to do with a person: it cannot refer to ideas, objects, and other nonpersons (they cannot be Jews). Only a person can pass the essential criterion, to have the "essence," that would make one a "Jew." Obviously, we can also identify a relevant group identity here (that of Jews) but this would not necessarily amount to much more than many persons being each a Jew. It goes without saying that a nationalist ideology would tend to view this group as an entity in and for itself.

The word "Jewish," on the other hand, an adjective (that can also be inflected as to be an adverb, i.e., when we mark a certain act as being done "Jewishly"), suggests a quality, a style, a content—and, only remotely, if ever, a being. While it, too, might be seen as ultimately referring to a certain essence (this is an almost trivial fact of the way we identify things as having a certain quality; as Daniel Boyarin puts it, we tend to be "closet Platonists" whether we realize this or not), it is of a different order from the existential matter of being (or not being) a Jew.[2] In the usage I have in mind, "Jewish" is explicitly subjective, evaluative, even judgmental, as it designates certain things (e.g., people, ideas, ethics, law, philosophy, way of life) as corresponding positively to a certain quality, the exact nature of which is obviously a matter of interpretation and judgment and given to debate and negotiation—that is to say, it has to do with some sense of tradition, which is manifestly "an argument extended through time" regarding practice, meaning, boundaries, and so forth.[3]

In a narrower sense, "Jewish" may simply be the adjective inflected from "Jew," meaning that it only designates that which is "of a Jew." In this case, one's being a Jew would be the aforesaid quality that allows for one's actions, beliefs, creations, and ideas to be designated "Jewish."

Here, "Jewish" would simply mean "belongs to a Jew" (or Jews), "held by a Jew/Jews," "practiced by a Jew/Jews," and so forth. It is the subject or agent (a Jew or Jews) doing/owning/holding the object that renders the latter Jewish. In the context of this usage, there is practically no limit to what this container may contain, as anything done by Jews could be considered "Jewish."

Needless to say, this narrow meaning of the adjective misses much of what we often refer to when we identify someone or something as "Jewish." While there are obviously many instances when "Jewish" is used exactly to allude to this narrow sense (including, I would hasten to mention here and will discuss in more detail later, instances in which we refer to the "Jewish state" and to "Jewish politics"), I nevertheless think it can be convincingly argued that more often than not we use "Jewish" to refer to a quality that is of a historical, sociocultural, or traditional nature. And it is this usage I want to stress in the context of the duality of Jew versus Jewish. This usage of the term would suggest that there is some correspondence of *meaning* (and not just attribution) that justifies or demands that we identify something as "Jewish." As such, it necessarily involves evaluation and judgment; it alludes to a (necessarily evasive, contested, and negotiated) sense of *authenticity.*

I should stress here that in this thicker-in-meaning usage, "Jewish" can quite naturally refer to nonpersons. Ideas, institutions, collectives, objects, rules, attitudes, and so much more can all be identified as "Jewish" by virtue of their meaningful correspondence to horizons of significance that we may consider (most probably building on and engaging in an ongoing debate or argument: i.e., tradition) as part of the Jewish universe. Note that this designation is also quite indifferent to the question of the acting agent's identity as a Jew or non-Jew. In other words, for an idea or a life-form (to take just two obvious examples) to be Jewish, they do not have to come from the mind of a Jew, or to be lived by Jews. Just as Jews can live by a Protestant ethic, so, too, non-Jews may live by a Jewish ethic.

These two usages—the narrow one, by which "Jewish" means "of a Jew," and the more expansive one, where it refers to a constructed and negotiated quality—are not necessarily mutually exclusive. We may conclude, if we are so inclined, that it is the mere fact that a certain attitude has been prevalent among people "who are Jews" that ultimately

THE JEWISH STATE VERSUS THE JEWS' STATE | 11

constructs it as a "Jewish attitude." But these two usages are also not necessarily mutually dependent: as just noted, for something to be "Jewish" (in the more expansive sense of the term), it does not have to be "of a Jew" or "of Jews." Even if we insist on the validity of the notion of a "Jew" as having to do with some objective essence of being, we may conclude that non-Jews may be holding ideas that are Jewish, adhere to Jewish values, and practice Jewish practices. Similarly (and maybe more judgmentally) we may also conclude that people who "are Jews," as in possessing this so-called objective trait, fail to adhere to Jewish values, ideas, practices, and so forth. In other words, both the notion of "Jewish non-Jews" and that of "non-Jewish Jews" would make good sense in the context of this usage of the term.[4]

Now, as I already noted, this may all seem rather trivial. But I suspect that some of the more problematic *political* consequences of these two contesting understandings often go unnoticed, as a certain—problematic—reading of them has become a taken-for-granted assumption of many discussions on such notions as Jewish politics and Jewish collectivity, and especially on Zionist nationalism and Israeli nation-statehood.

A Jewish State versus a Jews' State

Applied to politics—or, more, specifically to nationalism and nation-statehood, which is our focus here—the distinction between "Jew" and "Jewish" ultimately holds (or even hides and confuses) at least two, very different, often conflicting ideas, outlooks, or programs. One outlook may be described, following its spokespeople's own self-understanding, as "objective," while the other is explicitly "normative." Needless to say, as I suspect the above already suggests, and as I shall expand later on, there is nothing normatively neutral in either of these two outlooks. In any event, one is objective, since it takes Jewishness to be a given datum of one's being: a fact (of nature, or of history) of which one has no meaningful control. The other is normative, since it demands a loyal, active, and practical commitment to a value-laden horizon as a precondition of the (authentic) playing out of this Jewishness.

Let us focus at this point on the modern nation-state and spell out the basic difference between these two outlooks via a more explicit distinction between a "Jewish state" (which would be the notion carrying an explicitly normative charge) and a "Jews' state" (whose advocates would present as objective and normatively neutral, reifying the nation-statist order of the world as a given element of our reality).

The notion of a (or the) "Jews' state" would seem to be suggesting a simple, direct application of the so-called objective criteria of the person's biological origin or descent (and the collective identity built upon it) to the politics of nation-statehood and of sovereignty.[5] This is indeed the prevalent generic notion of nation-statehood: a (sovereign nation-) state of Jews would "simply" be defined or constituted by the objective fact of the biological/ethnic/racial/national makeup of the subjects represented by its sovereignty. If we follow the main fiction of modern sovereignty, that of the popular, national will constituting itself as sovereign via the nation-state, then we can describe the Jews' state as the sovereign who is constituted by or on the collective will of "Jews." Supposedly, the logic here is quite straightforward: a Jews' state would be the simple, direct equivalent of the State of the French, or the German, or the Serbs, and so on. (I am inclined to use here European examples exclusively, since the conceptual and ideological bed of this reading nourishes directly from the development of nation-statist ideology in Europe of the eighteenth and nineteenth centuries. Indeed, as will become evident, our discussion, which follows the cue of dominant, triumphant Zionist readings of Jewish politics, is confined to a European frame of reference.)[6]

Looked at from a normatively concerned point of view, the notion of a "Jews' state" would seem to be quite neutral, as, at least in principle, there is no normative or ethical directive immediately and explicitly imposed on such a state. (Needless to say, this idea only makes sense if we accept the nationalist, or nation-statist, political order of the world, on its European, colonial, and imperial roots as normatively neutral; I do not suggest that we do so, but I would nevertheless not delve into this argument here.)[7] Once the God-like event of self-creation of modern sovereignty (of Jews, in this case) has taken place, the sovereign and its politics do not have to abide by any normative principle, *Jewish* or otherwise, to be authentically exercising their constitutive reason. The "Jews" (let us suspend for now the question of what this designation may mean, or how it is determined) can—rather, *should*—make of their state whatever they choose to. They can, of course, prefer a certain type of social or political contract to guide the state's politics (e.g., to abide by a republican ethos or a liberal one), but there is no outside perspective that would normatively judge the authenticity, ethics, or purpose of this politics. All that is required is that the collective body present at the core of the fiction of the popular will (or represented by it) that allegedly constitutes the sovereign is identified as a group of Jews. Importantly, this necessarily forces the "Jews' state" to be preoccupied with "demography," or the preservation of an imbalance between a majority (of Jews) against a minority (of non-Jews) to uphold its constitutive reason; we shall return to this point later on.

Note that this conceptualization of the Jews' state or a state of Jews assumes as given and obvious matters that are in effect highly contested and far from clear, especially if we put them in a *Jewish* framework. Specifically, arguments for Israel's being "simply" (and "only"; see below) the Jews' state—and *not*, that is, a *Jewish* state—fail to, or maybe just prefer not to, seriously reflect upon the uneasy application of the modern European Christian-in-origin categories of nation, state, ethnos, race, and religion to the case of "Jews." Probably the most obvious aspect of this neglect is the in-effect highly contested matter of the alleged objective criteria that would determine who counts as a Jew and who does not.

The notion of a *Jewish* state, on the other hand, would suggest, at least in the framework of the distinction outlined above, some normative, ethical, and constitutive worldview as determining the state's identity or constitution as Jewish. Looked at from this point of view, for politics, economics, diplomacy, social care, and many other such elements of the workings of the state to be considered (authentically) Jewish, they would have to positively, meaningfully, correspond to what the historical conversation or argumentation would mark as "Jewish."

I must note that a Jewishly concerned point of view would most likely also question the idea of the modern sovereign nation-state and may very well arrive at the conclusion that a Jewish notion of ethics and the conduct of public life is simply incommensurable with the political configuration of the modern nation-state.[8] In this regard, as in many others, Wael Hallaq's judgment that traditional Islamic notions of governance, ethics, subjectivity, and law (among others) are so incompatible with the foundational notions of the modern sovereign nation-state so as to render the idea of an "Islamic state" an impossibility in principle, is highly informative to our discussion here.[9]

Yet, in the context of the predominant political discourse we are considering here, most references to Israel's being a Jewish state do not address this fundamental question. They seem to take as given the basic "form" of the politics of the nation-state and focus exclusively on the question of the "contents" that would make such a state authentically Jewish. We would be encouraged, in the context of this discourse, to ask questions such as: What Jewish principles should guide the conduct of the state? In what sense is the conduct of a Jewish army and especially the waging of war by such an army different than non-Jewish armies? What is—or should be—Jewish diplomacy? What are the principles of a Jewish economy? and so on. Much of the Israeli political debate has revolved around "second order" questions, such as: How should the public sphere in a Jewish state correspond with (a certain, limited interpretation of) Jewish religion? and, To what extent should the state nurture in its subjects a sense of Jewish tradition?

To reiterate: the discourse discussed here necessarily limits the scope of the discussion and focuses it on matters of the reality of the modern sovereign nation-state. In other words, the argument for a *Jewish* state accepts as given, usually without acknowledging this, the basic premises of a political form or configuration of power that is borne out of a specific history (modern European, Christian, largely Protestant) and seeks to apply it to the Jewish case.[10] The Jewishness (or the form) of the state is thus necessarily limited to an understanding of Jewish history, values, meanings, and ethics that is not fundamentally incommensurable with this form.[11] This leaves unexamined a whole range of questions that would amount to a Jewish critique of the idea of the modern nation-state—questions that would nourish on Jewish horizons to challenge the idea of sovereignty upon which the modern nation-state is constituted, for example.[12]

Note also that in the case of the notion of a "Jews' state," it would seem that form alone is of relevance: as long as the configuration of power, or political form of the nation-state, is seen as constructed by and for Jews, there is no point (or, in some formulation, it is nonsensical, if not even illegitimate) to ask questions of content, such as what is Jewish about the economy, diplomacy, or social care of the state. From this point of view, whatever Jews do with their economy, army, diplomacy, and social welfare is, ipso facto, Jewish.

What Is the State of Israel?

By way of exemplifying these two distinct and more often than not incompatible understandings of the very meaning of Israel's identity and the politics derived from it, let us consider two not unrepresentative exemplars.

The first comes from Hamid Dabashi's pioneering exposition of the intellectual and ideational infrastructure of the Islamic Revolution in Iran. Dabashi ties the history of the 1979 revolution in Iran and the formation of the Islamic Republic into a regional and global history in which the idea of a Jewish state plays a crucial role. As he puts it, in order to understand the events culminating in the establishment of the Islamic Republic,

> it is imperative to consider the geopolitics of the region. The partition of India and Pakistan in 1947 created the first religiously bifurcated states in the region. . . . A year later, in 1948, the establishment of the state of Israel created the first modern Jewish state in the region in specifically religious terms. The first Arab-Israeli war turned the Palestinian problem into the cornerstone of the regional conflicts—and the Jewish nature of the state of Israel was bound to intensify the Islamic disposition of opposition to it. . . . It is critically important to keep in mind that precisely at a time that both a Jewish state in Palestine and a Hindu-Muslim bifurcation in the Indian subcontinent was taking shape, Iran was experiencing the most momentous part of its modern history.[13]

This suggests a very specific understanding of Israel's being a Jewish state, and the way this impacts the Middle East at large. Specifically, as Dabashi puts it, Israel's "Jewish nature," which introduces into the geopolitics of the region "specifically religious terms," such that are "bound to intensify the Islamic disposition of the opposition to it," and that put Israel on par also with a "Hindu-Muslim bifurcation" of the South Asian subcontinent, must necessarily be referring to a normatively laden, traditional (or, to use Dabashi's term, "religious," regardless of the Zionist founder's self-identification as fierce secularists) sense of Jewishness that guides the state's conduct in the Middle East.

It is interesting to note that Dabashi considers all of these cases—postpartition India and Pakistan, as well as Israel and revolutionary

Iran—as belonging to the same "type" of state. This type may be termed "religious nationalism," but as any survey of the complicated interplay between nationalism and religion would show, many more other nation-states would fit the bill, even if we tend to consider them "secular."[14] Indeed, Dabashi seems to be suggesting a direct parallel between post-1979 Iran's Islamic "nature" or constitution and Israel's "Jewish nature." I do not read this to mean that he sees both as theocracies; rather, that in both of these cases of modern nation-statism, the political theology at play—a foundational element of this political form—makes a claim of direct relation to what we may call "traditional" theology.[15]

In any event, for this affinity between Israel and Iran to make sense, what Dabashi calls Israel's "Jewish nature" simply cannot amount merely to the demographic makeup of the state's population. This affinity assumes that there is something foundational about the polity that makes it *normatively* Jewish. This, of course, is not to suggest that Dabashi argues that this is a necessarily authentic or accurate political expression of Jewish normativity; nor does he clearly explicate (interested as he is primarily in the Iranian case, the question clearly falls out of the bounds of his discussion) what this something would—or does—amount to. Yet the gist of the argument is clear: Israel's Jewish identity refers to the same conceptual realm where Iran's Islamic nature is to be found. It clearly has to do with a political configuration that nourishes on traditional/religious normativity, and not "only" a matter of the genealogy (be it ethnonational or biological) of those in whose name the state is sovereign.

Other references to Israel's Jewish identity/nature do, of course, dive deeply into the matter of what this normativity or authenticity should or would amount to, and we will consider the matter in more detail. But before we do so, let us compare—or, rather, contrast—the view suggested by Dabashi's comments with a rather straightforward explication of a secularist, liberal Zionist proclamation. This was made by an unsigned editorial piece in Israel's *Haaretz* newspaper, presumably representing the principled stance of the paper's leadership, and in effect voicing a dominant tone among liberal, secularist Israeli Jews: "Zionism dreamed of a state for the Jews, not a Jewish state: a refuge for members of the Jewish people, not a state with an official religion like Muslim Saudi Arabia. The Balfour Declaration promised a national home, not a religious one. On Israeli identity cards, 'Jewish' describes a nationality [i.e., *not* a religion]."[16]

Coming in the context of decrying governmental initiatives to "strengthen" Israel's (and Israeli Jews') Jewish identity, which the editorial views as amounting to illiberal religious coercion, the thrust of the argument here goes directly against what could be deduced from Dabashi's comments: Israel is not (or, rather, was never meant to be) a "Jewish state." Any such designation, which would put it on par with "state[s] with an official religion like Muslim Saudi Arabia," would necessarily amount to a betrayal of the very founding *Zionist* notions of Israeli nation-statehood, or the statehood of Jews. Note also the implied affiliation of Israel with the "secular" West, in opposition to the "religious" East, in *Haaretz*'s statement; while Dabashi firmly positions Israel within a Middle Eastern context, *Haaretz*'s editorial makes a point of tying it to Western ideals of liberalism and secularity. (Furthermore, given the prevalence of what Haggai Ram has termed the "obsession" of "Iranophobia" in liberal, secular Israeli political culture, one is tempted to speculate why the editorial resisted the temptation to repeat the admittedly trite comparison of Israel to Iran as a rhetorical tool to warn against "religious coercion."[17])

According to this liberal-secularist reading of the very meaning of the Israeli polity, the assumed religious identity of the state, suggested (or explicated) in Dabashi's comments is either a misreading or an outright, determined (especially when made by "religious" Jewish Israelis) distortion of the state's raison d'être. The state is meant simply—and more importantly: *only*—to be defined as *medinat hayehudim*, the Jews' state. That is to say: the state must be (only) built on the datum of the genealogy of the people whose collective will constitutes its sovereignty. Any normatively Jewish prescription for the polity beyond this "objective" fact amounts to religious coercion and a distortion of the state's founding principles.

Demographics is at the core of this argument, as it focuses almost exclusively on the (nation-statist) arithmetic of a majority versus a minority. As this argument was separately reiterated by a resident *Haaretz* commentator (again, arguing fiercely against another case of what he saw as religious coercion): "Israel is a Jewish state only in the sense of it being a state in which a solid majority of people from a Jewish origin live, and not in any other sense. . . . Israel shall be a Jewish state only if a majority of its citizens is of a Jewish origin, and not because of laws that dictate certain lifestyles."[18]

The argument entailed is clear enough. First, the designation "Jewish" is primarily—if not solely—a matter of peoplehood, or nationality, in the sense of being a member of a nation, as the latter is constructed by the nationalist ideology; the discourse here, clearly, is a (liberal-)nationalist, Zionist one, bound to the idea of the nation-state. Being Jewish has to do, in other words, with one's "origin"; it has to do with the fact that Jewish peoplehood is seen as pertaining primarily to *ethno*nationality, hence as determined primarily by this matter of origin. Second, the State of Israel is understood here to be the nation-state of the Jews—that is, of the people who compose this peoplehood. Once a majority of Jews—as in "people of Jewish origin"—come to constitute a polity, there is no need (if it is not outright illegitimate) to expect or demand that the polity, its citizens, its cultural producers, and so on actively dialogue with and uphold what the outlook at hand considers "religion." Specifically, such a dialogue with tradition or religion would be considered illegitimate if it is conducted in a manner that would have practical implications for the conduct of public and political life in the state. Any such initiative must ultimately amount to an encroaching of the religious realm (seen as by definition irrational or arational, and most often also as archaic) into the realm of (secular, rational) politics. This may well end up with the enforcing of a religious lifestyle on a naïve majority of secular Jews, who pay heed to the religious demand that the Israeli polity carries some Jewish hues.

Importantly, the latter suspicion highlights the high degree to which the discussion at hand is bound to a prevailing sense of a Kulturkampf between secular and religious Jews as a founding feature of modern Jewry. More recently, this sense has motivated increased alarm, if not outright panic, regarding an alleged rapidly growing process of "religionization," by which religious ideas, practices, and worldviews permeate the otherwise secular (national, Zionist) spheres of education, culture, and politics.[19]

The overarching outlook from which this argument arises draws a distinction—which is clear and coherent in theory, but in practice is confused and inconsistent—between matters that are categorized as having to do with religion and others that have to do with culture, history, ethnicity, nationhood, folklore, and so on, which are seen as secular in essence. This argument starts from what it sees as a given fact—namely, that there are elements of Jewishness, or Jewish peoplehood, that are secular in nature. It sees these secular elements' presence in the public sphere, including the fundamental fact of their legitimizing the configuration of power where Jews hold sovereignty, as fully justified. Other elements, which have to do with Judaism as a religion, are, according to this argument, forbidden from shaping the Israeli polity.

The problem, of course—as almost all spokespeople for this stance would usually readily admit—is that the theoretical distinction at hand is far from being clear and easy to employ in practice. In the vivid formulation of the author and essayist A. B. Yehoshua, a vocal proponent of this liberal, secularist Zionist stance, religion has "melted into" the national Jewish body; a clear-cut "amputation" of the religious member from the national body, desired as it may be, cannot be easily achieved.[20]

The Roots of the Tension, or: What Is (Culturally, Spiritually) Jewish about the (Political) *Judenstaat*?

There is, then, a rather obvious tension between two competing understandings of the very meaning of Israel's "Jewishness." The roots of this tension can be found already at the formative stages of the Zionist idea, vividly captured in the bitter dispute between two of the most influential Zionist ideologues in Europe at the end of the nineteenth century and the early twentieth century, Ahad HaAm (the pen name of Asher Ginsberg) and Theodore Herzl, over the very meaning and nature of the Zionist vision, or program. This tension is represented most lucidly in what Hillel Halkin titled "the most contentious Jewish book review of the [twentieth] century"[21]: Ahad HaAm's essay from 1902,[22] a purported review of Herzl's *Altneuland* (a utopian tale, published earlier the same year, in which Herzl imagines a future return of the Jews to Palestine), which ultimately amounts to a "caustic attack" on Herzl's vision or political program for the Zionist movement.[23]

This debate has been discussed quite thoroughly in the past, most usually framed as expressing the contest between two outlooks for the Zionist project: Herzl's "political" brand of Zionism (i.e., Herzl's relentless insistence on a political solution to what was viewed in Europe of

the time as the "Jewish question," in the form of establishing an independent polity for the Jews, preferably in Palestine) versus Ahad HaAm's
"cultural" or "spiritual" brand (i.e., Ahad HaAm's insistence that the solution to this same purported Jewish question or problem must focus on
a cultural rejuvenation of the people, prior to any attempt at establishing
a state).[24] Another interpretation convincingly frames Ahad HaAm's critique of Herzl and the wider controversy surrounding it as feeding on
the cultural differences between the Eastern and Western (European)
worldviews the two men had held:[25] Ahad HaAm, a Russian Jew, formulated an "ethnicist" view of Jewish nationalism,[26] which fed on prevalent,
organic, or "Eastern" (European) notions of nationalism.[27] Herzl, a Vi-
ennese Jew, nourished on Central and Western European readings of the
nationalist imperative.

Without dismissing or disputing these convincing interpretations, I
would suggest that the debate between the two ideologues can also be
seen as capturing most vividly the sharply diverging understandings of
a polity that is identified as either "of Jews" or "Jewish." In other words,
Ahad HaAm's essay in question can be read as a normatively charged,
Jewish-polity-oriented critique of (Herzl's rendition of) a supposedly
objective notion of a "Jew's polity." Importantly, these two conflicting
visions both emerge from an allegedly *secular* perspective, complicated
or contested as the meaning of this secularity may be. Neither Ahad
HaAm's "Jewish state" view nor Herzl's "Jews' state" vision claims to be
motivated by religious or theological considerations, and both visions
are explicitly committed to what may be very crudely described as the
(secular) tradition of the European Enlightenment.[28]

One way to understand what is at stake here is to frame the argument
as a debate over *authenticity*—national, Jewish authenticity, to be precise. If we follow Ahad HaAm's cue, we will surely come to think that in
order for a polity's Jewishness to be meaningful, it must exhibit a rather
"thick" cultural sense of Jewish authenticity. And it should come as no
surprise that he does not see Herzl's envisioned polity as passing this
basic test; Ahad HaAm judges Herzl's vision in *Altneuland* harshly exactly because his (Ahad HaAm's) vision of a Jewish polity renders Herzl's
polity of Jews inauthentic. Moreover, seen from the point of view advocated by Ahad HaAm, the very concern for authenticity would not seem
to be equally shared by both sides of the debate at hand: this concern

emerges almost instinctively from the (admittedly normative) "Jewish polity" point of view, while the (allegedly objective) "polity of Jews" perspective would seem to be largely indifferent to this matter.

Not for nothing, the notion of "imitation" is dominant in Ahad HaAm's critique. He sees the main theme of Herzl's utopia as having to do with the Jew's imitation, adoption, and adaptation of gentile ways. Whatever angle he looks at this "New Society" (the Jewish polity imagined by Herzl) from, Ahad HaAm sees the same picture: "European people, European customs, and European inventions. Nowhere do we find any specific 'Jewish' impression." In Ahad HaAm's view, the overall image is necessarily one of inauthentic replication and lack of originality: "Everything in the Land of Israel [in Herzl's utopian New Society] was not originally created in the Land of Israel, but in England, America, France and Germany."[29]

This lack of authenticity has to do primarily with the New Society's indifference to (Jewish) tradition. In Ahad HaAm's understanding, there cannot be a genuine modern (secular) Jewish authenticity without a meaningful dialogue with Jewish tradition—a dialogue consisting of reading, studying, knowing, and reinterpreting this tradition, on the vastness of its scope and depth. Yet in Herzl's vision (as it is read by Ahad HaAm, of course) the Jews' imitations (or adoption) of and improvements on the European and more generally Western precedence are enabled exactly by the lack of a meaningful contact between the modern Jews and their past.[30]

What for Herzl is a foundation of the cosmopolitan nature of the New Society, Ahad HaAm sees as alienation from the collective selfhood. Take, as an example, the "question of language," which so preoccupied Ahad HaAm: for him, there can be no national Jewish authenticity that is not founded on a revived and renewed Hebrew as the national language. Yet for Herzl, it would seem, this is an irrelevant matter altogether. As much as Ahad HaAm is searching for a clear answer, he cannot find Herzl to deal seriously with this question, leaving the reader with only an implied sense that "we may conclude from various hints here and there that the masses in the villages and also in the cities use the German jargon that it brought along from the exile [i.e., Yiddish], and the educated [use] the European languages, and especially German, which is the language of the leaders."[31]

Ahad HaAm's guiding question in judging matters of authenticity seems to be almost obvious yet fatally devastating, if we accept his basic point of view. Simply put, he asks, *What is Jewish* about Herzl's imagined New Society? More elaborately, the question he poses in relation to Herzl's depiction of a flourishing publishing industry (manifested in the proliferation of scholarly periodicals) in the New Society is paradigmatic to his overall critique: "Do these periodicals also have any Jewish quality? Is there a place in them for questions that are specific to Jews, since they are *Jewish*, and how do the periodicals in the Land of Israel relate to such questions[?]" Ultimately, Ahad HaAm's search for a consideration of any "internal question of Judaism" in *Altneuland* finds "not even a hint."[32] Being a polity of Jews alone does not suffice; It is the Jewish consideration that demands attention.

Maybe the most interesting element, in this regard, is the sarcastic manner in which Ahad HaAm notes the cosmopolitan nature of the New Society. Herzl clearly celebrates its tolerance, expressed in its ability to freely build on diverse traditions and to appeal to people with various backgrounds, and he makes a point of stressing the New Society's liberal stance of being agnostic toward one's origins (notwithstanding the very foundation of this society by a collective of Jews, for Jews). Ahad HaAm, however, reads this liberal and cosmopolitan character as an outright expression of the lack of Jewish authenticity. He finds confounding, if not outright ridiculous, the fact (stressed with emphasized letters and an exclamation point) that "the fundamental principle of the New Society is this: *regardless of differences of religion and nationality* [*beli hevdel dat ul'om*]*!*" What liberal democracy would take to be a matter of the highest value is for Ahad HaAm almost laughable. Ahad HaAm incessantly notes the prominent presence of gentiles in *Altneuland*, reading this as amounting to Jewish self-alienation.[33]

This may be perplexing, especially given Ahad HaAm's contemporary image as epitomizing a more tolerant and sensitive form of Zionism (especially credited to his early attentiveness to the problematic attitude of the Zionist settlers to the Arabs in Ottoman Palestine).[34] His contempt—sometimes verging on disgust—of Herzl's notion that the state will be free and equal to all, regardless of difference of race, religion, and nationality, is apparent. It is here that Ahad HaAm's readiness to challenge Herzl's critical stance toward "national chauvinism" emerges most forcefully. Ahad HaAm does not hesitate to cynically suggest that what he himself is most concerned with can indeed be labeled as "chauvinistic"—or, at the very least, he is happy to note that this is how a Jewishly concerned point of view would be depicted by Herzl.[35]

Ahad HaAm's rhetoric notwithstanding, it is rather apparent (a point made repeatedly by his critics; see the documents curated by Joseph Goldstein) that it would be wrong to assume, as Ahad HaAm clearly implies, that Herzl is wholly indifferent to the question of authenticity, or that he values imitation.[36] Rather, Herzl represents another notion of "Jewish" authenticity, by which it suffices that Jews—specifically, working together as a national collective—are the active agents at play. The fact that Jews do/produce/run the matter at hand (specifically in this case, the polity as a corporate liberal society) renders it authentically Jewish. Herzl expressed this logic quite straightforwardly when he sought to convince the Sixth Zionist Congress, in 1903, to support what came to be known as the "Uganda plan,"[37] by stressing that the proposed Jewish protectorate in British East Africa would be "an autonomous Jewish settlement . . . , with a Jewish administration, a Jewish local government, and a Jewish official at its head."[38] The main question at hand is whether or not Jews become masters of their (political) history; whatever they may ultimately produce in such conditions of self-rule will necessary be authentically Jewish, as it would be the product of Jewish agency, as in having Jews as its acting subjects.

Viewed from this point of view, what Ahad HaAm sees as laughable imitation is indeed laudable, especially in a liberal-democratic frame of reference. It would make Herzl's celebration of the eclectic European nature of his imagined New Society to be a sign of its strength and innovation, not of imitation and inauthenticity. This stance is forcefully articulated in a reaction by Max Nordau, one of Herzl's staunchest allies, to Ahad HaAm's critique of *Altneuland*.[39] Nordau's passionate response suggests that Ahad HaAm's normative concerns are misplaced, since what he seeks but fails to find in Herzl's utopia (e.g., Hebrew spoken, Jewish culture taught and practiced), is simply taken for granted. However, more important is Ahad HaAm's complaint that "Altneuland is too European." Nordau answers this allegation with a resounding reply (in paraphrase): Yes, indeed! "It is true: Altneuland is a European section inside Asia." Moreover, this "Western-ness" is undoubtedly, Nordau reaffirms, what the Zionist movement under Herzl's leadership has been striving for. Yet Ahad HaAm's accusation of imitation is wholly misplaced, since the European civilization that Zionism nurtures in the New Society is equally a *Jewish* civilization:

> We imitate no nation; We only utilize and develop what is ours. We took part in the development of European culture, more than our numerical share; it is ours as much as it is the German's, the French's, the English's. We will not allow that someone will contrive an imaginary contradiction between Jewish culture, our Jewish [culture], and European culture. . . . We will never agree that the Jews' return to the land of their forefathers will be a retreat to barbarity, as our enemies and detractors argue. The Jewish people shall develop its special essence inside the general framework of Western culture, like any other civilized people, but not outside of it, not from a savage, philistine Asiatic-ness, as Ahad HaAm apparently wants.[40]

This text, often quoted to highlight the sheer orientalist outlook of Nordau's (and Herzl's) Zionism, is also important for the matter under consideration here, for its clear articulation of the sense of what we might term "objective authenticity." According to Nordau's view, European culture and civilization are as much Jewish as they are European, since Jews—or, rather, agents who "*are* Jews"—have taken an active (and even numerically or demographically disproportionate) share in creating this culture or civilization. The correspondence between this culture and any horizon derived from a Jewish normativity is secondary in relevance, if it is relevant at all. What is relevant is that people "who are Jews" created it.

A most telling expression of this view is captured in an address Herzl delivered in 1896 under the heading of "Judentum." While the title of the address could suggest an engagement with Herzl's understanding or construction of the meaning of Judaism, which is a possible translation of *Judentum* ("Judaism" is in fact the title chosen by the English translator of this address),[41] Herzl clearly refers to a different usage of the term, meaning "Jewry," "Jewish peoplehood," or "Jews as a collective."[42] Ultimately, the address does not offer any clear sense of what Judaism is about, but instead outlines (in very rough lines) what a biographer of

Herzl terms a "functional" definition of what Jewry is or what the Jews "are."[43] Crucially, Herzl's sense of "Jews" as "*what* they are" is determined primarily by antisemitism. Thus, it is this "foe" or "common enemy" that emerges as definitive of Herzl's sense of Jewish *nationhood*:

> We are a group, a historical group of people who clearly belong together and have a common enemy; this seems to me an adequate definition of a nation. I do not think a nation must speak only one language or show uniform racial characteristics. This quite moderate definition of nationhood is sufficient. We are a historical group held together by a common foe. This is what we are, whether we know it or not, and whether we desire it or not.[44]

Note that matters of content, such as values, laws, traditions, ethics, and culture are only secondary (Herzl fails to make any reference to such matters in the discussed address) to the determinant of unity by force of a common enemy. Whether or not one knows or desires it, it is beyond the individual's choice; they, as members of the nation that is Jewry, are determined by an outsider's hate and historical persecution. Herzl clearly subscribed to the idea that what Jews/Jewry do as a national group united by this force is authentically Jewish. It is the fact that the people involved do what they do "as Jews" that makes it authentically "Jewish."[45]

Furthermore, this allegedly objective infrastructure (i.e., a given sociohistorical condition, the condition of antisemitism) is exactly that which allows for a liberal tolerance of difference. To fully appreciate this, it may be worth reminding the reader that all parties to the debate at hand are taking part in it primarily as leading Zionist ideologues, as nationalists. Theirs is a debate over a political framework built primarily on Jewish agency, or the agency of Jews. I am stating here the obvious, because it is this taken-for-granted bed upon which a liberal tolerance of the Other is debated. Herzl's liberal vision "bears" tolerance exactly because it envisions an objective Jewish infrastructure (demographically determined) as its bedrock.[46] Once a numerical majority of members of the group (Jews, in this case, but it is not difficult to see the general pattern in play here) has been established—and this majority is constantly sustained by the polity—the polity can adhere to the liberal rule of neutrality, of adhering to the principle of "regardless of differences of religion and nationality."

It is not the case, then, that the Herzlian view is agnostic when it comes to the issue of Jewishness or Jewish authenticity. Rather, Herzl and Nordau are taking a leading part in a discourse in which it seems quite clear and obvious—to them, to their audience, and to their supporters and distractors alike—who (or what) the Jews are (they are those the antisemites hate), and their primary focus is on envisioning this taken-for-granted Jewishness as transformed via its political self-determination.

This necessarily paints the notion of cultural assimilation in a wholly different color. If in Ahad HaAm's view the active adoption of contemporaneous European forms of life, values, and so on—what falls under an expansive reading of "culture"—by Jews on expense of their traditional lifestyles, values, and cultures amounts to their assimilation and loss of authenticity, Herzl's and Nordau's sense of objective authenticity reverses the picture altogether. As put by one student of Zionist ideology:

> According to Herzl, it was not the Jews who passively and obsequiously assimilated into the cultures of the European powers. Instead, the Jews actively absorbed the European cultures as a matter of collective choice, and these cultures thus became Jewish collective assets in precisely the same way that they belong to the European Christian nations. . . . In other words, though the participants of this collective social reality never defined it as a "national" Jewish one, it was nonetheless a collective experience "of Jews" on the objective sociological level.[47]

The closing sentence in this quote captures the argument quite vividly: the focus of the Zionist view at hand is on the so-called experience "of Jews," on the "objective sociological level"—read: antisemitism—which (pre)defines the actors/agents (individually or collectively) as "Jews." Henceforth, their creation is rendered Jewish.

It may be not wholly redundant to note here also the taken-for-granted Eurocentric view at hand: all parties to this debate assume the European Jewish experience to be a universal Jewish feature that necessarily also applies to non-Europeans, disregarding not only the Jewish histories and experiences in Muslim and Arab countries but also the role of the Islamic world—the "not-Europe"—in shaping Jewishness itself. This is but one aspect of the Zionist view's indebtedness to European, Christian epistemology, and worldview more generally.

In any event, the Herzlian "Jews' polity" view at hand presupposes that there must be some predefinition, a certain something that defines the actor/agent as "a Jew" prior to our consideration whether this agent's cultural creation is to be viewed as Jewish. Once the former (i.e., Jewishness) is established, the latter (i.e., the Jewish nature of her creation) is a given, on an "objective sociological level."[48] Note: this cultural production is to be considered Jewish as in "of Jews"—even if it would not be judged as authentically Jewish from a point of view concerned with Judaic normativity. This is further complicated by the shifting of the focus away from the Jew and toward the antisemite whose hatred interpellates or fixates the Jew into his or her identity. To put it more crudely, given that, as Herzl himself suggests, it can be neither race nor language that defines the Jew, it is the enemy, the antisemite, who is granted the role of defining who is a Jew. The antisemite is given the agency of determining Jewish authenticity.

Ahad HaAm himself was painfully aware of this constitutive, generative role of antisemitism in the (political) Zionist project, and he lamented this fact. In his (cultural) Zionist critique of Herzl Ahad HaAm argued that since Herzl's "Western" Zionism is the child of antisemitism, it is bound to dissolve with the fading of antisemitism. As he provocatively put it: "Antisemitism begat Herzl, Herzl begat 'Der Judenstaat', Der Judenstaat [begat] 'Zionism', and Zionism [begat] the [Zionist] Congress. Antisemitism is then the cause of all causes in this movement." Antisemitism, he says, is the very "soul of this [Zionist] movement"; Herzlian Western political Zionism requires the "emanation" of its antisemitic forebearer to exist, "as the infant constantly requires its mother." Without antisemitism, (political) Zionism "could not survive even one hour."[49]

This is indeed a lamentable fact for a committed (Jewish) nationalist, for it suggests that one's identification as a Jew cannot self-sustain, instead having to "feed daily from the source of antisemitism." Resisting this Herzlian thinking, Ahad HaAm insists that even if antisemitism may have been a necessary condition for the emergence of national Jewish self-consciousness, it should not remain the condition for its survival. Instead, national consciousness should be based on "shared memories

and assets, shared thoughts and feelings, shared hopes and aspirations."
This, he argues, is what his own Eastern (European) Zionism, concerned
at it is with matters that are essential to Jewish tradition, provides. And
this is the reason why this Eastern cultural or "spiritual" nationalism
(i.e., what we may call a "Jewish polity" outlook for the national movement) will persist even if antisemitism somehow disappears.[50]

Note that Ahad HaAm seems to be less preoccupied with what we
may call, following Elad Lapidot's cue, the political-epistemological
problem at hand—namely, how opposition to antisemitism shapes the
very way we view reality, the reality of Jewish existence itself, getting
trapped, as it were, in the antisemitic worldview.[51] Writing in the context of fighting for the nature of the Zionist project in its very formative years, Ahad HaAm's critique of Herzlian Zionism is understandably
focused on matters of the Zionist program itself. But the thrust of the
critique he formulates goes much deeper than the immediate questions
debated at the Zionist Congress in 1897. As Lapidot's work shows, this
critique gains a powerful relevance after the Nazi genocide, as the opposition to antisemitism has sometimes led paradoxically to the effacement
of Jewish identity and of Judaism or Jewishness—of Jewish existence
per se. Being determined by one's "anti-" has grave consequences. Thus,
to take but a snippet of the rich world of "post-Holocaust philosophy"
that Lapidot surveys, in Jean-Paul Sartre's construction of the notion of
Jewish authenticity: "we have shown," writes Sartre, "that the Jews have
neither community of interests nor community of beliefs. They do not
have the same fatherland; they have no history. The sole tie that binds
them is the hostility and disdain of the societies which surround them.
Thus, the authentic Jew is the one who asserts his claim in the face of the
disdain shown toward him."[52] Herzl would concur.[53]

These, then, are two contesting notions of Jewish authenticity—and,
directly derived from it, Jewish politics—that are premised upon two
rather incommensurable readings of Jewishness, or Jewish identity. One,
what I suggest we term the "politics/polity of Jews," retraces the steps
of European nation-statist liberalism, by assuming an alleged given (in
effect, powerfully constructed and maintained) racial/national/ethnic
uniformity as an objective infrastructure upon which a color/ethnic/
nationality-blind polity is constructed. A certain cultural normativity
"naturally" emerges out of this infrastructure and is taken to be an ob-

jective fact of reality, upon which a supposedly universalistic apparatus is being built. The color blindness is enabled precisely by a presupposed objective fact of a dominant normativity, that would otherwise be seen as parochial (or chauvinistic) normativity.

Logically, this would demand a clear sense of a distinction between Jews and non-Jews, an a priori definition, or predefinition, upon which the liberal inclusivity and tolerance of the Other, which accompanies a perception of the (national) self as safe from assimilation, is built. In other words, if we accept the notion of objective authenticity entailed in the polity of Jews, we would necessarily need to first know who (or what) the Jews "are." Antisemitism may be that which defines the Jew in Europe, but what is the Jew outside of European antisemitism, in the polity of Jews?

Herzl, quite obviously adopting the essentialist notions of Jewishness prevalent in Europe of his time, pays little attention to this issue—so much so that a reading of Herzl's utopia, especially in light of Ahad HaAm's criticism, "force[s] us to ask whether Herzl even considered the distinction between Jews and non-Jews to be valid in the context of the relationship between the old-new Jewish nation and languages, cultures, and ethnic groups of Western Christian civilization."[54] (To be clear, this lack of an explicit concern for a distinction between the Jew and the non-Jew only applies to the intra-European context. It is clear that the distinction is forcefully reiterated when the Jews are confronted with those others that are shaped by what Nordau terms "Asiatic barbarity.")

The choice not to give a clear definition of Jewishness is common to practically all main formulators of the Zionist ideology, including Ahad HaAm. They seem to all share a general sense by which Jewishness is something intrinsic to one's being, which is impossible to define, but is nevertheless tangible, and rather obvious.[55] Yet, as the debate reviewed above shows, these ideologues differ dramatically on the question of whether this intrinsic quality alone suffices for a meaningful construction of a polity.

The second notion of authenticity, captured in what I suggested we label as "Jewish politics/polity," would demand a certain, not insignificant level of loyal dialoguing with a Jewish and even Judaic normativity or tradition in order for it to be judged as authentic. It expects the polity to be constituted on what it views as Jewish knowledge, and from there also values, ethics, and so on (Ahad HaAm famously named these the Jewish "national morals").[56] It would also expect the polity to be guided by this Jewish normative framework in its policies and actions. Needless to say, different thinkers have quite different, not infrequently conflicting ideas as to the exact contents of this normative framework, but they all share the same basic view, by which it is exactly such a framework that would enable the polity at hand to be judged as authentically Jewish.

The Jewishness of the Israeli Polity

Let us jump forward, as it were, and consider some of the ways in which these conflicting ideological outlooks have played out in the politics of the State of Israel. Judged broadly, it seems almost trivial to assert that Herzl's political Zionism, with its focus on the establishment of a nation-state, has triumphed over Ahad HaAm's cultural vision. The latter would have demanded a much more gradual development (or revival, if we follow more closely the spirit of this ideology) of Jewish cultural, spiritual, and social life before it would allow for a drive toward the establishment of a nation-state. Indeed, this gradual re-formation of Jewish life is essential to Ahad HaAm's vision exactly because it is a precondition for the polity to authentically claim a Jewish identity. The Zionist movement has instead put most of its efforts into achieving the political aim of establishing a sovereign state. This is not to say that the Zionist elite has not also dealt with questions of Jewish tradition, history, and practice as part of its process of collective reinvention.[57] But this elite was quite content with leaving some fundamental questions arising from this process of reinvention unanswered as it focused its resources and attention on achieving the political goal.

Yet it is also quite clear—and maybe just as trivial—that this triumph of political Zionism was not accompanied by a decisive preference of the "polity of Jews" outlook. The Jewish polity concern for knowledge of and dialoguing with tradition has clearly lingered on. If Herzl's was the triumphant political outlook, Ahad HaAm's held strong on a cultural level, with its insistence that the polity of Jews must also be of Jewish, even Judaic, authenticity.

While these two outlooks could be seen as mutually oppositional, the Zionist movement, on its culmination in the State of Israel, tended to

THE JEWISH STATE VERSUS THE JEWS' STATE | 31

constitute itself on an uneasy combination of the two. As put by Ahad HaAm's first biographer, Moshe Glickson, himself a leading ideologue of the Zionist community in Mandatory Palestine, Herzl and Ahad HaAm have charted two unique paths that are nevertheless, he argues, complementary. History, he writes (less than a quarter-century after the publication of Ahad HaAm's critique of *Altneuland*) has reconciled these "two paths for the Jewish salvation, which are one: The redemption by action [i.e., Herzl's political Zionism, aimed at the establishment of a polity of Jews] and the redemption by wisdom and popular education [i.e., Ahad HaAm's cultural Zionism, aimed at reviving Jewish tradition]. . . . We are following Herzl's dream of kingdom by the shining light of Ahad HaAm's."[58]

Regardless of the triumphalist, overly optimistic spirit of this proclamation, it still captures a foundational truth about the Zionist project in Ottoman and Mandatory Palestine, also manifested later in the State of Israel—namely, the continuous skipping between these two differing, often conflicting readings of the very meaning of Zionism's and Israel's Jewishness and of Jewish politics more broadly. In the context of a budding Zionist community under the sovereignty of the Ottoman Empire and later the British Mandate, this duality could prove to be an intellectual and sociopractical stimulus that may well encourage collective self-examination, innovation, and reformation. This is so specifically since, at that stage, the debate had been primarily cultural and intellectual. It did not bear upon the "identity" of the sovereign; it had not had, in other words, the apparatus of the nation-state at its disposal.

This has changed dramatically, of course, with the establishment of the state in 1948. From this point on, the question at hand has gained a unique importance, as it came to pertain to such matters as the legitimacy of the sovereign, the ways in which this sovereign shapes the public sphere, dictates elements of its subjects' private and public lives, sets the borderlines of inclusion and exclusion under its rule, and—most fundamentally—kills and demands the sacrifice of its subjects' lives, all in the name of its (Jewish) sovereignty.

We may safely generalize and state that Israeli politics is determined by an uneasy upholding of both and at the same time an objective sense that Israel is primarily a polity of Jews and a normative notion that it is (or, rather, should act as) a Jewish polity. This combination is upheld

regardless—or in spite—of the fact that, as we have seen, these two outlooks may end up directing the polity in different ways, not infrequently
conflicting with each other. Maybe more importantly, as I argued earlier,
the tension entailed in this uneasy combination is often overlooked or
outright denied. While there is much talk on matters pertaining to the
politics of Jewish identity in Israel, often categorized under "religion and
politics," much of this talk fails to directly address the tension between
the two differing understandings or outlooks of Israel's Jewishness. This
tension itself is in effect a key to understanding Israeli politics, in the
most extensive sense of this term.[59]

Put schematically, we may say that while the state is founded—as a
matter of its political constitution—on a Herzlian notion of a "polity of
Jews," important segments of the cultural and especially the educational
sphere within the state have been shaped by an Ahad HaAm–inspired
notion of Jewish politics (a project overseen by the very same elite who
led the foundation of the state along Herzlian lines).[60] Importantly, both
the state and the culture/education it has promoted have been viewed
as "secular." In other words, both the idea of an objective determinant
of being a Jew and the subjective notion of Jewish culture are seen as
independent—at least in principle—from religion. Yet the agreement
seems to persist that much of the substance of Judaism as a culture, as
well as the essence of a hereditary determinant of Jewishness have been
historically dominated by a religious tradition.[61] This transforms the as-
cription of Jewishness and Jewish culture as secular into a self-professed
revolutionary act.

The tension entailed herein shapes much of the actions, debates, and
analyses of the matters at hand. I have elsewhere discussed in more detail the rather curious notion of a state's identity, and the ensuing debates
surrounding Israel's identity as a Jewish state.[62] For the sake of the current discussion, let me briefly recap here how the debates over the quasi-
constitutional identification of Israel as a Jewish and democratic state
and as the nation-state of the Jewish people capture this tension between
the two competing readings of Jewish politics.

These debates have gained momentum following the legislation in the
early 1990s of two Basic Laws (the supposed building blocks of a future
written constitution for the Israeli polity) the purpose clauses of which
include a reference to "the values of the State of Israel as a Jewish and

democratic state." The debates have reached an apogee of sorts (surely they have yet to conclude one way or another), with the legislation in 2018 of the controversial "Basic Law: Israel the Nation-State of the Jewish People."[63]

The declaratory identification of Israel as Jewish and democratic fell far short of spelling out the meaning of this identification, either in concrete legal terms or in the more general political terms discussed above. It does little, in other words, to solve the tension between the two outlooks of Jewish politics. And it has fed what many see as a constitutional crisis that gained further momentum since 2023.

The president of the Israeli Supreme Court at the time of the legislation of these Basic Laws in the 1990s, Aharon Barak, has since gained the status of either a national villain or a liberal-democratic saint among Israelis—depending, of course, on how they view or understand his interventions on the matter. Guiding his court with an activist ethos, Barak has famously interpreted the legislation of the 1990s Basic Laws as amounting to a "constitutional revolution"—that is, as offering for the first time in Israel's history a written constitutional framework for the Israeli legal system.[64] This would logically mean that the court is put in a position that requires it to interpret Israel's values as a "Jewish and democratic" state, and Barak's court has indeed taken upon itself to review the legislator's and the executive's acts in light of its interpretation of these values. It was the ensuing decisions by the court with respect to this principle that have made the court the object of fierce political argumentation.

Thus, to give but one famous example, Barak's court has ruled the practice of allocating state lands for the establishment of settlements for Jews only unconstitutional. Consistent as it may be with Zionist basic principles of redeeming and "Judaizing" the land,[65] the court found such a discriminatory practice to be incommensurable with the value of equality, to which, the court decided, the state is bound by its *Jewish* character. As Barak himself put it in his decision:

> Indeed, the return of the Jewish people to its homeland is derived from the values of the State of Israel as both Jewish and Democratic state. . . .
> "The State—is the state of the Jews; the regime that exists in it—is an enlightened democracy, which grants rights to all citizens, Jews as non-

Jews alike."[66] ... Moreover: not only do the values of the State of Israel as a Jewish state not dictate discrimination on the basis of religion and nationality, they in fact proscribe such discrimination, and demand equality between religions and nationalities.[67]

It is telling, but far from surprising, then, that Barak's reflections on the ambiguous nature of the phrasing "the values of the State of Israel as a Jewish and democratic state" betray exactly this tension between competing readings of the very meaning of Jewish politics and of Israel's Jewish identity. Barak explicitly reads Israel's Jewishness to be a matter of its Zionist character. This refers, it appears, to Israel's being both a state of Jews and a Jewish state. "A Jewish state is a state that expresses the Zionist vision," Barak writes; in his admittedly mainstream (but maybe surprisingly Zionist, especially to those who take him to be a scion of universalist liberalism) reading, the "world of Zionism" that the state manifests consists of such nationalist basic principles as the Jews "return" to "their land," the site of the "national homeland of every Jew," and their redemption. Israel as a Zionist, Jewish state, he writes, is "a state that redeems the land for Jewish settlement" (read: a Jews' state). But this "world of Zionism" also consists, in Barak's rendition, of Jewish culture that is imbued with what the liberal discourse would call religion (read: a Jewish state). Thus, the list of resources he offers for deciphering Israel's values as a Jewish and democratic state also include "traditional" values, which are manifested in religious Jewish law.[68]

Writing after his retirement, the president of the Supreme Court insists that the task of outlining what these competing commitments or characteristics of the state should amount to is not the court's to carry. Rather, it is a social, cultural, and political task that would naturally be carried by the people's representatives. Yet the Israeli legislature's attempt at doing just that ended up only further highlighting the tension between these competing readings of Jewish politics. I am referring here to the legislation of the "Basic Law: Israel the Nation-State of the Jewish People," another quasi-constitutional building block that had been the focus of a continuous debate within Israel for over a decade before its final approval by the Israeli parliament in July 2018. (Interestingly, the relevant Wikipedia page suggests that this Basic Law has "overruled" the afore-quoted ruling of Barak's in the Ka'adan case.[69] While clearly motivated in part by this ruling, it seems an oversimplification to declare the Basic Law as overruling the principles enunciated in this judicial decision). This legislation was the culmination of a heightened political tension surrounding Israel's Jewish identity, which has come to dominate Israeli politics. Since clearing the last legislative hurdles it has also attracted much international attention and has been given to multiple legal challenges.

To understand the history of this law, which allegedly aims to enshrine Israel's identity as *the* Jewish nation-state, we should read it as an initiative motivated by concerns of the "state of Jews" kind (meaning, an attempt to constitutionally reiterate or reinstate the preferential status of the majority of Jews over Palestinian Arabs within the state), which was somewhat unintentionally transformed into an apparently confused debate over the meaning of a "Jewish state" (meaning, an attempt to explicate what a normative adherence to "Jewish heritage" may amount to).

The debate over the bill has offered a clear view of the essential tensions at the very roots of the Israeli polity. Specifically, it highlighted the tension between Zionism's rebellion against what it has viewed as Jewish religion and Zionism's foundational claim to a Jewish history and identity that are, by the Zionists' own account, saturated with the same religious elements. More critically, it has exposed the Zionist inability to construct a full-fledged independent-from-religion (i.e., in Zionism's own terminology, "national" and "secular") positively *normative* sense of Jewish identity. Such an ideological construction could have been the source that would clearly identify Israel's values as a Jewish state, hence, ultimately, the Israeli meaning of Jewish politics. Instead, the law directs much of its impetus toward a *negative* construction of Jewish-Zionist nationhood, by way of refuting the Palestinian claims to nationhood and attempting to buttress the preference of Jews over non-Jews in Israel.

Two issues emerged almost instantaneously as the flash points attracting most commentators' attention: the implied preference of Israel's Jewish identity over the polity's (liberal-)democratic principles when the two are understood to be in conflict, and the assertion of Jewish nationhood through the blunt negation of Palestinian national self-determination.

In the critical liberal Zionist (oppositional) reading of the law—a reading that, as we saw above, is nevertheless principally committed to a "state of Jews" framework—the main motive behind the law has been an attempt (which the critics clearly see as racist) to firmly establish the collective inferiority of Palestinian-Arabs in the nation-state of Jews. In this reading, the internationally accepted rightful affirmation of the Jewish majority's determination of Israel's Jewish identity masks a more sinister, less acceptable practice of what *Haaretz*'s editorial names "apartheid," in which this affirmation is built primarily on the negation of the national "Other."[70]

The centrality of the Palestinian challenge to political Zionist nationhood is most clearly explicated in a draft proposal to the original legislative bill (first presented to the Israeli Parliament in 2011), published by the Institute for Zionist Strategies (IZS) in 2009. This document's authors justify the legislative initiative as a countermeasure to what they decry as a gradual erosion—and ultimately a "perversion"—of the Zionist vision, entailed in the idea (which, the document bemoans, has clearly gained traction) that the preference of Jews over non-Jews in Israel is illegitimate. If left unopposed, they warn, this trend would lead to the transformation of Israel into the opposite of "a state of Jews"— namely "a state of all of its citizens," a liberal-democratic state, where all citizens, regardless of their national(ist) belonging and aspirations, enjoy equal status not only in face of the law but also in the allocation of material and symbolic resources. Doing so, the authors of this draft bill clearly expose the fundamental dependency of the "state of Jews" outlook on an a priori "demographic" calculation of a privileged majority versus a tolerated minority. In this framework of nationalist political philosophy, the Jewish character of the nation-state must amount to an explicit preference of people who are Jews over those who are not, at least in collective terms.[71]

The authors of this document directly identify the liberal threat to the "state of Jews" outlook as they warn against a "radical liberal interpretation": the "elevation of equality . . . to an exclusive supreme value in Israel" that "distorts the intention of the Founding Fathers of the State of Israel." Such interpretation/application of equality "denies the Jewish People its right to self-determination" and "leads to the warped conclusion that all laws contributing to the Jewish character of Israel are undemocratic (except for now, the Law of Return) and must therefore be annulled."[72]

As Avi Dichter, the member of the Knesset who presented the bill to the Israeli parliament, has triumphantly put it, the Basic Law was aimed at "preventing even a shadow of a thought, not to mention an attempt, to transform Israel into a state of all of its citizens."[73] *Haaretz*'s editorial highlighted the impetus of this assertion: "The ugly, naked truth has been exposed: The nation-state law was meant to make it clear to Israeli Arabs that the state views them as second-class citizens. Admittedly, they have 'equal rights just like the rest of us,' but they should know that the state doesn't belong to 'all its citizens.'" [74]

The liberal alarm that this Basic Law is meant to constitutionalize the preference of Jews gained more straightforward support in a proposed resolution considered by the Israeli government in late May 2023. Dubbed by some in the Israeli press the "Zionism Law," the resolution would require that "the values of Zionism, as they are expressed in Basic Law: Israel the Nation-State of the Jewish People will be guiding and deciding the policy of the public administration, foreign and domestic policy, legislation and governmental actions."[75] Explaining that at times the government takes into account "various professional considerations" that "ignore basic Zionist values," the proposal seeks to amend this by reaffirming the "values [that] express the right of the Jewish people to self-determination in the Land of Israel, among them settlement, security, culture, and Aliyah."[76]

The minster who proposed the resolution explained that it "will enable us to give preference to IDF soldiers and army veterans, entrench the Jewish people's connection with its land and strengthen the Negev, the Galilee and Judea and Samaria."[77] Critical commentators have noted that the resolution "would encourage ministers to advance policies that place Zionist values over others that should have the same status, such as equality before the law."[78]

In any event, it is easy enough to see why a liberal-democratic mindset would oppose the "Nation-State" basic law (although the debate over it has clearly exposed some of the more pressing logical inconsistencies of liberal Zionism). Other oppositions to the bill also shed light on the ways in which it has played into the debate over the meaning of Jewish politics. Throughout the almost-decade of debate over the bill, it has been insistently opposed by two groups who are usually considered to be on the sidelines of mainstream Israeli sociopolitics: Palestinian Arabs and ultra-Orthodox Jews (the two groups also opposed the abovementioned proposed governmental resolution, or "Zionism Law"). As for the former group, the reasons for rejecting the bill seem quite obvious: Palestinian Arabs object to a political configuration of power that puts them in a precarious position of a tolerated minority who lacks equal protection of its rights. Yet, in the context of the current discussion, it is the ultra-Orthodox Jewish opposition to the bill that sheds light on what is at stake between the two readings of Jewish politics discussed here.

This opposition may indeed seem perplexing. Wouldn't a reaffirmation of Israel's Jewish identity be something naturally favored by those who conservatively observe Jewish law? Yet the wider ultra-Orthodox discourse on the matter makes it clear that the opposition was not aimed at the law per se (ultimately, parties representing the ultra-Orthodox communities in Israel helped the bill pass its final legislative hurdles, most probably motivated by coalitional considerations), but rather at the overall epistemology from which it derives. Simply put, the ultra-Orthodox view rejects the very notion that Israel is a "Jewish" state, since in the ultra-Orthodox view the Jewishness of the state must amount to more than the Zionist understanding of Jewish politics (i.e., mainly the "state of Jews" calculation of demographic imbalance). The challenge here is not against the intended strengthening of Israel's Jewish character, but against the Zionist understanding or construction of this character. In other words, the ultra-Orthodox opposition suggests a (critical) "Jewish polity" view of the Israeli state, judging it to be fundamentally lacking exactly in being indifferent, if not outright hostile, to what the nationalist view designates as "Jewish religion" and the ultra-Orthodox critique sees as the very essence of Jewishness.

Conclusion

The debate over the "Nation-State Law" and the discourse from which the law arises capture a foundational trait of the Israeli polity. This debate may be described as an epistemological argumentation over how to approach the very constitutive notion of Israel's Jewish character. The unresolved nature of this law, the fact that it manages to be seen by critics and supporters alike as both and at the same time "obvious" or "redundant" and "radical" or "dangerous," compounded by its ultimate failure to positively instill this designation (i.e., "Jewish state") with explicitly positive meaning all reflect some of the foundational tensions in Zionist ideology and Israeli nation-statism.[79]

These tensions all touch upon the Zionist taken-for-granted claim for *Jewish* nationalism—that is, the reading of Jewish identity as pertaining to "nationality," in the ideological meaning of the term—and the just-as obvious Zionist failure (or neglect) to construct a positive meaning of a "secular" (as in not related to what Zionist ideology would see as "religion") Jewish identity. Instead, Zionism and the Israeli polity have shifted the discourse from a "Jewish state" to a "Jews' state", from asking, "What makes someone or something Jewish?," to constructing a polity based on a majority of "Jews."

Ultimately, the law was following a much wider ideological and discursive trend, which this chapter has sought to explicate. Among other things, it has exposed how the Zionist taken-for-granted understanding of Jewish nation-statehood—framed as a "state of Jews"—is found to be undermined by its inconsistency with basic democratic principles of equality. Furthermore, like much of the wider discourse on these matters, the debate over the law was transformed into a discussion on the meaning of Israel's identity as a "Jewish state," a discussion that some of the main protagonists of this debate never attempted to hold (they are satisfied with viewing it as solely the Jews' state).

The questions that this chapter has tackled—about issues pertaining to the very meaning of Israel's Jewishness—are time and again forced on the Israeli public sphere by the basic statist imperative of preserving the political Zionist taken-for-granted understanding of Jewish nationhood. In this, the crippled debate over the Nation-State Law echoes a foundational trait of political Zionist ideology, which, confronted with the dilemma of its own Jewish identity, preferred to forgo the discussion and focus instead on establishing a configuration of power in which Jews hold sovereignty. The fact that many participants in the debate, as well as many of those analyzing, criticizing, or celebrating it have not identified, acknowledged, or explicated the tension, if not outright contradiction, between these two outlooks has overshadowed our understanding of a foundational aspect of Israeli nation-statism.

2

Zionism as Supersessionism

Introduction: The Confusion about Zionism and Judaism

Zionism's claim to Jewish history and identity, as we have seen, is complicated. On the one hand, both the movement and the ideology tend to be confrontational, defining themselves as revolutionary and adopting a rebellious attitude toward Judaism, Jewish tradition, and Jewish history. On the other hand, Zionism sees the very things it rebels against as its own: Jewish history—as in the history of Jews and Judaism alike—is part of Zionism itself; Zionism defines itself as a *Jewish* national movement. How are we to understand this simultaneous combination of negation and appropriation?

As Arthur Hertzberg puts it in what remains one of the most penetrating analyses of the Zionist idea, the question of how to account for Zionism's place within Jewish history when the ideology itself sees very little "meaning and validity" in the Jewish past presents the students of Jewish history with "the most debated, and least solved problem of Jewish historiography."[1] The importance of this question can hardly be overstated: "The issue at stake in this discussion is not merely the correct understanding of Zionism, though that alone is a matter of prime importance. It involves the fundamental question of the total meaning of Jewish history."[2]

Furthermore, this question is not only historiographical in nature; it is also key to understanding Zionist ideology and its political embodiment in the State of Israel, shedding light on the wider Jewish world and the politics of the Middle East, as Israel's struggle with its own claim to Jewish identity shapes how the state and its society view their position vis-à-vis other Jewish communities in the world, as well as Palestinians and other Arabs (the 2018 Nation-State Law, as discussed in the previous chapter, being a recent blunt manifestation of this sociopolitical fact). Yet the discussion of this issue seems to be mired in confusion.

The tensions surrounding Israel's Jewish identity are, as we have seen, derived directly from Zionism's confrontational appropriation of the Jewish past, and even of Judaism itself. This chapter discusses the complicated matter of Zionism's relation to Judaism in more detail by exploring the viability of the framework of supersessionism to understand this relationship. The chapter first articulates the conceptual, interpretive puzzle at hand—namely, Zionism's "Jewish problem." Following a short discussion of the Christian notion of supersessionism and its prevalence in the context of Christian Zionism, the chapter goes on to consider the applicability of supersessionism to Zionism, and to Israeli political culture. Employing a distinction between "hard" and "soft" supersessionist stances, the chapter also considers Jewish or Judaic responses to what could be viewed as Zionist supersessionism.

In what follows, I suggest that we might have a better understanding of Zionism's claim to Jewish identity if we frame the relation between Zionism and Judaism as one of supersessionism: a (political) theology of replacement, where Zionism is understood to be taking over the role and place of historical, traditional Judaism, rendering the latter not only anachronistic and inadequate but also superfluous and even inauthentic. This framing might help us to better understand Zionism's complicated, conflicted claim to Jewish identity and to appreciate differing Jewish reactions to Zionism.

This chapter is meant to be an exercise in what might be termed, following Mary Midgley's insightful comparison of philosophy to plumbing, a "conceptual de-clogging": an overcoming of a fault in a conceptual scheme that has functioned as a largely hidden infrastructure of our understanding of history and of present sociopolitical reality.[3] As Midgley puts it, "When the concepts we are living by work badly," they "quietly distort and obstruct our thinking." But it is hard to see these malfunctions of our conceptual infrastructure:

> We often don't consciously notice this obscure malfunction, any more than we consciously notice the discomfort of an unvarying bad smell or a cold that creeps on gradually. We may indeed complain that life is going badly—that our actions and relationships are not turning out as we intend. But it can be very hard to see why this is happening, or what to do about it. We find it much easier to look for the source of trouble out-

side ourselves than within. Notoriously, it is hard to see faults in our own motivation, in the structure of our feelings. But it is in some ways even harder—even less natural—to turn our attention to what might be wrong in the structure of our thought.[4]

Yet sometimes this conceptual self-reflection becomes necessary, almost forced upon us. "When things do go badly," Midgley says, "we have to do this":

> We must then somehow readjust our underlying concepts; we must shift the set of assumptions that we were brought up with. We must restate those existing assumptions which are normally muddled and inarticulate—so as to find the source of trouble. And this new statement must somehow be put in a usable form, a form which makes the necessary changes look possible.[5]

In Alasdair MacIntyre's phrasing, such a conceptual impasse can result in an "epistemological crisis," an inability to understand the world, as the stories we have been using to do so prove no longer fit for purpose.[6] The "de-clogging" exercise thus necessitates the forming of new, updated narratives that capture not only how we should view current reality and its history but also what was wrong with the stories we had been telling ourselves about it.

It is my contention that much of the discussion on Zionism's relation to Judaism—the attitude of the ideology and of the state it has brought to life toward what both ideology and state see as their Jewish history and identity—is mired in such conceptual confusion and misunderstanding.[7] And I propose that framing this relation as an attitude of supersessionism would allow us to both see the source of the trouble (the misunderstanding of the relation between Zionism and Judaism) and think of possible ways out of it.

The often hidden confusing and faulty conceptual infrastructure of the case at hand follows Zionism's self-understanding or self-fashioning as a modern movement of Jewish nationalism. It describes the relation between Zionism and Judaism as one of modernization, secularization, and politicization. Zionism, in this reading, is a "*modern* answer" to questions of Jewish identity,[8] the outcome of "a quest for self-determination and liberation under the modern conditions of secularization and liberalism."[9] Zionism is seen here as a revolutionary remaking of Judaism, "the most fundamental revolution in Jewish life," that is at the same time a re-formation or re-creation of the authentic, original, political-national meaning of Judaism—a meaning that has allegedly been corrupted in exile, in the state of lacking sovereignty.[10] This reformulation achieves its fulfillment, so the argument goes, in the sovereign nation-state of Jews, which fills a historical void in Jewish public life, becoming "a normative center for Jews all over the world."[11]

This view, while still holding strong as an almost default option for describing and explaining Zionism's convoluted relation to what this ideology sees as its own Jewish roots, has won its share of criticism, coming even from writers who adhere to Zionist ideology and to the epistemological underpinnings of it, often captured under the heading of "the Enlightenment."[12] These critiques dismiss the bipolarity of a "conservative, medieval" religion pitted against a "modern, secular" nationalism as a "stereotypical and one-dimensional understanding of human history."[13] Instead, scholars call for a more nuanced understanding of the mutual dependence and influence between Zionism and Judaism. Zionism emerges in this picture as "modern yet not secular," while Judaism (read here as a more limited-in-scope "religion . . . on its various aspects") is understood to be a "component in the historical manifestation of Jewish nationalism, but not its subject."[14]

Often, such misgivings regarding the validity of a naive secularist view remain committed to the Enlightenment's epistemology and the conceptual tool kit it has bequeathed to us. They tend to read Judaism as fitting (roughly, at the very least) the category of religion and to see politics and nationalism as essentially secular realms of human conduct; they also adopt the Enlightenment's notion of history as continuous progress.[15] Yet they challenge a one-dimensional narration of history where the secular (i.e., Zionist nationalism) and the religious (i.e., Judaism) cannot cohabitate. The two realms might be seen, then, as caught in a "dialectical relationship": "Far from being a clear break with the past, national movements are essays in reinterpretations of the past and its retrieval. And since one element of this past has to deal with religion, every national movement has to deal in an innovative and transformative way with the religious dimension of its past."[16]

More substantial critiques interrogate the epistemological roots of Zionist nationalism, highlighting its commitment to modern European, post-Reformation Christian, and Hegelian notions of nationalism, politics, and religion. These critiques highlight the indebtedness of the Zionist idea to the system of thought that emerges from the configuration of power of the modern sovereign nation-state and in turn works to legitimize the state's claim to absolute sovereignty. They problematize the view of the state as secular, exploring the ways in which the political theology of the modern state generally and of the State of Israel more particularly correspond with, negotiate, appropriate, negate, and reinterpret what the state itself would see or define as "religion."[17]

This chapter frames Zionism's relation to Judaism as supersessionism. Its aim is not to argue that Zionism *is* supersessionism; rather, it makes the case that the concept of supersessionism can help us better understand the relation between Zionism and its own Jewish history—or its claim to Jewish identity. Note that the argument that Zionism can or should be viewed as supersessionism does not have to carry negatively judgmental implications. Just as in the case of Christian supersessionism, it can be celebrated as the emergence (dialectical or otherwise) of the *true* nature of Judaism; indeed, this, as we will see later, is exactly the position taken by Zionist ideologues who celebrate the dual action of appropriation and negation of Jewish tradition by Zionism, even if they do not use the term "supersessionism" itself. At the very least, viewed positively, the argument that Zionism "fits the bill" of supersessionism can be read in light of an appreciation of Christian supersessionism as manifesting a less problematic (compared to a Christian antisemitic negation of Judaism) sense of filiation that in effect opens the space for Judeo-Christian dialogue and *convivencia*.[18]

But it is also clear that for people concerned primarily with a Jewish view or appreciation of Zionism and the State of Israel—people who see their commitment to Jewish tradition and other matters of Jewish identity as constitutive of their identity while not necessarily un-self-reflectively subscribing to the Zionist rendition of these—this view would encourage a renewed engagement with the notion of Judaism not only outside of the context of being bound to, or defined by, the political ideology and the state it has established but also independently from the state, and even vis-à-vis or against it.

Supersessionism

Simply put, supersessionism, sometimes also referred to as "replacement theology," names the theological notion that the Christian church has superseded—as in replaced, took the place of—the Jewish people, assuming what they traditionally see as their role as God's covenanted people, Israel: "As God rejected Israel for their refusal of Christ's messiahship, so the church represented the ultimate fulfilment of their mission. The church was therefore the 'true Israel', inheriting, and in the process spiritualizing, the promises of the Hebrew prophets."[19]

Judging or evaluating supersessionism is far from simple. There are differing interpretations of the notion and its implications, specifically in terms of Christianity's relation to Jews who deny Christian theology. According to one influential reading, for example, this "theology of displacement" may be seen as posing, especially to Christian theologians, a "theological problem, because it threatens to render the existence of the Jewish people a matter of indifference to the God of Israel," ultimately "engaging in a massive theological contradiction."[20]

On another, "psychological" level, "supersessionism is problematic because it instils feelings of hatred and contempt toward Jews."[21] Hence, a recent critical-theological (Christian) engagement with the scourge of antisemitism points the finger directly at "the evils of supersessionism" as the root cause of antisemitism across the generations.[22] By this reading, supersessionism must logically amount to "erasure," an "implausible vilification of a tradition in order to supplant it." The historical implications of "the consuming error of Christian supersessionism" is nothing less than a violent, patricidal, and genocidal manifestation of a Christian suffering "from an Oedipus complex" and the ensuing attempt "to slay the father."[23] The idea behind this "patricidal liberation" holds that "to celebrate the son" (Christian faith) "one must slay the father (Judaism)."[24] This notion is based on an "anxious logic, that in order for me and mine to live 'the other' and 'the burdensome' must die."[25]

Furthermore, reading supersessionism in this way negates any viable notion of filiation between Christianity and Judaism because the "very welcome . . . suggest[ion] that Christian anti-Semitism is plausibly seen as a kind of sibling rivalry" proves historically untenable: "Only 'patricide' (or 'matricide') does justice to the numerous ways the Christian church has sought to erase its forebear."[26]

No wonder, then, that, following the Holocaust, Christian churches who "have begun to consider anew their relation to the God of Israel and the Israel of God" have "revisit[ed] the teaching of supersessionism after nearly two thousand years" and "now publicly confessed that fidelity to the gospel requires the rejection of supersessionism."[27] Interestingly, the same critical Christian theological reading of supersessionism finds "secular treatments of religious identity" to be similarly responsible for the same act of erasure entailed in supersessionism's double act of appropriation and negation. Not coincidentally, it is Sartre's treatment of antisemitism and Jewishness, discussed briefly in the previous chapter, that attracts much of this reading's attention.[28]

Approached "as an analytical category," supersessionism may be seen as "mak[ing] a positive contribution to the discussion" on Christian antisemitism by shifting our attention to "the issue of self-definition, which in many ways is antecedent to any attitudes, speech or actions directed against (anti-) the Other. Since Christian treatment or Jews and Judaism—whether expressed in verbal, social, or political terms—was rooted in the church's own self-conception with respect to the tradition and heritage of Israel, our understanding of the former will be enhanced by a clearer perception of the latter."[29]

Offering a Jewish view of Christian supersessionism, David Novak helpfully suggests that we distinguish between "hard" and "soft" renderings of it. The former type prevents dialogue between Christians/Christianity and Jews/Judaism, while the latter allows it:

> Hard or maximal supersessionism asserts that God has elected Christians to displace the Jews in the covenant between God and His people. Christianity is taken to be Judaism's necessarily total successor or "fulfilment." For hard supersessionists, the only option for Jews is conversion to Christianity. This means an abandonment of Judaism. Hard supersessionism of this sort kills Jewish-Christian dialogue before it even starts. Jews faithful

to the Jewish tradition cannot accept this categorical dismissal of Judaism's theological validity.[30]

Soft supersessionism, Novak suggests, is more tolerant, since it "accept[s] the historical fact that Jews have remained with the 'unsupplemented' ancient covenant while Christians have been called by God to a higher level."[31]

Andrew Crome's insistence that the common reference to supersessionism as "replacement theology" is somewhat inaccurate helps to highlight how supersessionists make a claim to foundational *authenticity*. The move from Israel to the church is hence not a replacement per se, but a return to the true meaning of Israel: "The church does not replace Israel, but has always been the true Israel by faith (cf. Rom. 9:6). The difference rests in the way the church is used (as a spiritual, rather than a national body) as God's prime instrument, and the access now available to gentiles. Supersessionists would therefore argue that their theology promotes continuity: the prophets and patriarchs are therefore as much a part of the church as the contemporary believer."[32]

The matter at hand relates, then, to contested notions of authenticity, appropriation, and negation or erasure. As Brian Klug points out, while much of the tension surrounding practices and ideas that we would usually label as "supersessionist" has to do with the issue of appropriation, supersessionism cannot be reduced to mere appropriation, as it often also involves exclusion and (at least implied) elimination. Considering, as an example of supersessionism, the practice of Christian seders, Klug notes that labeling this practice supersessionist "is a much more comprehensive indictment than criticizing Christians for purloining a particular ceremonial meal":[33]

It goes deeper. It amounts to saying that the Christian seder appropriates Judaism as such, relegating it to the pre-Christian past and treating Jews (as Rebecca Cynamon-Murphy puts it) "as relics rather than people." . . . Supersessionism, you could say, excludes Judaism not by shutting it out but by incorporating it, dissolving it into Christianity. Seen as supersessionist, the Christian seder makes a meal of Judaism itself, devouring it whole and assimilating it into its sinews. Only the bones are left on the seder plate. No act of appropriation could go further than this.[34]

Indicting the "theological exercise" of supersessionism as "deeply out of place," Cynamon-Murphy interprets supersessionism as depicting "the entire narrative arc of the Jewish people as simply a preamble to the main act." It is noteworthy that, like Klug, Cynamon-Murphy sees the practice of Christian seders as an especially telling example of supersessionism, since these seders manifest what she calls the "objectification of our Jewish neighbors."[35] (Tellingly, a "play" on the Jewish seder also constitutes a part of what I would suggest we may see as Zionist supersessionism. I will get to this point later on.)

Crucially, supersessionism is not a one-sided relationship. Judaism does not remain mute in the face of the Christian claim. In Novak's formulation, Judaism's reaction to Christian supersessionism, or, more broadly, the diverging ways in which Judaism views Christianity and the relation between the two sides, might also be defined as hard and soft formulations of *Jewish* supersessionism: a range of attitudes oscillating between denial of a relation and silencing of dialogue to allowing some form of cohabitation and conversation.[36] As I will argue, the same would be true with regard to Judaism's relation to Zionism in light of Zionist supersessionism.

Christian Zionism and Supersessionism

The association of Zionism with supersessionism is anything but novel when the qualifier "Christian" is added to "Zionism." A plethora of works interrogating Christian Zionism allow us, among many other things, to appreciate the degree to which foundational notions of (nominally secular) nationalist ideologies, which Jewish Zionism obviously shares, have their roots in Christian theology and, especially, in supersessionism.[37]

As Crome notes, the very concept of "elect nationhood," which has played a major role in the shaping of multiple collective and national identities and (theo)political ideologies, has its roots in supersessionism.[38] Spokespeople for various collectives see their respective groups as having replaced Israel as "elect," a supposedly secular nationalist idea that is rooted in the Christian theological concept of supersessionism.[39]

The general phenomenon at hand has resulted in a wide array of concrete readings of the relation between Christian Zionism and Judaism or the Jewish people—that is, in the context at hand, the practical, political, and theological meaning of the supersessionist aspect of Christian Zionism:

> Differences on almost every issue can be found within the varieties of Christian Zionism. For example, while most Christian Zionists expect the Jews to convert and follow Jesus Christ at the end times, not all do. Some think that the majority will die at Armageddon, and only a small remnant will convert. (The Rapture means that Christians will be out of the picture while the battles rage.) Others want active evangelism in Israel to herald the end days. Some argue that conversion will only come about when the messiah returns, rendering any present mission to the Jews inappropriate. It is not always clear whether "conversion" requires forgoing Jewish cultural and religious identity.[40]

It is important to note that Christian Zionism tends to preserve a distinction between Christians/Christianity and Judaism/Jews. It suggests courses of future histories involving Jews and their polity (the Jewish state), directing Jews and Judaism in certain political trajectories whose eschatological, messianic end is Christian. Indeed, this distinction—and the interpretive space it opens up (Jews and their state still have their own course of real history to follow before this eschatology is to happen; they are not simply swallowed up and disappear within Christianity "in this world")—is what allows Jewish and Israeli Zionists to work in tandem with Christian Zionists to promote the very "this-worldly" interests of the State of Israel, suspending or simply ignoring as irrelevant the Christian theological underpinnings of this type of Zionism.

Furthermore, "the standard supersessionist position in which the Christian understood herself as the 'true' or 'fulfilled' Jew" was undermined (at least in the reading offered by Crome) by a "Judeo-Centrist" (Christian) insistence that "Israel remained God's elect nation, and that his primary focus therefore remained on the Jewish people." As Crome's study of English Christian Zionism shows, "Judeo-centrists repurposed this narrative by drawing a firm boundary between God's promises for Jews and his promises for Christians, and by viewing England as having an important role as an auxiliary 'chosen' nation." Moreover, this combination of "a covenantal and a missional element, in which England had a higher moral calling because of her eschatological destiny" has translated into concrete political, nation-statist programs that are very much in line with what the Zionist movement has ultimately amounted to, in its devotion to restoring the Jewish people to Palestine.[41]

But how are we to understand the relations between Christian Zionism, Jewish Zionism, and Judaism? Specifically, what are the political (defined expansively) implications of supersessionism in the context of Zionism, Christian or otherwise? Commentators have offered a wide array of readings, from an enthusiastic advocacy of (at least implicitly) supersessionist Christian Zionism as speaking the ultimate theological or political truth, through careful warnings of the sometimes unintended consequences of an alleged enthusiastic Christian endorsement of Jewish nationalism, to outright delegitimization of supersessionism as racist (i.e., antisemitic) and of Christian Zionism as missionary.

Consider, as an example of the first, positive stance, Gerald McDermott's advocacy of what he terms the "New Christian Zionism." Formed in the context of the dominance of an assertive, politically successful Israeli nation-statehood, this New Christian Zionism sees the State of Israel and the Zionist enterprise at large as part of the *Christian* story of salvation:

> We [i.e., the "New Christian Zionists" McDermott speaks for] are also convinced that the return of Jews from all over the world to their land, and their efforts to establish a nation-state after two millennia of being separated from controlling the land, is *part* of the fulfilment of biblical prophecy. Further, we believe that Jews need and deserve a homeland in Israel—not to displace others but to accept and develop what the family of nations—the United Nations—ratified in 1948. We would add that this startling event climaxed a history of continual Jewish presence in the land going back at least three thousand years.[42]

In McDermott's formulation, this New Christian Zionism follows the Israeli theopolitics quite loyally: "We *do* know that the state of Israel, which includes more than two million non-Jews, is what protects the people of Israel. Support for this state and its people is eroding all over the world. Israel lies in a region of movements and governments bent on its destruction."[43] Yet, as he is quick to stress, this is not merely a matter of worldly politics; neither is the New Christian Zionism "merely nationalism." Ultimately, it is about theology: "The purpose of these prudential arguments—political and legal and moral—is to undergird a new *theological* argument for the twenty-first century."[44]

While most scholars agree that dispensationalism is a central source of Christian Zionism, dominated by a detailed eschatology of rapture, McDermott judges this version of Christian Zionism to be inadequate, since it "puts Israel and the church on two different tracks, neither of which runs at the same time." The New Christian Zionism he speaks for dispenses with this parochial theological baggage. Arguing that "the people and land of Israel are central to the story of the bible"—contrary, that is, to the fact that "Israel has not been central to the church's traditional way of telling the story of salvation"—the New Christian Zionists offer a Judeo-centrist (Christian) Zionism. They "believe that the Bible claims that God saves the world *through* Israel and the perfect Israelite; thus the Bible is incoherent and salvation impossible without Israel." This makes the "history of salvation" a continuous, present matter: "The people of Israel and their land continue to have theological significance."[45]

Viewed more critically, Christian Zionist supersessionism emerges as a problematic (to say the least) case of appropriation, even when it is not delegitimized outright as antisemitic. Brian Klug, for example, who offers such a critical analysis, remarks that "the permutations are bewildering" when we consider this appropriation in context. To start with, considering the deep, early roots of the Zionist idea (read here to mean the political project of the Jews' "return" to Palestine and the "restoring" the Jewish state there) among Christians, it is far from clear "who is appropriating what from whom."[46] As demonstrated by Shalom Goldman's argument for what he calls "a wider and more inclusive history" of Zionism, "one that takes the Christian involvement with Zionism into account," Jewish Zionism was clearly "influenced by—and cannot be understood in isolation from—Christian culture generally and Christian Zionist culture specifically."[47] General calls and specific programs for the restoration of Jews to their ancient homeland and the establishment of an independent polity there have circulated among Christians for centuries prior to the emergence of the (Jewish) "forerunners of Zionism" and the formation of the Zionist movement in nineteenth-century Europe. Furthermore, when the (Jewish) movement finally emerged, its leaders were clearly influenced by Christian correspondents, whose role in shaping the Zionist idea, Goldman shows, cannot be dismissed. Klug summarizes the point: "You could perhaps argue on this basis that Jews appropriated Zionism from Christians."[48]

Moreover, even if we prefer to avoid the argument that Christian Zionism was a direct source of inspiration for secular Zionism, the latter's indebtedness to what we may call the conceptual or ideational legacy of Christian Zionism is difficult to ignore. The Zionist "definition of the Jewish collectivity as a territorial nation, using the terminology of modern nationalism and the concept of the modern state, was meant to follow and internalize the same understanding that had guided the Christian Zionists."[49]

As Klug notes, Christian and Jewish Zionists alike approach the Hebrew Scriptures as the original source of the (political) idea at hand, and both employ questionable hermeneutical exercises in doing do.[50] In the Christian case, this amounts to "a Christian appropriation from Judaism with an apocalyptic sting in the tail": a reading of a traditional tie between the Jews and Zion that is "folded into" the doctrine of the second coming and the end times, prophesizing the ultimate wiping out of Jews who have not converted to Christianity. In the Jewish Zionist case, this misreading or appropriation amounts, at the very least, to a conflation of the biblical, prophetic, almost-otherworldly promised land and the modern, political, this-worldly State of Israel.[51] Furthermore, driven by a forceful sense of collective reinvention and rebellion against ("religious") tradition, (Jewish) Zionists would offer a politico-historical-legal—as opposed to theological—reading of the biblical text, amounting to what Amnon Raz-Krakotzkin has aptly summarized as the claim "God does not exist, but he promised us the land."[52]

Zionism, the Jewish Past, and Messianism

The driving force of the argument that Zionism's relations to Judaism may be considered one of supersessionism is captured in the Zionist claim to be a revolution—or even a Trotskyite-like "permanent revolution"—against the Jewish past.[53] At the same time, it is of crucial importance that Zionism does not seek to simply secede from Judaism, but instead insists on appropriating and creating what Nahman Syrkin, a leading ideologue of Socialist Zionism, has explicitly called "a new *relegia*," which was nevertheless seen as Jewish.[54] Zionism fashions itself as a revolution that confrontationally, aggressively seeks to redefine and appropriate the very meaning of Judaism.

That is to say, the argument at hand would make less sense were Zionism to present itself as speaking from within the long history of the development or evolution of Judaism. Clearly, what we now call "Judaism"—a problematic term to employ here, since "the very name 'Judaism' . . . has Christian supersessionism written into it. . . . There could not be a more profound Christian appropriation of Judaism than the name 'Judaism' itself"—is an ever developing, changing tradition, or modes of being in the world more generally.[55] Were Zionism to view itself as a mere turn in this same tradition, the notion of supersessionism might be quite inadequate. This has been the case with those authors commonly identified as the "forerunners" of the Zionist idea, "pious rabbis like Alkalai and Kalischer, who insisted on standing within the tradition [and] had to prove before the bar of the classical religious heritage"[56] that their proto-Zionist program for Jewish self-help was fully compatible with the teachings of this tradition.[57] And it is exactly their conversation or debating *within* the tradition, the sense of Jewish continuity that their interventions have offered, that renders them mere forerunners of Zionism, and not Zionists per se.

The "proper" Zionist ideologues, on the other hand, are identified as such by, among other things, their aggressive confrontation with the Jewish past, to which they could assign no positive "meaning and validity."[58] The Jewish past was especially a "problem" to the "extremist" (Hertzberg's terms) or revolutionary Zionists, who came to dominate the Zionist movement by the 1920s: "Their program of total revolution, of a complete break with the entire earlier career of the Jew in favor of purely secular national life ('let us be like all the gentiles'), required the assumption that the eighteen centuries of life in exile had been a barren waste."[59] Their attitude toward this Jewish or Judaic past was captured in the Nietzschean call (cited by M. Y. Berdyczewski as a motto to his essay discussing the proper Zionist relation to the Jewish past) that "if a temple is to be erected a temple must be destroyed."[60]

The building of this new temple was likewise explicitly religious, and, indeed, supersessionist. In Syrkin's formulation, for example, a Manichean image of a (Socialist) Zionist "war . . . in the name of the light" against the "forces of darkness" (namely, the guardians of the old religion who "hold the masses in their benighted state") is rapidly concluding with the invention of a new ("Hebrew") religion. While traditional Judaism is for Syrkin (quoting Heinrich Heine) "not a religion but a disaster . . . corrupting the Jewish mind and the Jewish soul, hindering any independent action, [and] chaining the people in bondage," his prognosis is not only about the breaking of the old yolk: it is also, primarily so, about the "resurrecting" of Judaism by way of remaking it in the image of Zionism.[61] A new kind of Judaism, one that "stands as a total opposition to medieval Judaism, to religious Judaism, to the Judaism of the exile," is nothing short of an all-encompassing "new religion [*relegia ḥadasha*] that will hover over all aspects of life" and that is nevertheless the most authentically Jewish.[62]

Zionist supersessionism can be better understood when put against the background of "the two Jewish philosophies which dominated the first half of the nineteenth century," and against which Zionism vehemently preached—namely, "assimilation and religious Reform."[63] As Syrkin is keen to stress, this comparison proves that the Zionist confrontation with the past is more forceful than those offered by its ideological or sociopolitical competitors. Zionism, he proclaims, "does indeed uproot religious Judaism in a more forceful and deeper manner" than these competitors:

> This is so since while Reform and assimilation uprooted Judaism from the outside in an artificial way [i.e., in terms of the current discussion, they did not present supersessionist claims], and their result was either absorption [among the non-Jewish communities, in the case of the assimilationists] or a revival of Talmudism, of traditional Judaism [in the case of the Reform movement, which is, at the end, a Jewish religious phenomenon], . . . Zionism uproots traditional Judaism from the inside, as it creates new contents of Judaism, as it changes the people's spiritual values of life,—uproots and eradicates it for once and for all.[64]

This (Jewish-)Zionist anti-Judaic stance has also clearly put some of these rebellious ideologues in an existential bind, bringing them to wonder, in Y. H. Brenner's formulation, "How can we become not-us?"[65] The striving to outgrow one's own past additionally touches upon a decisive matter of supersessionism: that the supersessionist party aims to eventually mark a break from that which it replaces. This bears important implications regarding the nature of the relations between the two sides of the supersessionist relation. Thus, for example, Jacob Klatzkin—who depicts the sovereign state as that which ought to define the new, Zionist Judaism and Jewish identity—expects that, once accomplished, this (Jewish) sovereignty would amount to a clear break from traditional Judaism. After the sovereign state of the Jews is established, he writes (decades prior to the establishment of the state), the Jews will be "parted into two collectives: a Hebrew collective [in the newly established state] and a Jewish collective in exile."[66]

Of course, not all Zionist ideologues spoke the language of rebellion. Theodore Herzl and Leo Pinsker are two prominent examples in this regard. But they, too, offered a vision in which the Jewish past is something to be overcome, generally void of positive meaning for the present and future. They "could make their case [for the relocation of Jews to a separate territory] only by interpreting the whole of postexilic history as an otherwise insoluble struggle with anti-Semitism."[67]

The story of Zionism's relation to its Jewish past is obviously a complicated one, and the above is but an anecdotal focus on one aspect of it. I have offered elsewhere a detailed discussion of the matter, which cannot be exhausted here.[68] What emerges from this complicated picture is that Zionism's resentful, revolutionary attitude toward its Jewish past—a past for which Zionism, viewing itself as a Jewish national movement, nevertheless makes a claim—holds a key to appreciating its supersessionist attitude. Zionism rebels against its past, and against what it sees as an outdated meaning of Jewishness captured by this past, while seeking to appropriate this past to promote its politics and ideology. Hertzberg summarizes the point: "On the one hand, history was invoked to legitimize and prove the need for the Zionist revolution; in another dimension, as it followed the pattern of all revolutions in imagining the outlines of its promised land, the mainstream of Zionism sought a 'usable past', to act as guideline for the great days to come."[69]

This forward-looking usage of the past also directs our attention to Zionism's messianic impetus, which is, "from the Jewish perspective . . . the primary element in Zionism."[70] As Hertzberg notes, this messianism has been used to tie Zionism in a narrative of Jewish continuity, in which "Zionism is made to stand in an unending line of messianic stirrings and rebellions against an evil destiny. . . . The bond between the people and its land, which it never gave up hope of resettling, was thus never broken, and Zionism is, therefore, the consummation of Jewish history under the long-awaited propitious circumstances afforded by the age of liberalism and nationalism."[71]

But this narrative (by which measure, it must be noted, it would be hard to claim that Christianity does not fit the same *Jewish*-messianic bill), "a kind of synthetic Zionist ideology presented as history," its chief proponent being Ben-Zion Dinur,[72] "must be subjected to serious criticism."[73] This is due not only to the fact that the promised political end-of-time has failed to arrive; this criticism is also, primarily, motivated by the fact that Zionism understands the very notion of messianism in a substantially, radically—I would say "supersessionistly"—new manner. While the premise "that Zionism is Jewish messianism in process of realizing itself through this-worldly means" might be seen as fitting "that stream of Zionist thought which remained orthodox in religious outlook, and therefore limited its tinkering with the classical messianic conception of the Jewish religion to the question of means," it is, at best, "artificial and evasive" when it "pretends to apply" to the mainstream of the Zionist movement. "What is being obscured," an issue that is "the crucial problem of modem Zionist ideology," has to do with the relation between Zionism and Judaism, here exposed as "the tension between the inherited [i.e., traditional, Jewish] messianic concept and the radically new meaning that Zionism, at its most modern, was proposing to give it."[74]

The "Copernican revolution which modern Zionism announces," a revolution that amounts to "a fundamental change not merely in the concept of the means to the Redemption but in end values." has to do with the shift from theology to theopolitics. If traditionally, Jewishly, "messianism had always imagined the Redemption as a confrontation between the Jew and God," leaving the gentile with at best a supporting role,

in the cutting edge of Zionism, in its most revolutionary expression, the essential dialogue is now between the Jew and the nations of the earth. . . .
The Messiah is now identified with the dream of an age of individual

liberty, national freedom, and economic and social justice—i.e., with the progressive faith of the nineteenth century. . . . The scheme of Jewish religion had seen the messianic problem as one of resolving the tension between the Jew and his Maker—the Exile is punishment and atonement for sin; for the new doctrine [i.e., Zionism], at its newest, the essential issue is the end of the millennia of struggle between the Jew and the world.[75]

Like Jewish tradition, Zionism speaks of a "remaking" of the Jewish people as a preamble to redemption, but Zionism—at least in its mainstream currents—shifts the role of redeemer from God to politics (defined expansively). Zionism represents this new, revolutionary notion of redemption on its "sweeping and passionate demands" by employing "a language reminiscent of the prophets," rendering its designation as secular at best wanting. Needless to say, this Zionist theopolitics, its notion of redemption-by-means-of-modern-nation-statist-politics, offers a radically new, revolutionary reading of the Jewish messianic tradition: "Every aspect of Jewish messianism has been completely transmuted by this new absolute."[76] But it does not simply vacate the theological or religious realm; rather, it replaces it.

The supersessionist impetus of Zionism is apparent even if we follow Arieh Saposnik's suggestion and suspend, as it were, the discussion of Zionist messianism and instead focus on the "redemptive spirit and vision that animated much of Zionism."[77] Importantly for the current discussion, Saposnik, who seems to suggest that a focus on this "redemptive *faith*" of Zionism will also redeem the ideology or the enterprise it has led, releasing them not only from unwarranted critique but also from unrealistic expectations, would argue that such a distinction between messianism and redemption would allow us to see that Zionism is *not* supersessionist.[78] He insists that this focus will help us to appreciate Zionism's basic commitment to Judaism—that is, to see that "Zionism in many respects aspired to what it conceived as a Jewish return to history rather than a retreat from, or supersession of it."[79] Zionism, Saposnik argues, "sought a reclamation and a reshaping of Jewish historical consciousness," its vision of redemption and liberation offering those whom Yosef Hayim Yerushalmi called the "fallen Jews" a remedy for the European "betrayal" of socialist and liberal ideas that promised them liberation. This was part of what Saposnik calls, following Yosef Gorny,

Zionism's "utopian realism," which, among other things, has saved Zionism from "slip[ping] down the path to totalitarianism."[80]

Yet the Zionist relation to its Jewish past is much more complicated than what Saposnik seems to suggest. This is entailed specifically in the Zionist sense of history, which we will discuss shortly. At this point, it is worth noting that, as Yael Zerubavel shows, the construction of Zionist collective identity and memory—as is the case with many other modern nationalist movements—has been as much about establishing discontinuity with the assumed nation's past as it is about the "imagining" of the nation.[81] In other words, Zionism's construction of Jewish nationhood (or, more specifically, nation-statehood) is shaped not only by the "return," "reclamations," and "reshaping" (to use Saposnik's terms) of the Jewish past,[82] but also in its interruptions of the flow of tradition—the breaking from this past.[83]

In this, Zionism may be seen as simply following a well-trodden, modern-nationalist path. As Pierre Nora notes, commenting on modern European national movements in general, the "modern metamorphosis" encapsulated in collective national memory is characterized by "distance memory." In this metamorphosis, "our relation to the past . . . is something entirely different from what we would expect from a memory: no longer a retrospective continuity but the illumination of discontinuity"; a relation of continuity with the past is "broken."[84] This is most lucidly captured in the notion of national revival or (re)birth, which symbolizes "at one and the same time a point of separation from another group and the beginning of a new life as a collective entity with a future of its own."[85] As Zerubavel shows, this is forcefully exemplified in the genre of myths of origins (in the Zionist case, embodied in the myth of Tel Hai), which "requires the twofold strategy of emphasizing a new beginning as well as discontinuity with an earlier past. 'For something genuinely new to begin,' Eliade notes, 'the vestiges and the ruins of the old cycle must be completely destroyed.'"[86]

This Zionist interruption is most famously captured in the combined notions of negating the "exilic" past and its subject, the "old" Jew, and the creation—or birth—of a "New Man" or a "New Jew" (or, preferably for many Zionist ideologues, a "New Hebrew," marking a clearer break not only from the "old" but also from the "Jew"), an ontologically distinct subject of Jewishness or Judaism. As Rina Peled's study of the European roots of the Socialist-Zionist movement shows, this "New Zionist Man" is premised, "like the Zionist movement in its entirety on the 'negation of exile,' both on the political-national plane and on the personal-existential one." Among other things, this negation, a cornerstone of Zionist ideology, means "not only the normalization of the Jewish People and its return to history as a national-political-territorial collective, but also the abolition of the Jewish individual, the 'foreign' or 'Other.'"[87] The relation between this "New Zionist Man" and its Jewish ancestors forcefully captures the eliminatory impetus of the Zionist replacement or supersessionism. "Zionism's 'New Man' is in effect the absolute opposite of the exilic type," the "old" Jew. As Peled shows, all Zionist ideological streams shared the "common basis of the negation of the exilic Jew," "internalizing antisemitic stereotypes," and ultimately developing their "different variants of a 'New Man,'" fed by contesting European ideologies of the time.[88]

The invention of this new identity—captured in a mythic notion of the Sabra,[89] and expanding in its more radical interpretations and ideological embodiments into a decidedly anti-Jewish identity in the style of the "Young Hebrews"—while it argues for a "rebirth" of the past, marks a break from it.[90] As Zerubavel notes, for the Zionists "the use of the adjective *ivri* (Hebrew) to reinforce the tie with the ancient past and to dissociate from the concept of *yehudi* (Jewish) . . . is particularly appealing as a way of marking the symbolic discontinuity between the period of Exile and the modern National Revival. Zionism wishes to present the 'Jew' with an opportunity to transform into a 'Hebrew' or, as Berdyczewski puts it, to be 'the last Jew or the first member of a new nation.'"[91]

This "desired transformation of the Jews and the construction of 'the New Jew'" also directs us to the complicated relationship of Zionist supersessionism to the Christian supersessionist hope or wish to convert the Jews. Needless to say, while many Christian Zionist visions of the restoration of the Jews to their land also entailed a necessary stage of the Jews' conversion to Christianity, Zionism, of course, lacked such a stage. Yet the creation of the "'the New Jew,' redeemed, powerful, rational, and productive who stands against the 'exilic Jew'—the representative of irrationality and decadence" is clearly indebted to the supersessionist, "Christian distinction between the new Jew and the old Jew" and preserves its basic outlines.[92]

Zionism and History

The Zionist negation of exile also sheds important light on its sense of history, which is permeated with a supersessionist outlook on its "Christian ambivalence" toward Judaism and the Jews.[93] This is captured by what David Mayers identifies as the Weberian legacy of interpreting secularism—namely, "what we may call with more than a tinge of irony—given its religious overtones—a *supersessionist* perspective." This developmental, evolutionary perspective of "progress" presents secularism as "the triumph of a modern, secular, rational, disenchanted sensibility over mystical, enchanted, and superstitious religion."[94] If we return to the suggestion that supersessionism may be approached "as an analytical category," shedding light on "the issue of self-definition," we can easily see how the secularist Zionist self-image is based exactly on this sense of a modern, secular, rational, and disenchanted sovereign self.[95]

As Amnon Raz-Krakotzkin and Jonathan Boyarin—each approaching the point from a different angle—both show, this secularist self-image is deeply indebted to a specifically Christian, Protestant, supersessionist reading of history.[96] Indeed, as Raz-Krakotzkin notes, following Carlo Ginzburg,[97] "Christian ambivalence towards the Jews" plays a constitutive role in shaping modern historical, so-called secular consciousness per se, encompassing far more than the case of Zionism and Jews. Nevertheless, this Christian ambivalence has a "unique significance" for understanding Zionism: it highlights the degree to which the Zionist project of modernizing, secularizing, and politicizing Judaism and the Jews is "a process that in reality took place through an internalization of Christian perceptions of the Jews and their exile."[98]

Viewed from this point of view, secular Zionism emerges as

an extreme manifestation of the theological-Orientalist dimension of secularism, and as a conscious internalization of Christian ambivalence toward the Jews. The "return" of the Jews to Palestine, to the East, was based on complete identification with . . . the Christian imagination of the land of the ancient Hebrews—and through it, the denial of both the Arab East and of historical Judaism. Thus, despite the Zionist rhetorical rejection of "assimilationist trends," the movement can in fact be read as an extreme expression of the desire to assimilate the Jews into the Western narrative of enlightenment and redemption. This is manifested in the various meanings of the term "negation of exile," the concept that embodies the fundamental aspects of Zionism as an ideology and as a political-cultural phenomenon.[99]

Once again, the supersessionist claim to authenticity, of being the "true Israel," emerges as a critical matter here. The Zionist acceptance of the "Protestant theological . . . terminology of originality, authenticity, and return" means Zionism's "accommodation into the Christian perception of history, and particularly to the Protestant theological imagination." Thus, paradoxical as this may sound (at least to those who neglect to account for the Protestant roots of European secularism), "the secularization, that is to say nationalization, of Jewish consciousness meant its articulation according to the millenarian Christian vocabulary."[100]

It emerges, then, that what Zionist discourse depicted—betraying its heavy indebtedness to Hegel,[101] "prophet of the state as bearer and apotheosis of history" — as the Jews' "return to history" captures much of its supersessionist impetus.[102] As Jonathan Boyarin perceptively notes, the dominance of the Hegelian philosophy of history in Zionist thought is of crucial importance, "because he [Hegel] formulates nation-statism per se, rather than just being an Enlightenment Figure or a particular nationalist."[103]

It is exactly the combination of "Enlightenment progressivism and romantic nationalism," which is, critically, also devoid of racism or "ethnic chauvinism," that made Hegel's thought attractive to multiple nationalist programs, "including those of Jewish-state nationalists."[104] More specifically, it is the combination of the idealization of nation-statism and territoriality with a "supersessive view of history—the notion that the intellectual limitations of the past are always overcome in time"—that highlights Hegel's importance for Zionism.[105]

This "supersessive view of history," or "what might be called his [Hegel's] chauvinism of the present, a consignment of the past, whatever may have been its virtues in its time, to the dustbin of history," is reflected, of course, in the Zionist negation of the exilic past.[106] This negation creates a rupture, denying "panchrony," the view of tradition as a living, viable entity in the present.[107] The past must be overcome, the present (and future) being its superiors.

Viewing Zionism through its indebtedness to this Hegelian thinking allows us, then, to see Zionism's "thoroughly modern nationalist thrust and its progressive, Enlightened prejudices. Whereas we are used to seeing nationalism in terms of an identification with a hypostatized collective past, Zionism entails an explicit rejection of an immediate past that no longer works as the ground of Jewish identity."[108]

Zionism and Divine Election

The Zionist confrontation with and appropriation of Jewish tradition (what Hertzberg nevertheless calls "secularization") also reformulated the biblical notion of a "holy nation" or the "chosen people."[109] Here, too, God was replaced by the "national genius" in the role of the (nevertheless theological) agent anointing or choosing the nation for the task of being "light unto the nations." Yet this has clearly conflicted with the Zionist wish to "normalize" the Jewish nation—again, by means of nation-statist politics. "If the new messianism meant the normalization of the place of the Jew in the world, what unique destiny was ultimately reserved for him? If his 'end of days' is to be an honorable and secure share in the larger liberal society of the future, what remains of his 'chosenness'?"[110]

The "solution" to this dilemma was to avoid it by means of (modern) mystical reasoning. Thus, for example, in Moses Hess's thought, offering "the only apparently logical resolution to this tension between the heart and the head" and seeking to "define some grand 'modern' and 'progressive' role that Jewry alone was destined to play in fashioning the world of tomorrow."[111] Hertzberg's harsh treatment of this intellectual exercise is illuminating:

> With characteristic lack of systematic exactness, he [Hess] speaks mystically of new transcendent values which are to issue from a restored Zion (an idea in the older religious key) and of a new Jewish nation to act as the guardian of the crossroads of three continents and to be the teacher of the somnolent peoples of the East—i.e., he imagines a distinguished, *but not a determinant*, part for the Jew to play in the general *mission civilisatrice* of an expanding West.[112]

The same "doctrine" of political mysticism was also "preached" by other Zionist thinkers, offering various interpretations (fed, in turn, by the ideologues' competing political commitments, from liberalism to Marxism) of this metaphysical calling of the Jewish nation, assigning it "the role of the mentor of the Middle East, or the most blessedly modern small state, or the richest of the reviving national languages, or the most ideologically correct socialism."[113] Yet this cannot distract us from seeing how the allegedly secularized, modernized, and politicized notion of chosen-ness appropriates the traditional Jewish source.

This was most fully articulated in Ahad HaAm's writing. Seeking to assert "the continuing chosenness of the Jew in this-worldly terms," Ahad HaAm "had to claim much more"—namely, to more fully appropriate the notion of divine election (while still remaining "secular"). He thus shifted the focus of the discussion to matters of "national morals" and "national genius," arguing that these "would always remain uniquely sublime among all the creations of man." His brand of "spiritual" Zionism thus articulated a variation of the notion of messianism and chosenness where Jewish "morals" or ethics (rather vaguely defined) "comes to full flower in a national community in Palestine living as a moral priesthood whose authority is accepted by all mankind."[114]

Arthur Hertzberg's conclusion that "Zionism represents a crisis not solely in the means but in the essential meaning of Jewish messianism" holds a key to understanding Zionism's relation to Jewish history, and to Judaism more generally, allowing us to "place Zionism in its proper historical frame." Zionism, as leading advocates and students of the ideology have argued (regardless of the fact that some may find it difficult to square this with a "secularly committed" worldview), "is, indeed, the heir of the messianic impulse and emotions of the Jewish tradition, but it is much more than that; it is the most radical attempt in Jewish history to break out of the parochial molds of Jewish life in order to become part of the general history of man in the modern world."[115]

It would count as "the most radical" only if we ignore the Jewish roots, or supersessionist claims, of Christianity. Importantly, Zionism's relation to Judaism is not detached from a wider context, where gentile agency plays a major role in the shaping of this movement of Jewish nationhood. Here, too, the impetus of the influence is far from unidirectional.[116] As Saposnik argues, the Zionist "redemptive faith" nourished not only on

Jewish messianic or redemptive traditions but also, equally so, on "Christian notions of salvation" and "secular political messianic ideologies":

> Christians, Christian institutions, and Christian theologies and eschatologies, bound up with the Holy Land, remained a central—indeed, at times the central—other, from which Zionism often drew as a sounding board and as a rival. The question of redemption, and in particular redemption as bound up with the Land, was a central concern in this encounter between Zionist and Christian undertakings in Palestine and has been neglected by much of the scholarship to date.[117]

In Hertzberg's final analysis, "the tangible successes of Zionism as a movement have not . . . been widely and unquestioningly accepted as proof of the validity of Zionism as secular messianism." This is so since, regardless of what Hertzberg identifies as "the realization of some of Zionism's direst predictions, like the destruction of European Jewry," as well as its success at achieving statehood, Zionism has failed to solve what the European nationalist terminology of its time identified as the Jewish question. In other words, Zionism has failed to reframe (or, to be more attuned to the language of supersessionism, replace) Judaism and Jewishness by way of modernizing, politicizing, and secularizing them. "On the contrary, the last half century," writes Hertzberg in the late 1950s, only to be proven especially prescient in the decades since, "of Zionist thought has been marked by increased wrestling with the meaning of the Messiah ideal and by an ever-growing trend toward some kind of marriage between the religious vision and the need for Jewry to become, as best it can, an easily understandable part of the contemporary world."[118]

Zionist Supersessionism and Israeli Political Culture

When it comes to the politics of the nation-state of Israel, authors are much more ready to posit it as having replaced "old" Judaism. Thus, for example, in Shlomo Avineri's summary of the narrative, as secularization and political emancipation in modern Europe have undermined traditional, religious structures or infrastructure of the collective Jewish forms of life, "the State of Israel put the public, normative dimension back into Jewish life. Without this having ever been defined or decided upon, it is a fact that to be Jewish today means, in one way or another, feeling some link with Israel." The state becomes the core of modern Jewish identity, "the new *public* dimension of Jewish existence. . . . Israel not only is the focus of identity for those Jews who live there but also defines, more than any other factor, the Jewish identity of those Jews who do not live there but view it as central to their own self-definition as Jews."[119]

A subtitle of a recent triumphalist formulation of the same point is unequivocal: "The Zionist revolution changed history and reinvented Judaism."[120] Since the establishment of the state, the author argues, "the entire Jewish people has undergone a metamorphosis. Israel has gradually become the most important force in all areas of Jewish life. . . . Israel has consolidated its hold as the most dominant entity in the Jewish experience, defining and determining Jewish identity, memory and the place of Jews and Judaism among the nations."[121]

The impetus of this replacement or supersessionism is most fully expressed by the theopolitics of the state, in which sovereignty takes the role of the quasi-divine agent who not only protects the Jew but also completes her or him. This is expressed most clearly and provocatively in A. B. Yehoshua's typology of "full" or "complete" versus "missing" or "incomplete" Jews. As I have discussed in detail elsewhere,[122] in Yehoshua's political theology (which has its roots firmly planted in mainstream political Zionism) Jews who live under Israeli sovereignty are kind of a new, improved being, surpassing the exilic, incomplete Jews living outside of the sovereignty of Jews.[123]

In a rather obvious reference to the notion of a new covenant, Yehoshua's typology also echoes the Christian denouncement of Jewish parochialism or particularism while celebrating the "total" Zionist-Jewish identity as universal.[124] This is captured in his provocative pronouncement that non-Israeli, or diaspora ("exilic") Jews, "are partial Jews, while I [Yehoshua] am a whole Jew; In no way are we the same thing—we [Israeli Jews] are total and they [non-Israeli Jews] are partial; we are Israeli and they are Jewish. In recent years, my fellows and I have needed to defend Israel vis-à-vis the issue of the state, as if it were merely an issue of citizenship, while Israel is the authentic, deep concept of the Jewish people. . . . And it is about this deep matter that we must defend against the Jewish offensive."[125]

Here, then, the negation of exile and the creation of a "new man" is woven into the supersessionist picture, in which the authentic, total, complete, universal-in-his-nationalism New Zionist Man takes over the place of the inauthentic, incomplete, particular, and parochial old, exilic Jew, whose nationalism is "diminished."[126] Yehoshua is clearly echoing here the equally Zionist and Hegelian notion that "genuine existence is uninational and collective," that "each *person* is to be realized or to realize herself in *one* collective. The individual can be happy, reconciled to history, only when his actions are in harmony with the historical force of the nation."[127] The exilic, partial, *multi-* or non-national Jew, Yehoshua suggests, is akin to a prisoner:

> A jailed prisoner is a partial human being, in the sense that a considerable part of the horizon of human activity is blocked from him. . . . In his feeling and consciousness he is surely a whole human being, but in his reality he is lacking, he is a defected human being. The feeling and consciousness of the Jewish person in exile as a Jew is, no doubt, one and whole as a Jew, but in his *reality* as a Jew . . . he is limited, lacking and blocked. Exile is a partial, defected, and lacking situation, according to Judaism's very perception of itself.[128]

Not for nothing, Yehoshua's formulation was identified as showing "the internalization of typical anti-Semitic imageries."[129] Yet note how he claims a *Jewish* authority in positing his provocation; it is Judaism that justifies his political theology.

Yehoshua's is obviously a "hard" supersessionism that also provokes (as he himself notes) a "Jewish [counter] offensive" against which he is calling to arms. His is an absolute, binary image of either/or, where Judaism is bound to fit itself to Zionism (ideally, by way of "amputating" the sickening "religious" outgrowth of the national body) if it is to survive.[130]

Tellingly, Yehoshua's frustration with the fact that he needs to debate what for him seems obvious belies the fact that Israeli sociopolitics has sometimes dealt with Zionist supersessionism in differing ways. If we follow Novak's suggested distinction, focusing specifically on the varying degrees of dialogue between the replaced and the replacing parties, a more nuanced picture emerges: both Israeli political culture and the practical choices of Jewish Israelis show the varying ways in which the Zionist supersessionist stance is interpreted, resisted, and adapted.

On the ideological and official level, we may mention in this context the shift from the Socialist Zionist confrontational, aggressive rewriting of (Jewish) tradition to the less confrontational, more selective (in its approach to Jewish tradition) statism advocated by David Ben Gurion.[131] The Socialist Zionist movement has undertaken an aggressively combative form of supersessionism, captured most lucidly in the literal rewriting and re-forming of Jewish holidays. The Kibbutz movement's redoing of the Passover seder ritual meal and its traditional text—which brings immediately to mind the Christian seders mentioned above—is an obvious case in point. The seder and its Haggadah were neither merely abandoned, nor religiously reformed. Rather, they were resolutely rewritten and forcefully appropriated, becoming an important marker of Socialist Zionist identity.[132] Ben-Gurion, who understood that such an ideologically committed supersessionism would not resonate well with many of the Jewish communities relocating to the newly established state, many of them motivated by traditional notions of Jewish identity and Judaism, has sought a less confrontational, somewhat more dialogical—but nevertheless supersessionist—stance, in which the sovereign state is elevated to a sacred status.[133]

The development of the Israeli political culture since the ascendence of the Likud party in the late 1970s has been characterized by a further "softening" of the supersessionist stance. The vision offered by such political leaders as Menachem Begin and Benjamin Netanyahu was one in which the sacredness of the state is deemed a genuinely traditional Jewish value, sidestepping or, rather, repressing the supersessionist impetuous of the Zionist ideology they have advocated. Religious Zionism has further developed this stance into a deification of the state, in a manner where Zionist political theology becomes the only Jewish theology worthy of its name.[134]

On the sociocultural level, the softer supersessionist stance seems to have appealed to the Israeli Right's largely traditional Mizrahi constituency, for whom much of the secularist slogans accompanying the "harder" Zionist supersessionism have sounded "foreign and insipid."[135] Similarly, a movement of a (largely secularly minded) "return to the Jewish bookcase," a reclamation of Jewish texts and rituals, dubbed by one commentator a "Jewish renaissance," suggests that many Israeli Jews believe that this supersessionism might—and should—be mitigated by a reaffirmation of its commitment to certain, mostly textual, aspects of Jewish tradition.[136]

Clearly, Zionist supersessionism feeds what Joyce Dalsheim has called "Israel's Jewish problem."[137] And one of the maybe surprising effects of this problem is what Gideon Katz has identified as "the fear from Judaism in Israeli culture." This Israeli "nightmare" is, expressly so, a replacement angst, a "deep anxiety expressed by many secular Israelis that Judaism is liable to efface their identity," most simply expressed by the terror "that secularism is a passing historical episode."[138]

Katz finds this to be "an inherent element of Israeli secularism," one expression of which is "the psychological representation of Judaism as a volcanic force deep within the collective unconscious which has threatened the seemingly stable secular identity of Israeli Jews."[139] As he shows, prominent representations of the (dominant, Jewish-)Israeli identity and culture depict these as being caught in a "bitter struggle with a titanic, persistent Judaism." Spokespeople for Israeli secularism see it as holding an "inferior and vulnerable" position vis-à-vis Judaism, fearing annihilation (or, as Dalsheim's subtitle has it, "self-determination" is made into "self-elimination").[140] "In the more optimistic scenarios," Katz writes, "[Judaism] is an inherent force that threaten [Israeli identity] and undermines its foundations. It is pulled by the force of a reverse flow of time . . . and disappears in the exilic, despised Jewish past."[141]

Granted, this is clearly primarily a secularist-Israeli predicament. Yet, as Katz notes, we would be amiss to dismiss it as a merely sectorial matter. While there is obviously room to distinguish between secular Israeliness and Israeli culture more generally, the fact remains that "the secular public has been the dominant party in the creation of this culture, in the past and in the present"—hence there is every justification to "speak in the same breath of secularism and Israeli culture."[142] Indeed, the anxiety he unveils among secularist spokespeople ultimately deals with "the tension between Israeliness and Judaism" in the most general terms of both sides of this relationship. The cultural and intellectual leaders whose works Katz interrogates see Israeliness "as a version of secularism, probably its greatest achievement," as "the striving for a normal existence," a normalcy embodied in the secular political organization of life under the nation-state, as opposed to a "religious community." It is exactly the ghostly "emergence of Judaism" from the depths, prompted both by historical events and by Judaism's "untamable nature," that highlights the precariousness of this normalcy.[143]

While Katz avoids contextualizing the Israeli case in a wider theoretical framework, it is quite apparent that the phenomenon at hand fits within what Derrida has famously dubbed "hauntology," meaning a concern with the political and cultural effects of the "spectral," literal, or metaphorical ghosts of the past: apparitions, visions, and representations of that which once was and no longer is.[144] It is not hard to see how a supersessionist act of appropriation and erasure would give birth to a sense of being haunted, and there is ample historical evidence to suggest that this has been the case with Christian supersessionism.[145] Granted, Katz's analysis fits what Martha and Bruce Lincoln call a "secondary haunting,"[146] focused primarily on literary representations of the spectral, "things non-material or 'ghostly' by definition: the affective, the dead and not-quite-gone, the sensed but not seen."[147] But, clearly, for the subjects whose works he interrogates, the haunting is a "primary" one, the menacing presence of the Judaic past very real and present.[148]

This menace of the Jewish or Judaic past and the fear of its "volcanic" eruption in the Israeli, Zionist present was famously anticipated—one is tempted to say, "prophesized"—by Gershom Scholem. As he commented in his correspondence with Franz Rosenzweig (an admittedly oft-quoted letter; pardon me for quoting it here yet once again, and at length):

This country [Mandatory Palestine, or the Land of Israel, from whence he was writing to Rosenzweig] is a volcano! It harbors the language! . . . Much more sinister than the Arab problem is another threat, a threat which the Zionist enterprise unavoidably has had to face: the "actualization" of Hebrew.

Must not the conundrum of a holy language break open again now, when the language is to be handed down to our children? . . . Many believe that the language has been secularized, and the apocalyptic thorn has been pulled out. But that is not true at all. The secularization of the language is only a façon de parler, a phrase! It is impossible to empty out words which are filled to the breaking point with specific meaning—lest it be done at the sacrifice of the language itself! . . . If we could transmit to our children that language which was transmitted to us, and if we could revitalize the language of the ancient books in this transitional genera-tion, would it not then reveal itself to them? And then, would not the religious power of this language perforce break open again one day? . . . Is it not true that almost all of us live with this language over a volcano with the false security of the blind. Must not we or those who came after us stumble into the abyss when we fail to see again? And nobody can know whether the sacrifice of those who perish will suffice to close the hole and avoid the plunge into the abyss. . . . Today it seems weird to us and at times we are scared and frightened to hear a religious phrase quite out of place, in a totally unrelated context. *Fraught with danger is the Hebrew language!* . . . God will not remain silent in the language in which He has affirmed our life a thousand times and more. This unavoidable revolution of the language, in which His voice will be heard again, is the only issue that is not spoken about today in this country. Those who called the Hebrew language back to life did not believe in this trial yet they created it. May it not come to pass that the imprudence which has led us on this apocalyptic road ends in ruin.[149]

Katz's cultural explanation for this Israeli sense of being haunted by Judaism is indeed revealing. Consider, for example, the "demonic char-acter" of Judaism, as it emerges from this Israeli fear: Judaism, "as a religion," is "frozen, totalistic, as if it exists in another reality"; it is "un-familiar," and it "erupts." The encounter with it results in a "metamor-phosis" of the individual, who "does not remain in his/her identity but is displaced from it." This Judaism, Katz summarizes, is not something with which one can have a "vital" contact, yet it is taken to be somehow part of the individual: "Judaism is in us, nesting in us, belongs to us, and is just the same foreign and unknown." Referencing Barukh Kurzweil and Yeshayahu Leibowitz, Katz finds "the avoiding of contact" with Ju-daism to be "the most accurate description of Israeli culture, its sources and its distress." The self-perception of Israeliness, captured in Ahad HaAm's "basic proposition regarding the replacement" (i.e., taking the place of traditional Judaism, through appropriating and transforming or nationalizing, as in rendering it a national culture, its basic content and concepts), ended up rendering Israeliness "estranged" from Judaism. In

Katz's reading, given the fact that the Jewish people has traditionally carried an "intensive religious content," the Israeli "substitute" (*tahlif*) is "bound to remain insufficient."[150]

Conclusion

So what? What exactly is at stake in identifying Zionism as supersessionist vis-à-vis Judaism?

It all comes down to the *Judaic* question: What happens to Judaism—to these vast, varying, dynamic traditions of Jewish communities all over the globe and across millennia—in the process of being appropriated and allegedly superseded by a political ideology and nation-statist politics? Brian Klug's summation of the issue at the core of Christian supersessionism is informative in our case, too. Problematizing the identification of the Jewish people with the biblical Israelite nation, he writes: "It comes to this: Christians and Jews alike appropriate the Hebrew text—and it is a perfectly appropriate thing to do. What is not appropriate is to take one another's take away from each other, stamping our own brand upon it or erasing it altogether."[151] In other words, while appropriation alone may be tolerable, it is the ensuing erasure that accompanies it that highlights the problem at hand. The supersessionist party not only "replaces" the "old"; it also negates and erases it.

The discussion of supersessionism, appropriation, and erasure is necessarily a complicated one. Any simple, naive suggestion that one side ("traditional Judaism," in our case) stands by idly, passively witnessing another party (Zionism) going about actively and self-assertively appropriating and claiming to have replaced it and made it redundant, is bound to be found lacking, even misleading. Here, it may be helpful to return to Novak's typology of hard and soft supersessionism, and especially to his suggestion that this is not a one-sided relation, nor is it one-dimensional; rather, there are also hard and soft *Jewish* supersessionist stances vis-à-vis Christianity.

Jewish hard supersessionism, Novak writes, "is the inverse of the Christian version. This Jewish position holds not that Christianity has superseded Judaism; instead, it is Judaism that has superseded Christianity." Obviously, this is not a temporal but a theological argument:

"For Jewish hard supersessionists, Christianity is not *progressive* in relation to its Jewish origin. Instead, Christianity *regresses* to the pagan or
idolatrous past that Judaism has superseded." These Jewish hard supersessionists (it might be better to call them "countersupersessionists," as
they formulate their stance against the background of Christian supersessionist dominance) are thus "often vociferous opponents of contemporary Jewish-Christian dialogue." In effect, they deny that Christianity
has Jewish roots (something the Christian supersessionist cannot do),
"assert[ing] that Judaism has no connection to Christianity whatsoever."
Hence, while "Christians cannot deny their origin in Judaism however
much they might claim to have superseded Judaism," the Jewish stance
at hand prefers to shut down dialogue and to "ignore Christianity, treating it as a regrettable and theologically regressive offshoot of Judaism."[152]

Novak, who himself is calling for a Jewish-Christian dialogue in the
face of a common enemy—that of the militant secularism, who "in a real
sense . . . claims to supersede both Judaism and Christianity, insisting
it has the sole right to legislate public morality"—nevertheless believes
that some sort of ("soft" or "inner") Jewish supersessionism is nevertheless needed. This Jewish supersessionism, he suggests, is essential for
Jewish self-preservation, since, "without some kind of supersessionism
on our part, Jews like me would have no cogent reason for not going
forward into what Christians regard as Judaism's fulfillment." It is this
supersessionism, an "*inner* Jewish matter," that allows Jews "to explain
to ourselves why we remain Jewish and do not become Christians."[153]

It is tempting to ask whether (self-professed secularist) Zionist
nationalism should be read as part of this "common enemy" of both
Christianity and Judaism—namely, the "hostile . . . militant secularism"
that "lumps together" Jews and Christians, "imagin[ing] that humanity
has 'progressed' beyond divine authority and biblical morality."[154] The
confrontational Zionist stance of ideologues like Brenner, Berdyczewski, and Syrkin would obviously lend itself to such a reading. Yet more
important is the notion that the two types of what Novak calls Jewish
supersessionism vis-à-vis Christianity can be employed to also understand two types of Jewish (or Judaic) reactions to Zionist supersessionism, between which a spectrum of variations opens up. Limits of space
and scope dictate that the following consideration of these reactions is
necessarily only preliminary and generalized in nature. I will also refrain

from calling these reactions (as might be suggested by Novak) "superses-sionism," instead simply noting the varying degrees of rejection of—or dialogue with—Zionist supersessionism they offer.

The first, hard, rejectionist Judaic stance against Zionism can take both an Orthodox and a progressive (to use, in both cases, the self-professed identities of the actors involved) shape.[155] The former, Ortho-dox stance is captured rather forcefully by ultra-Orthodox anti-Zionism, as formulated and practiced by the likes of Joel Teitlebaum, his Satmer Hassidim, and the Neturei Karta group.[156] In the straightforward formu-lation of Yisroel Weiss, these parties offer Judaism as an "alternative to Zionism."[157] Adhering to Orthodox interpretations of Jewish theology and history, their critiques are explicit in positing Judaism *against* "the pseudo religion of Zionism,"[158] arguing that "Judaism and Zionism are antithetical and contradictory," and that "Zionists are misinterpreting Judaism."[159] Blaming "the aftermath of the Enlightenment" for Zionism's success, Weiss speaks directly against Zionism's basic ideological funda-mentals, such as "changing the definition of Jewry from that of a people of faith, intent on achieving closeness to the Creator in this world, to that of a barren secular, ethnic identity." The Zionist anti-exilic stance is rendered theologically heretical, damaging "both exilic missions (re-pentance and serving as a 'light onto the nations')." The Judaic rejection of Zionist supersessionism accordingly sees the "the total dismantling of the Israeli state" as the only potential reconciliation of these opposites. Clearly, no room is left here for dialogue.[160]

The progressive anti-Zionist position draws its sources largely from a wide array of modern Western philosophical engagements with ethics and aims explicitly to draw on a variety of Jewish/Judaic sources (e.g., "Jewish secular, socialist, and religious traditions") to critique Zion-ism.[161] Thus, for example, in Judith Butler's call for Jews and Zionism to "part ways," showing that "Jewish critique of Israeli state violence is at least possible, if not ethically obligatory" and "affirming a different Jewishness than the one in whose name the Israeli state claims to speak." For Butler, it is essential to escape the "claim to [Jewish] exceptionalism," encapsulated in a reliance on Jewish sources to make an ethical claim against Zionism. In other words, she would be explicitly critical of a Jew-ish reaction to Zionist supersessionism that is not ultimately "refused in favor of more fundamental democratic values." For her, "the opposition to Zionism requires the departure from Jewishness as an exclusionary framework for thinking both ethics and politics."[162]

Both variations of Judaic anti-Zionism are at pains to break apart the identification between Jews/Judaism and the State of Israel—to show, that is, that Israel does not represent the Jewish people and its histories, and that not all Jews support the state "by default." Much attention is given in this context to Zionism's attempt at "normalizing" the Jewish people as opposed to fulfilling its covenantal mission. A rather striking example of this comes from "a writer who is concerned with the spiritual substance of Jewish tradition in terms of modern thought," writing under the pen name Yehudi Adam.[163] Starting with an explication of the covenantal meaning of the biblical notion of the "chosen people" and the history it entails, and contrasting this meaning with nationalist readings of chosen-ness and history, the writer posits Judaism and political Zionism as total opposites:

> Bearing in mind that "Jewish" may mean "of the Jews" and "of Judaism", we may say: political Zionism is a negation of all that Judaism has stood for since the Hebrew tribes became a nation at Mt. Sinai. . . . For anyone who is sufficiently familiar with the Jewish sources and with Jewish history to know that dedication to a spiritual task and destiny is the very essence of Judaism, which has made the Jewish people unique and immortal, it is a plain fact that Judaism and the ideology of political Zionism are mutually exclusive. Whoever affirms the political Zionist's aim to normalize the Jewish people repudiates Judaism, and whoever understands what Judaism is and stands up for it implicitly rejects political Zionism, whether he is aware of it or not.[164]

Soft Jewish reactions, on the other hand, are less ready to break the tie between Zionism and the Jews. This is so since, in most cases, they tend to accept the reading of modern history, and especially the Holocaust, as proving the basic Zionist premise right. In other words, if the common enemy uniting Christian and (soft-supersessionist) Jews, in Novak's formulation, is militant secularism, then in our case it is antisemitism that pushes Jewish reactions to Zionist supersessionism to allow varying degrees of correspondence between Israeli or Zionist nation-statism and Judaism. Sometimes this lands those who present such soft reactions in the position of adherent Jewish/Judaic critics of Zionism. Writers such as Yeshayahu Leibowitz, Barukh Kurtzweil, Simon Rawidowicz, and Leon Roth come to mind as fascinating examples of such commentators who have employed a Judaically informed ethical judgment of Israel (in chapter 5 of this book I discuss the case of Leon Roth's interventions).[165] They have often noted the price exerted from Judaism itself by actions of the Jewish state, often embracing a "Jewish exceptionalism" view by which, to paraphrase Roth, it is perfectly reasonable to expect a Jewish polity—that is, a polity committed to Judaic ethics—to behave more ethically than the gentile norm might suggest.[166]

We may also identify a soft Judaic reaction among adherents of what we may term as "Zionistically agnostic," mostly denominationally Orthodox Jews, who seem to believe that the State of Israel, with all its problematically secular Zionist underpinnings, can nevertheless promote the interests of Judaism. This attitude is best captured, if I am not mistaken, in the pragmatic stance of parties representing the ultra-Orthodox communities in Israel, cooperating and coalitioning with Israeli governments ruled by Zionist parties, even when their rabbinical or spiritual leadership professes an uncompromising critique and even rejection of Zionism. A forceful expression of this stance was the assertive declaration by Aryeh Deri, then the political leader of Shas, before the 1999 elections that Shas—with its commitment to an Orthodox observance of Sephardi Judaism—represents the real Zionism. While confrontational, it is not hard to see how such a stance could offer a dialogue between the two sides.[167]

As noted earlier, an exhaustive discussion of these and other Jewish or Judaic reactions to what emerges as Zionist supersessionism is obviously beyond the scope of the current discussion, and the above is admittedly rendered with only wide brushstrokes. What it nevertheless shows is that a reading of Zionism as supersessionism does not leave Judaism mute or passive in face of the Zionist appropriation of the meaning of modern Jewishness. A detailed exploration of these reactions must remain to be explored elsewhere.[168]

3

Israeli Nostalgia

Introduction: The Problem of the Israeli Past

The State of Israel—or, to be specific, the political culture prevalent in the state—has a problem with history: being the culmination of the Zionist ideology and the political project it has propelled, it cannot "simply" tie itself to its immediate, Jewish histories, which are carried by its population. As we have seen, the Zionist bedrock of this political culture has been preoccupied with breaking away from what it has viewed as exilic, defeatist Jewish history. It sought a "rebirth" of a "New Zionist Man," and, ultimately, a new national identity, and even, in the more extreme renditions of erasure, of a new nation (Israeli, Hebrew), separated and distinguished from the "old" Jewish one. In light of this, Israeli identity has been shaped as something of a new creation, formed in opposition to the exilic Jewish past. Yet the state still claims to be a "Jewish state," and the nation in the name of which it claims sovereignty is the Jewish, not Israeli, nation.

Much of this tension is captured in a certain prevalent and influential Israeli nostalgia. This nostalgia and its correspondence with other Israeli nostalgias shed further light on "Israel's Jewish problem." To appreciate it, we may begin with some comments made by the renowned philosopher Avishai Margalit, who addresses this matter in the context of discussing the ethics of memory. Being concerned with collective memory, Margalit turns naturally to discuss the political significance of nostalgia, and his judgment is unequivocal: nostalgia is politically dangerous and morally deficient. As a "moral sentiment," Margalit notes, nostalgia can turn dangerous, since it "tends to distort the reality of the time past . . . in a morally disturbing way." Nostalgia "idealizes its object . . . and locates it in a time of great purity and innocence, thus the object . . . is enshrined with purity and innocence."

More immediately relevant to the political frame of reference are instances where nostalgia becomes "vicarious memory," in which one's memory is "plugged" by the memories of others. Margalit singles out what he calls "nostalgic kitsch," which he judges to be a "manifestation of moral failure." This failure has obvious political imports: "Memory, like any other form of knowledge, is power. Whoever controls memory and forgetting gains in power." Nostalgia "can easily be put in service of brutality," justifying acts (such that, for example, would aim to restore the presumed purity of the past) that would otherwise be indefensible. More specifically, there is the matter of the "*politics* of memory, namely, the means and the ways in which memory—especially collective memory—is shaped and manipulated by political agencies, for political gains." Importantly, "the politics of *memory* is also the politics of *forgetting*; creating and maintaining social amnesia by political agencies."[1]

Margalit, who was born in Mandatory Palestine, grew up in Jerusalem, and has lived most of his life in Israel, offers two corresponding examples of nostalgia derived from his experiences as an Israeli. He suggests that they are equivalent in their "systematic distortion" and "idealizing [of] the past," their promotion of "sentimentality" and "kitsch morality." These examples have to do with what Margalit calls "the conflict in our contested debatable land Israel/Palestine." Identifying all main actors in this conflict as "saturated with vicarious nostalgia," Margalit ties together and in effect equates, in terms of their ethical insidiousness, two remembrances of the past that are prevalent among Israeli Jews, and that he sees as exemplifying the "pernicious nostalgia in our promised/punished land":

On one hand, some people of my generation and upbringing nourish Ashkenazi nostalgia for the pristine society of the Yishuv (the pre-state Hebrew community in Palestine) and to the early days of Israel, before the invasion of immigrants from Islamic countries. On the other hand, there is the counter nostalgia of some immigrants from Islamic countries, saying, we lived happily in our innocent and pure communities in Marrakesh, and Bagdad, based on respect for parents and elders, till you soulless Ashkenazi transposed us to your state and ruined, beyond repair, our innocence and beautiful form of life.[2]

It is safe to assume that no student of Israeli society would argue with Margalit about the prevalence and basic outlines of these two nostalgias; they are common currency in Israeli culture. Yet, contrary to Margalit's bundling together of the two cases (I will dub these, for the sake of simplicity, the Ashkenazi and the Mizrahi nostalgias, respectively) as exemplifying the same ethical-political import of nostalgia—and a matter that is out of Margalit's frame of reference but is of interest to our discussion here, the same attitude toward their respective Jewish histories—it is not hard to see that there are some obvious, politically crucial differences between the two. The two nostalgias are held and propagated by groups that occupy different social classes and have distinctly different access to power and privilege. To put it simply, one is the nostalgia of the dominant, the other of the dominated (at least as far as we focus solely on the Jewish-Israeli majority; as I will mention shortly, the Palestinian minority's presence also looms large here, but rather implicitly so).

Needless to say, the two nostalgias both remember and forget or silence elements of the pasts they valorize. Looked at politically, however—that is, with a consideration of the political, power-related implications of this remembering/forgetting—they clearly differ from each other. While the Ashkenazi nostalgia forcefully erases or silences the Palestinian presence in the "purity" of the "pristine" Good Old Land of Israel, the Mizrahi nostalgia at best silences chapters of discord between a Muslim majority and a Jewish minority in Arab and Muslim lands. (It is interesting to note that Margalit himself, while immediately situating these nostalgias in the "contested debatable land Israel/Palestine" leaves this silencing out of the story, making it primarily about the relation between Ashkenazi and Mizrahi Jews in Israel.)

The two nostalgias engage with the Jewish past in different manners. For the Ashkenazi nostalgia, the Jewish (European or otherwise) past is absent; it yearns for a Zionist, so-called Israeli (even though the reference is usually to the pre-1948 past), post-rupture-from-Jewish-exile, pristine origin. The Mizrahi nostalgia, on the other hand, is explicitly a yearning for a "diasporic" *Jewish* past, which it valorizes. Each of the two nostalgias also offers a rather radically different political horizon (even if not a political program per se) than the other. They each provide, in other words, a view into motivations for political action, allow us an understanding of how the political agents involved view themselves and their political counterparts, and teach us something about potential future courses of action they may be prone to take. And these, quite clearly, are of different political import.

The Ashkenazi yearning for the "good old times" of the "pristine society" of the Yishuv and early Israeli statehood, "before the invasion of immigrants from Islamic countries" (and, we may add, when it comes to the period of early Israeli statehood, after the expulsion of Palestinians from the land) has an obvious eliminatory aspect to it, both in its remembering and in its forgetting. A political embodiment of this nostalgic remembering/forgetting would conceivably also yield a striving for silencing those disturbing Mizrahi Others, who have gradually become more vocal in the Israeli public and political spheres while maintaining the silence(ing) of the Palestinians. What one is nostalgic for here is exactly the absence of these disturbances (if we wish to stick to the purity metaphor, we may see them as no less than contaminations). The group who shares this nostalgia has held the privileged position in the Israeli configuration of power, and its members bemoan a sense of the cohort's undermining by newcomers and other Others. To jump straight into the political hotbed of what Margalit calls the "conflict in our contested debatable land Israel/Palestine," the political message entailed in this Zionist Ashkenazi (settler) nostalgia is that a so-called solution to the conflict—the very meaning of peace—would aim to yield these silences, to recreate a political reality where Mizrahim (and Palestinians, always present but often only implicitly so, in matters of Israeli political culture; and here simply erased from the picture, their dispossession composing the background of the pristine past) are absent, and Ashkenazi Israelis are able to enjoy undisturbed the good of the land that is now theirs. "Pernicious" indeed.

On the other hand, what Margalit labels the "counter nostalgia" of Israeli Mizrahim (to use the common although not uncontested term for Israelis who hail from Islamic and Arab countries) offers as a political horizon an inclusivity that is gravely missing from a political reality determined by what is often called—a misnomer nonetheless—the "Jewish-Arab conflict." The memory of a generally (relatively, even) peaceful conviviality in Arab and Muslim countries that was violently disrupted by the nationalist project of establishing a nation-state for Jews in Palestine suggests political trajectories that are indeed *counterintuitive* to the nation-statist, eliminatory mindset: it yearns for a time of cohabitation and mutual respect between Jews and Muslims, even if it does not go all the way to question the basic Jew versus Arab binary, the Zionist construction of which preceding and enabling the actual uprooting of Arab-Jews from their homelands and the dispossession of the Palestinians. The range of solutions to the Israeli-Palestinian conflict such a nostalgic horizon may offer (although this conflict is not its primary concern, and it, too, leaves the Palestinians silent) is indeed starkly different politically, as well as morally and ethically, from what the Ashkenazi yearning for the "Good Old Land of Israel" may yield.

Needless to say, the Mizrahi nostalgia is no less liable to being appropriated by a nation-statist set of interests. While it valorizes a pre-Zionist, Jewish past in the lands of exile, it can still be adapted and adopted to serve the state. This is quite apparent in the advocacy of certain civil society organizations that claim to speak for Mizrahi and Sephardi Jews, who maintain a dual agenda of simultaneously celebrating the Jewish past in Muslim and Arab lands and valorizing the Israeli state as having redeemed these communities and as protecting Jewish existence itself. Recent attempts at asserting a Mizrahi identity politics and a Mizrahi approach to Judaism similarly tie the advocacy of what we may term Mizrahi "traditionism"[3] with outright Zionist chauvinism.[4] Nevertheless, it is not difficult to see that, at root, this nostalgia opens up a political horizon that transcends nation-statism.

It may not be out of place to ask why Margalit labels this Mizrahi nostalgia a "counter" memory. What does it stand contra to? If the original (Ashkenazi) nostalgia is about the Mizrahi (and, less directly but as forcefully, Palestinian) absence from the scene, then this Mizrahi nostalgia agrees on the basic distribution: it, too, yearns for a time when Mizrahim were not in Israel (it leaves unattended the question of the Ashkenazi presence there). Here, in the Mizrahi nostalgia, the nationalist frame of reference falls apart. The national "us" is no longer uniform or united, and what the nationalist perspective would see as a "return" and "ingathering of exiles" is portrayed as uprooting and colonization. Moreover, the uprooted-turned—colonializers, those who were brought into the national/ colonial project after its course has been set, yearn to leave the colony and to return to what they dare call their (old) home. Their nostalgia directly, even if not explicitly, challenges the notion of Israel being a ("national") home for Jews the world over.

Why, then, call this a "counter memory"? On one level, it clearly speaks against Zionist Ashkenazi hegemony and its "settler memory," remembering (or dreaming; here lies the political impetus of this memory, invented or otherwise) a time outside of this hegemony.[5] In this sense, "counter" here bears more immediate political import: the nostalgia at hand speaks contra power, or at least longs for a configuration of power different from the present one. It is about the yearnings of the dispossessed, the marginalized, to be less so.

On a deeper level (which Margalit must be attentive to), the Mizrahi nostalgia also stands in contradiction to a certain narration, and negation, of the Jewish past, which lies as a somewhat hidden geological layer of the Ashkenazi nostalgia. Salo Baron called it a "lachrymose" narration or memory of the Jewish past as one long, continuous list of persecutions, pogroms, and all-out misery, a (meta)historical background against which the Zionist idyl in Palestine (including its justification of the dispossession of Palestinians) is defined and shaped.[6] The Mizrahi nostalgia contrasts this bleak image with a generally rosy (or maybe simply less catastrophic, more nuanced) image of cohabitation that renders the ethnonationalist upheaval of life in what Zionist ideology derides as "exile" less urgent, if not outright needless, its price, paid both by the uprooted Jewish communities and the dispossessed Palestinians, unjustified. The message here could be read as unquestionably subversive. No wonder, then, that another author, offering an explicitly political Zionist consideration of the sources of Zionist thought, labels this "counter-narrative" of Jewish history (countering, that is, the Zionist negation of exile)—what he cynically terms "an idyl of Muslim-Jewish 'coexistence' in the Arab world"—as anti-Israeli Arab propaganda: "This false myth of a Jewish-Muslim idyl should be denounced as what it really is: a political trick aimed at delegitimizing Zionism and Jewish nationalism. It is a shame that from time-to-time Jews, too, fall prey to it."[7]

Nostalgia and the Study of Israeli Politics

Allow me to digress here for a moment from the immediate concern with Israeli political culture and reflect upon what these particular nostalgias can tell us about the value of nostalgia for studying politics more generally. As we have seen, the two instances of Israeli nostalgia offer competing—conflicting, even—political horizons that could potentially be translated into political action. More importantly, they offer the observer of Israeli society a detailed look into such foundational aspects of political reality as the way in which political agents understand their being-in-the-world; their relation to their past; their grievances, preferences, and yearnings. Crucially, the point of view offered by the study of these nostalgias spells out such attitudes toward these matters that may be otherwise unpalatable or unacceptable to certain mindsets (say, a self-perceived enlightened, liberal-democratic point of view) and would most likely be denied when addressed directly (in public opinion surveys, for example).

In this regard, nostalgia proves to be a valuable tool for political analysis. The Israeli case suggests a more general notion, by which the study of nostalgia can yield an insightful view of politics that other approaches to the study of politics may fail to expose. Nostalgia is often approached dismissively; historians tend to judge it as shallow, kitschy. In this, it is just like myth: both are obviously "distortions" of the past, but both have obvious political import. And it is my suggestion that we should study nostalgia with the same level of seriousness that we have come to study myth as an important element of sociopolitical reality.[8]

To be clear: our concern here is not with the politically concerned critique of nostalgia, but with its analytical usage for the study of politics. It goes without saying that nostalgia is far from a neglected topic of commentary and study, and it would be futile to try and survey the literature on the subject, which covers such diverse fields as psychology, history, literature, art, and anthropology. Furthermore, as an object of political criticism, nostalgia has sparked many a brilliant intervention, some of which enjoying a lasting impact on political discourse—especially so, it seems, in the American case.[9]

Closer to the aim here, nostalgia is also often evoked to explain certain political developments. These explanations often suggest (and rarely explicate) a causal scheme, where nostalgia, or the yearning entailed in it, motivate political action.[10] Yet these are often retrospective scholarly exercises, seeking to explain, in hindsight, how certain political programs have triumphed, contradicting what many commentators thought would happen. Often, commentaries identifying these and other cases as instances of nostalgia employ the concept to highlight the irrational nature of the motivations behind these developments.

What I would suggest instead, following the lessons offered by the Israeli case, is that we approach nostalgia as we would other cultural forms to understand how agents instill their reality with meaning, how they understand their world and their place within it, and how they might choose to act in pursuing the horizons opened—or narrowed—for them by these understandings and meanings. As Richard Hofstadter has noted, dealing with what he saw as the American obsession with nostalgia, the constant, sentimental, and distorting reference to the past speaks volumes about how the agents involved see their future: nostalgia can be both retrospective and prospective.[11] As Barbara Cassin puts it, the "nostalgia of the past" is also a "strange memory of the future."[12] Or, in Svetlana Boym's phrasing, "Fantasies of the past determined by needs of the present have a direct impact on realities of the future. Consideration of the future makes us take responsibility for our nostalgic tales."[13] Nostalgia, then, allows the observer a view into a prevalent worldview, an outlook of what is to come, against the background of which the agents shape (also) their politics. In the context of the current discussion, nostalgias can help us see some potential futures of Jewish politics.

To a certain degree, the critique of nostalgia is trivial, even tautological: it goes almost without saying that we tend to embellish our pasts, and to call something "nostalgic" is by a certain prevalent definition to identify it as a mirage, as an image of something that never really was, a cleansed and beautified version of our pasts. But this is not to say that a critical study of nostalgia—or, more importantly, the study of a political culture through a study of its nostalgia(s)—is without merit. On the contrary, it is my argument that exactly because of its naive nature, nostalgia offers us a clear insight into the political self-perception of the group sharing this narrative, or image, of its supposedly unblemished past.

Furthermore, given the "recreational" nature that often characterizes the practice of nostalgia (e.g., the cultural exercise of digging for the past, recreating it, celebrating it) demands resources, from time to money, nostalgia can prove to be helpful in studying those who benefit from the dominant configuration of power. Of course, Others, too, have nostalgias. But, given that the political study of the powerful is more challenging, since the prevailing configuration of power tends to hide behind the images, ideas, symbols, and myths it depicts as collectively appealing, nostalgia holds a potential of offering us an uncommonly intimate view of what the powerful tend to fantasize.

In short, the study of nostalgia should be an integral part of the tool kit of students of politics, standing alongside the study of political myths, symbols, and collective memory. The merit of the study of nostalgia for political analysis is clearly illustrated by the Israeli case at hand. Specifically, we will focus on manifestations and outgrowths of what Margalit identifies as the nostalgia of his generation and ethnoclass—that is, the middle-class Zionist Ashkenazi nostalgia. Given the prevalent configuration of power in Israel, which puts this ethnoclass at the center of power, it is safe to identify this as the nostalgia of the powerful.

Nostalgia, Meaning, and Power

Clearly, the very notion that the study of nostalgia can or should be part of political analysis is indebted to an interpretive approach to political science, committed to the notion that the main task of students of politics is to understand *why* people act the way they do. It is, in other words, part of a larger social-scientific worldview that sees social analysis as complete only when it allows an understanding of behavior. This necessarily involves a reconstruction and analysis of how the political agents view their world and instill it with meaning.[14]

Nostalgia is one of the cultural, social, and political forms that function to articulate and maintain this meaning-instilling process. As Kathleen Stewart puts it:

> Nostalgia is an essential, narrative, function of language that orders events temporally and dramatizes them in the mode of "things that happened," that "could happen," that "threaten to erupt at any moment." By resurrecting time and place, and a subject *in* time and place, it shatters the surface of an atemporal order and a prefab cultural landscape. To narrate is to place oneself in an event and a scene—to make an interpretive space— and to relate something to someone: to make an interpretive space that is relational and in which meanings have direct social referents.[15]

Moreover, like myth, nostalgia offers multilayered and multivocal narratives that speak to various audiences in divergent ways. As Svetlana Boym puts it, "Nostalgia speaks in riddles and puzzles, so one must face them in order not to become its next victim—or its next victimizer."[16] This suggestive nature of nostalgia's messaging highlights that whatever is the nature of our scholarly engagement with nostalgia, analyzing it necessitates interpretation.

The narratives—and their meanings—that nostalgia tells or propagates are often constructed *against* the prevalent sociopolitical reality, enabling an alienation or distancing of this reality, hence allowing us (at least potentially) to approach it without being immersed in it. Nostalgia "is a pained, watchful desire to frame the cultural present in relation to an 'other' world—to make of the present a cultural object that can be seen, appropriated, refused, disrupted or 'made something of.'"[17] As Kathleen Stewart explains, following Pierre Bourdieu, this allows us a view into how a certain "self" draws images of distinction that put that same self in a politically privileged position:

> Culture is "seductive" only from the "point of view" of a "self" whose (polemical) cultural practice it is to construct codes of distinction and good taste—a pure aesthetic that is rooted in an ethos of elective distance from the contingency of the natural and social world. Here the desire is to purify, reify, and miniaturize the social world and so to make a giant of the individual self. Here, individual life narratives dramatize acts of separation-freedom, choice, creativity, imagination, the power to model and plan and act *on* life. From here there is the danger of being drawn in by images that are "larger than life" or have "a life of their own."[18]

Yet, as Stewart is quick to note, there is an alternative approach to nostalgia, that of the "others": "In an 'other' place there are 'others' whose practice it is to speak from 'closeness' and contingency, to 'talk back' to codes with the informality of anticodes and to back talk 'distinction' with universalizing ethics of personhood." This is a quintessentially subversive stance, since it strives to reform the prevalent configuration of power by rendering it no longer obvious and given, but contested, offering alternative contexts in which to create meaning and to understand reality:

For these "others" on the "margins" the social world is not reified and fixed but thrown into flux and doubleness. Talk is double-voiced, codes are visible from one mode of attentiveness and quite invisible from another so that they refer, inescapably, to the context of their social use. Here it is recognized that everything "depends"; meaning can only be made and read in a "context" that is not just a "background" for the "text" but its very inspiration—its enabling condition. Here texts are contingent and they are *about* contingency. From here nostalgia is a painful homesickness that generates desire and not, in itself, "seductive" or debased; it would be said that seduction and debasing are things that *people* do and not things inherent in a cultural form. Like other cultural practices in places like this, nostalgia sets in motion a dialectic of closeness and distantiation; its goal is not the creation of a code based on empty distinctions but the redemption of expressive images and speech.[19]

This distinction between the nostalgias of the dominant and the dominated is echoed in Gayle Greene's insistence that we distinguish between, on the one hand, nostalgia that is primarily "a forgetting," a depiction of the past that is "merely regressive" and reactionary, and, on the other, nostalgia that allows a memory or a reconstruction of the past that is liberating ("feminist memory" is Greene's example).[20] It is important to note this distinction, since it can help us avert a "hostile critique" of nostalgia, as both Stuart Tannock and Michael Kenny warn against.[21] Rather, as Kenny insists, it allows room for studying "the different affective, sentimental and ideational roles that various kinds of nostalgia practice perform."[22] Granted, context plays a crucial role here, and there is no way to absolutely, clearly, preventatively distinguish between regressive or oppressive and liberating nostalgias. The very act of interpretation, noted earlier, is key here.

Nevertheless, it seems rather apparent that this distinction—between nostalgia that is primarily a regressive, reactionary forgetting, seeking to reify the prevailing configuration of power, a nostalgia that gives the self who sees itself as "larger than life" a life of its own; and nostalgia that undermines and subverts this configuration by contextualizing it and by remembering what the powerful wish to forget—can shed much light on the two nostalgias discussed by Margalit. The Ashkenazi dominance seeking to reaffirm (and re-create) itself as the "natural" order of things by propagating a forgetful nostalgia for the Good Old Land of Israel, for a time when everything was simple and pure, contested by a Mizrahi "dialectic of closeness and distantiation" propagating a nostalgia that seeks to "redeem" an alternative interpretation of political reality, where the prevailing configuration of power will no longer be a given.[23] Significantly for the current discussion, this subversiveness also calls for a different appreciation of, and attitude toward, the Jewish past.

Israeli Nostalgia

Arguing against what he saw as a certain contemporaneous political pre-occupation of his sociopolitical cohort, regular contributor to *Haaretz* Gideon Levy sought to contextualize this preoccupation within what he insightfully identified as a recurring pattern in Israeli political culture: nostalgia. There is, he argued, "a tried-and-true tendency in Israel: the longing for what used to be, and even more so, the longing for what never was." Identifying the dominant spirit of the time of his writing as "dystopian," Levy found that his cohort's reaction to it fits a pattern: "Israel has always longed for its past and embellished it . . . we were taught to miss the right things and not to know the rest." Levy offers a firsthand account of the prevalence of nostalgia in the very young years of Israeli nationhood, which correspond with his and his peers' childhood:

> Israel has always longed for its past and embellished it. In 1960, Hed Arzi Music issued a double album, "Hayo Hayu Zmanim" ("Once Upon a Time: Israeli Hit Tunes of Yesteryear"). . . . At barely 12 years old, the state was already longing for its past. They were the first records in most Israeli homes. We played them dozens of times, in a premature, over-the-top bursts of nostalgia. It's how we were taught to miss the right things and not to know the rest. Sixty years later and the song's the same.[24]

Levy identifies three core elements in this "nostalgia of deceit" and the embellished past it fantasizes, echoing or reformulating what Margalit summarizes as "Israel the beautiful and the just, before the scoundrel came to power": "The exemplary democracy, the free media and the glorious secularism that thrived here once and are no more." Yet, as must be the case with every nostalgia, "the truth is that things were . . . not as good as people say."[25] He thus goes on to contrast the message instilled in this nostalgia with the rather grim reality of the past it valorizes. But what is important for our purposes here is the obviously political nature of the message propagated by this nostalgia: it is about the political preferences, self-perception, and discontent of a liberal-Zionist class that views its predominance as waning.

What this nostalgia allows us is a view—an intimate one, at that—of the self-construction of the Israeli liberal secular Left, and, by implication, a view of what its political program may be aiming to yield. In other words, it is exactly this first-person plural, the "we" that dominates Levy's column, that must be interpolated: because it is nostalgia that defines—at least in this specific cultural-political context—the "we." Or, more accurately, it defines what the spokespeople of this "we" would want it to look like, shaping political agency and directing its hoped-for future. As Boym reminds us, the word nostalgia is a compound of *nostos* (we, us) and *algia* (longing). And this compound holds volumes in terms of political significance: *algia* can bring "us" together, create empathy with others, and motivate us to achieve goals that are quintessentially political. But it is exactly that "we," *nostos*, the first-person plural, that defines what the wider (national, social) "we" looks like, or should look like: who is in and who is not. Ultimately, it creates division when leaving those "strangers," the "not us," out.[26]

In the case at hand, the first-person plural offers a rather exclusionary notion of the collectivity that makes the Israeli "we." This can be seen, for example, in the geographical imagining of this nostalgia, since this "dreamy, idyllic re-imagining of the nation endorsed a selective relationship with the past and mapped it out onto the country's geography accordingly."[27] As Sharon Rotbard observes, the nostalgia's "selective relation to the past" is apparent in, among other things, the imagined geography of the Good Old Land of Israel:

> Except for the White City [the nostalgic imagining of Tel Aviv, which functions as the "capital city of the Good Old Land of Israel"] there are no other urban settlements in this land, neither of veterans nor of newcomers, there is no trace of the Baron [Rothchild] settlements [who preceded the Zionist colonies and did not fit the prevalent, revolution-

ary Zionist ethos], and of course there is no trace in it of the Palestinian places, present (including Jerusalem) or absent [i.e., erased—physically or mentally—following the 1948 war]. This land is composed mostly of the unique mythological frontier of the Labor movement's settlements.[28]

The temporal map of this nostalgia is of no less importance: it embodies the negation of exile and the relegation of the Jewish past into the bin of the forgone and forgotten. The longing here is for an "Israeli," or, more accurately, a Land-of-Israel-Zionist past, not a Jewish past in exile. Short as it may be, this past has no past: like the Sabra, it is "orphaned," being born "out of the sea," without parents.[29] It relates neither to the Jewish nor the Palestinian pasts.

As Rotbard further notes, there are common themes between the "selective" geography of the nostalgic "home" and the just-as-selective notion of the past it fantasizes:

> Just as the geography of this imaginary country . . . was (in the terms of Michel Foucault) "heterotopic," so its history was heterochronic—Good Old Eretz Israel was doomed to remain always "old" (that was what made it so "good"), but not so old as to encourage its inhabitants to actually investigate the period which preceded Labor[-Zionist] settlement, as this had already been declared ancient and antique. In any case, history should have been left far enough in the past that it would not interfere with today's reality, and therefore its time was never the present.[30]

The fact that only a fraction of the Jewish Israeli population can in reality claim a direct relation to the past that this nostalgia glorifies—the vast majority of this population having arrived in Israel after that supposed golden age has ended—only further compounds its manufactured nature and political import.

Music, too, plays a central part in this Israeli nostalgia. As Edwin Seroussi notes, "Israeli sonic nostalgia" was already ubiquitous in the years immediately after the foundation of the state.[31] This "relentless turn to the sonic past" (Seroussi mentions the same *Hayo Hayu Zmanim* musical revue and LP as epitomizing it) was dominated by a socially, politically, ethnically, and ideologically well-defined elite, "a group of canonic agents in the cultural scene . . . and state-controlled mass media . . . all of whom were related to the Palmach military units." The contents of its program were similarly distinctly sectorial, captured in "the song repertoire of the pre-state secular Ashkenazi Zionist settlements." Not much later on, the same Zionist sonic repertoire was further canonized by "Israel's ultimate pop icon," Arik Einstein, who, paradoxically enough, considering his and his milieu's role in perpetuating this authoritative nostalgia, was also taken to be representing Israel's counterculture, in a series of albums titled *The Good Old Land of Israel.*[32] This soundscape, too, worked to exclude and forget as much as it functioned to remember and define a "we." Via its various canonizations and symbolic fortifications (this soundscape became the soundtrack of Israel's civil, national holidays), this sonic repertoire "served as an agent in the delineation of the canonic Zionist repertoire by means of the exclusion of soundscapes that existed on the ground during the 'heroic' pre-state (*Yishuv*) and early state periods, such as those of private, religious, non-Western, and urban spaces."[33]

Critical commentators have directly addressed the political import of the Ashkenazi nostalgia. Tom Mehager, for example, argues that it serves as a cultural-political device meant to deny the secular-Ashkenazi sector's liability for the 1948 dispossessions and deportations of Palestinians. Positioning the Ashkenazi nostalgia squarely at the center of the Israeli configuration of power, Mehager ties the Palestinian catastrophe of 1948 with the emergence of an Ashkenazi secular elite in the early years of Israeli statehood. The advent of this configuration of power was driven by "the dispossessing of Palestinian lands and property after the 1948 war. The Ashkenazi group, who composed the demographic majority among Jews during the war and was the forefront of the actions of deportation and dispossession [of Palestinians], is the one who enjoyed the 'distribution of the loot' of the Palestinian catastrophe." The nostalgia at hand, then, functions to conceal, as it were, an inconvenient truth: "The systematic marking of the 1967 occupation [as opposed to the 1948 war] as the core problem—bringing an end to which will allow us to return to the 'Good Old Land of Israel,'" amounts to an attempt to "normalize and reify the power relations and distribution of resources in the 1948 lines [i.e., after the Palestinian catastrophe has taken place]." On the other hand, the collective interests and nostalgias of Mizrahim in Israel were shaped as a "mirror image" of the Ashkenazi group. "While according to Leftist Zionist Ashkenazi historiography [popularized and mythicized in the 'Good Old Land of Israel' nostalgia at hand] a fair and vibrant social-democracy was established here [in Israel], the Mizrahi public remembers the first decades of Israeli statehood as an era of resource deprivation and subjugation in all aspects of life."[34]

Focusing on contemporary politics, Amos Noy sees the Ashkenazi nostalgia as immediately driven by the perceived threat to the privileged position enjoyed by Ashkenazim from a resurging Mizrahi constituency. As he puts it, as soon as the Mizrahim appear on the public sphere, nostalgia shows up (*"mizrahim bashetah—nostalgia bapetah"*). The "deceiving, distorting, forgetting and erasing" nostalgia, "tightening the tribal lines in face of a common enemy" and decrying the loss of the good old homeland, is but a tool in the arsenal of the Ashkenazi upper class's fight to preserve its power.[35]

Similarly, Hani Zubaida and Benny Nurielli see this nostalgia as promoting a "justification for the Zionist-Ashkenazi cultural-political interests." Going back to the geographical representation of the nostalgia (the Good Old Land of Israel, with its epicenter in the "White City" of Tel Aviv), they highlight the ways in which this nostalgia functions to "cleanse" the space of "unwanted populations," aiming to achieve the "dream" of "a White City for white residents."[36] Zubaida explains this as the result of a conflict or contests between two types of Israeli-ness: the common, existing one, and the desired, ideal one. The common Israeliness is "the popular ['*amami*, a common code name for Mizrahi], or 'The Second Israel' [another common reference to Mizrahim], or the 'The Ugly Israeli.'" This type is the cause of "moral panic": "They supposedly could take over the state and bring about its destruction. They must be stopped! How? Well, for this we have the desired Israeli, 'Salt of the Earth' who built the state, the son of 'The Good Old Land of Israel.' . . . While the first type is clearly Mizrahi, the second [type] is Ashkenazi."[37]

A Zionist Nostalgia?

Perhaps the most illuminating aspect of this Israeli nostalgia is the fact that it exists in the first place, "persist[ing] tenaciously in Israeli cultural spaces."[38] If by "Israeli nostalgia" we mean a sentimental memory of an *Israeli* past, we must first confront the fact that the State of Israel itself is

relatively young, its society, having arrived in the country mostly after
the establishment of the state, even younger. Moreover, as Gideon Levy
testifies, this nostalgia was already a dominant feature of Israeli culture
in the early 1960s, barely a decade after the establishment of the state,
when its population was growing rapidly through waves of immigration. To a substantial degree, this yearning for a past long gone is taking
shape when the State of Israel and Israeli society do not have much of a
past to speak of in the first place. Moreover, as already noted, the longing at hand is not for the (long and real) Jewish past in Europe (or, more
specifically, eastern Europe, from where most of the Ashkenazi elite has
arrived) and other parts of the world.[39] Rather, it is focused on the Good
Old Land of Israel, a contested territory that has for generations been
home mostly to non-Jewish Palestinian Arabs. In other words, this Ashkenazi nostalgia (unlike the Mizrahi one, we must note) does not yearn
for the exilic places that were the original homes from which Zionists or
Israeli Jews left for Israel. Instead, it yearns for a place that has been—
distinctly so, given the context of an ongoing violent conflict over the
land—home to its Others.

Moreover, if we consider the nostalgia at hand as a yearning not exactly or primarily for a past but to a mythic notion of place—specifically,
one's "home," one's "nativity" (when Johannes Hofer coined in 1688 the
term and identified nostalgia as a medical condition, he described it
as "the sad mood originating from the desire for return to one's native
land"), this Ashkenazi nostalgia emerges as even more perplexing.[40] The
dominant ideology around which it coalesces, Zionism, argues exactly
that the subjects of this nostalgia, Israeli Jews, are now, in the present,
finally home, after millennia of exile (meaning here, specifically, being
away from home). Having advocated a nationalist outlook according to
which Jews are "out of place" in Europe and elsewhere and insisting that
they should "return" and be replanted in their historical homeland, Zionism was ultimately successful in bringing these members of the Jewish nation to their "real home." Moreover, as Hagar Kotef suggests, this
concept of home plays a major role in the construction of the settlers'
subjectivity, their very self.[41]

Note that the Ashkenazi nostalgia both Avishai Margalit and Gideon
Levy describe does not suggest that the object of yearning is home in
Europe. Zionism has taught its subjects that the Land of Israel—and

then, more importantly, the State of Israel—*is* their home. Even more so: *theirs*, in the sense of belonging to them, who are overwhelmingly either immigrants or settlers, and not to the contemporaneous inhabitants of the land. (Compare this with the Mizrahi yearning for home in the Arab or Muslim countries, which Margalit equates with the Ashkenazi nostalgia.)

So, why the nostalgia for home, which is the very same contested territory they have come to dominate, guided by Zionist ideology? Why is it that this cohort—a pioneering, leading class of the Zionist enterprise, an enterprise aimed at bringing about a bright future of strengthening national revival—are besieged by nostalgia? What is it exactly that they are missing?

Clearly, the Israeli case deals also with the problem of the contested nature of the Israeli claim to nativity in the Land of Israel, which has been, as a matter of historical fact, someone else's home. It is, in other words, about the colonial aspect of the Zionist enterprise.[42] As the party who has been newly settling in the contested land, Israelis have very little by way of "memorative signs" of their non- or (pre-)Israeli history.[43] In this, Zionism follows a rather well-trodden path. As Boym reminds us, there is something rather universal lying at "the very core of the modern condition," in "the [nostalgic] sentiment itself, the mourning of displacement and temporal irreversibility." The "promise to rebuild the ideal home," a motivation that "lies at the core of many powerful ideologies of today, tempting us to relinquish critical thinking for emotional bonding," is indeed powerful—and dangerous: "Unreflected nostalgia breeds monsters." Confusing "the actual home and the imaginary one," fashioning a "phantom homeland, for the sake of which one is ready to die or kill," nostalgia is simply too important a political fact to be ignored.[44] And the Israeli Zionist case is no exception.

This, then, is the political analytical aspect at play here: the prevalence of the Israeli Ashkenazi Zionist nostalgia betrays an unspoken uneasiness with the collective sense of home, or the apparent lack of such a homely sense. A contrast between a prescribed (by the dominant ideology) feeling of having finally arrived home and a reality of a violent contest over the land—and, maybe more latently, an Israeli sense that "we are not home after all"—is a key to understanding the Israeli collective being-in-the-world.

Furthermore, as I have noted, the Zionist project of modernizing the Jews and returning them to their home/land has been a self-consciously revolutionary endeavor, rebelling against what this nationalist ideology depicted as a two-millennia-long past of Jewish passivity and servility—captured, of course, in the Zionist negation of exile, meaning here both space (the not-Land-of-Israel) and time (the "Jewish" past). As we have seen, to a large extent Zionism builds itself *against* this Jewish, exilic past. Yet nostalgia, with its "affective yearning for a community with a collective memory," is "a longing for continuity in a fragmented world"; it emerges as a "defense mechanism" to counter the "accelerated rhythms of life and historical upheavals" of modernity.[45] Nostalgia's impetus is, in other words, counterrevolutionary.

The working of the nostalgic defense mechanism against upheavals of modernity can be seen in what we may consider as a Jewish diasporic nostalgia that stands, either implicitly or explicitly, against the Zionist negation of exile: a *Yiddishkeit* nostalgia that yearns for the lost (mostly European, but also early American) Jewish past. Such nostalgia can be detected, for example (at least according to some readings) in Philip Roth's *The Plot against America*.[46] It is also apparent in what Rachel B. Gross convincingly suggests we should view as a form of Jewish American lived religion.[47] Gross sees Jewish nostalgia as replacing (and not merely derived from) earlier loci of Jewish practice and identification. Her work locates this nostalgia in such spheres as genealogical exploration, which functions as an "emotional and spiritual experience of Jewish history. . . . As in Kurzweil's declaration, 'I was born in New York but came out of a shtetl,' Jewish genealogists merge ancestral past and individual present through nostalgic longing."[48] Similarly, she finds this nostalgia in visits to historic synagogues as heritage sites, in children's toys, and in Jewish delis.[49]

It would make a lot of sense, then, if the (Israeli) Ashkenazi nostalgia functioned similarly, as an attempt to *counter* the Zionist ideology by invoking a longing for a Jewish Ashkenazi past. This is indeed the case with the Mizrahi nostalgia recounted by Margalit, expressing a yearning to return to a (Jewish) home in the Arab or Muslim lands and in effect rejecting the Zionist notion of the ingathering of exile in the ancient homeland. It might be argued that this is also the case with *Yiddishkeit* nostalgia in Israel, but this is an obviously marginal and politically rather insignificant phenomenon to pose a challenge to Zionist political culture.

Yet the Ashkenazi nostalgia for the Good Old Land of Israel that presents itself as staunchly Zionist makes very little sense in such a counterrevolutionary, antimodernist context. The nostalgic Israeli Ashkenazim are mostly loyal heirs to a Zionist revolutionary ethos, and they are clearly benefiting from the fruits of this revolution. The status they are yearning for—that of being the supposed owners and masters of the land—was allowed to them exactly thanks to this revolutionary rupture from the past that precipitated those "accelerated rhythms of life and historical upheavals."[50]

In other words, the Ashkenazi nostalgia deals directly with what Edwin Seroussi calls Zionism's "time paradox"—its charged relation to its Jewish past—which feeds on the tension that arises from two contradictory impulses of Zionist ideology: "advocating the reintroduction of the Jews to the unilinear progress-oriented stream of (Western) history" while simultaneously "promoting a return to a mythical past of national independence conceived, of course, in modern terms."[51] This has motivated a grand cultural-political project of dealing with the past, aptly termed by Yael Zerubavel as the "re-covering" of roots.[52]

Nationalism, Nostalgia, and "Home"

It has already been noted as a staple of modern history that when the "we" at hand is a national collective—a collective formed around and under the pressure of the gravitational core of nationalist ideology, served by the apparatus of the sovereign nation-state—a preoccupation with the past and a glorification of certain elements within it as the golden age of national self-determination are discernible.[53] This preoccupation is a generative imagining of the national collective and its past,[54] culminating, in Eric Hobsbawm's famous phrasing, in the invention of its tradition(s).[55] Indeed, the past is the main pillar of most myths of nationhood.[56] This makes the fact that, "traditionally, the field of nationalism has not paid a great deal of attention to nostalgia" regrettable indeed.[57]

Here, Boym's typology, which distinguishes between "reflective" and "restorative" nostalgia, proves especially helpful:

Restorative nostalgia stresses *nostos* and attempts a transhistorical reconstruction of the lost home. Reflective nostalgia thrives in *algia*, the longing itself, and delays the homecoming—wistfully, ironically, desperately. Restorative nostalgia does not think of itself as nostalgia, but rather as truth and tradition. Reflective nostalgia dwells on the ambivalences of human longing and belonging and does not shy away from the contradictions of modernity. Restorative nostalgia protects the absolute truth, while reflective nostalgia calls it into doubt.[58]

Restorative nostalgia is the staple of nationalist ideology, and especially of national revivalist movements, who "engage in the antimodern myth-making of history by means of a return to national symbols and myths and, occasionally, through swapping conspiracy theories." It "puts emphasis on nostos and proposes to rebuild the lost home and patch up the memory gaps." Needless to say, this is not how nationalists would want to see themselves. Restorative nostalgics "do not think of themselves as nostalgic; they believe that their project is about truth." On the other hand, reflective nostalgia "dwells in *algia*, in longing and loss," preoccupied with the very remembrances of things past. Shying away from metanarratives, "inhabiting many places at once and imagining different time zones," reflective nostalgia "loves details, not symbols"; it "lingers on ruins . . . in the dreams of another place and another time."[59]

Note that both types of nostalgia have political and ethical import: while it should be clear enough why restorative nostalgia, the core of nationalist ideologies, *is* political, we should not relegate reflective nostalgia, with its obsession of longing itself, to the sidelines of the political, dismissed as "merely a pretext for midnight melancholias." Rather, "at best, reflective nostalgia can present an ethical and creative challenge," with obvious political implications. It in effect questions nationalist metanarratives, seeding doubt and offering competing points of view.[60] Based on this typology, Boym further suggests that we distinguish between "national memory," which is "based on a single plot of national identity," captured in restorative nostalgia, and "social memory," best captured in reflective nostalgia, "consist[ing] of collective frameworks that mark but do not define the individual memory."[61]

The interaction between these two types of nostalgia is discernible in the Israeli case: what both Margalit and Levy point to is the fact that

within a national collective and under a heavy hand of nationalist ideology—or, to use Boym's typology, under the heavy hand of "national
memory," serviced by a restorative nostalgia (i.e., the Zionist metanar-
rative of "return," "redemption," and "the ingathering of the exiles")—
various "social memories," serviced by "reflective nostalgias," may form,
pitting one sector of the allegedly unified nation against the other, offering competing evaluations of political reality and directing political
action in diverse ways.

The Mizrahi nostalgia follows rather loyally the outlines of what
Boym calls "off-modernist" nostalgia. As she explains, "The adverb *off*
confuses our sense of direction. . . . It allows us to take a detour from the
deterministic narrative of twentieth-century history." Off-modernism
is a contrarian stance to modernism, critiquing "both the modern fas-
cination with newness and no less modern reinvention of tradition."
This "off-modern tradition" combines longing for the past with a sense
of present estrangement. It fulfills a crucial function as a "strategy of
survival, a way of making sense of the impossibility of homecoming,"
for those "off-modernists" who came from traditions located on the
sidelines of the colonial West—that is, the traditions that the West has
viewed as marginal or provincial.[62]

The Mizrahi nostalgia of the "good old times in the Arab and Muslim lands" takes a similar off stance vis-à-vis the modernist nationalist
narrative of ingathering of exiles and redemption by way of modernization and politicization of the Jewish people. It is, in other words, the
off-modernist nostalgia of those marginalized by the dominant Israeli
political culture, a "strategy of survival" of those who find themselves
stripped of their identity and tradition by a newly invented national
tradition—especially so since for them a return home (in the Arab and
Muslim lands) is mostly impossible, due to the prevalence of a political conflict between sides that identify as mutually exclusive "Jewish"
against "Arab" (rendering, that is, the very notion of an Arab Jew politically oxymoronic). As Boym explains, reflective nostalgia is a mourning,
not a melancholia: the thing that is lost, that which is mourned, is lost in
concrete, not abstract, terms.[63]

In this, the Mizrahi nostalgia is complemented by the arguably more
politically successful nostalgia propagated by the Shas party and the sociocultural movement it has led—consisting mostly of Israeli Jews who

trace their roots to Arab and Muslim countries—of "returning the old crown to its glory." Famously, this slogan is open enough to interpretation to allow the party's leadership and its constituency to each read it differently. While for the Orthodox-rabbinical leadership it speaks mostly to its hope of restoring a certain interpretation and practice of Jewish law to prominence, for the party's constituency it reads mostly as propagating a "countermemory." It suggests that Jews in Arab and Muslim lands enjoyed a glory prior to a degradation caused by their immigration to Israel, painting the Arab-Jewish past in obviously nostalgic hues.[64]

Conclusion

Nostalgia tells us volumes about the ways in which individuals and the sociopolitical groups they belong to understand their world, their misgivings about the present, and their hopes for the future. Needless to say, it would be wrong to suggest any kind of causal and rule-like relation between nostalgia and political action; human reality is simply too complicated to follow such a path.[65] But it is exactly the interpretive opulence allowed to us by nostalgia that is of immediate political-analytical value; it allows us a view into a rather intimate collective self-perception, helping us to see the formation of identities and the articulations of conflicts that could otherwise be sanctioned as illegitimate by a predominant political culture and the ideology it derives power from. Furthermore, it directs us in multiple directions in our search for the meaning of politics. The media of nostalgia are numerous, and political meaning is to be found in countless arenas that are sometimes neglected by students of politics such as music, film, popular culture, and art.

There are also obvious limitations to the use of nostalgia for political analysis. Maybe the most obvious of these is the case of what Boym calls "reflective" nostalgia, the immersion of oneself in the longing itself, in *algia*, which functions, to a large extent, to postpone action. Here, the line between nostalgia and political behavior or action is too tangled to allow us to offer a convincing interpretation or understanding of real-world events. Indeed, to a large extent, the sentiment of this reflective nostalgia is "anti-political," reifying what Mary Midgley warned against as the (misleading) dichotomy of idealists versus realists.[66] It positions the nostalgic in a contrarian position to the "real world" of the present political machination in the context of which one is experiencing—and exercising—this *algia*. But this, too, is ultimately a form of being in the world that is clearly political. It expresses a misgiving about the present, a critical judgment of it. And in extreme cases it can even lead to a crisis of legitimation, where too many of a polity's subjects are busy longing for something else.

As is the case of interpretive political science more generally, the study of nostalgia is firmly grounded in a specific context—cultural, historical, lingual, sociopolitical, and so on. It resists an easy rule-generalization of the kind positivist political science tends to prefer. Yet, without diving into the vast epistemological conflict that has determined the shape of the discipline of the study of politics for almost a century, it is exactly this kind of analysis—the local, the particular—that allows us a glimpse into human truths that are universal.

The merit of this analytical tool is clearly demonstrated by the Israeli case. Looking at Israeli nostalgia, we are made privy to some of the more surprising effects of Zionism's negation of its Jewish past. Jewish Israelis, Zionists, are left yearning for something—a certain time and place—that is but a manifestation of their hopes for the future: a future in which the dominant, nation-statist Ashkenazi configuration of power reasserts itself and yields the silences of Zionism's "Others." Yet this is far from solving Israel's "Jewish problem": Zionist ideology forbids a yearning for an exilic, religious Jewish past, in effect depriving Jewish Israelis of their immediate past (as in their familial past, the past whose memories can still be carried and shared from grandparents to grandchildren). Zionism does, of course, as do nationalist ideologies generally, tell its subjects stories of their glorious past, a golden age that is to be re-created by the nation-statist order of things. But this past is ancient; it cannot, by definition, be related to in an unmediated manner (the mediation carried out by state agents, who promote a certain view of this past to match the statist interests).

It is not uncommon to hear American visitors to Israel, excited or overwhelmed by the opulence of the ancient archaeological sites they encounter on their visit, commenting on how privileged Israelis are to have this sense of history. Clearly, these visitors, members of the colonizing majority of North America, lack such access to sites of "their" ancient history. Yet the Israeli Ashkenazi nostalgia discussed above highlights a "deficiency" in the Israeli past, which this American excitement does not capture. Visit any Israeli antique shop or flea market, and the material reality of this nostalgia, of what it is missing, will be made apparent. There is very little, if any, material presence of what we may call the "intermediate past"—a pre-Israeli and pre-Zionist history, say, a century or two centuries back, that Israelis would want to or could claim (materially, in this case) as their own.[67] Similarly, there are famously very few physical or archaeological sites of this pre-Israeli, mostly non-Jewish past; Israeli roots are either too short (cut from their exilic Jewish ground) or too long, planted in an ancient, nationalized past.

4

Redemption Politics*

Introduction

As William Cavanaugh notes, soteriology is a key component of theo-politics: "the modern state is built upon a soteriology of rescue from violence," a foundational "myth of the State as Savior," the basis of the modern concept of sovereignty.[1] Among other things, this soteriology is constructed via and expressed by political myths, symbols, and rituals that "imagine" the nation and "invent" its traditions.[2] To do so, nation-statist ideologies and political cultures use a variety of sources, including such that originate in traditions that preceded the state, carried, practiced, interpreted, and updated by the communities from which the state shapes the nation in the name of which it claims sovereignty.

The so-called secular political tradition of the state would tend to label these preceding traditions as "sectarian," "parochial," and, most importantly, "religious," implying (or forcefully explicating) that they do not fit—at least prior to being reformed and nationalized—within the modern, inclusive, and secular framework of the nation-state.[3] Needless to say, the process of nationalizing these traditions is not always smooth, as the traditions might not be attentive to the needs or the views of the sovereign nation-state. Sometimes they contradict its theopolitics or forcefully negate what for the state must be beyond doubt (e.g., the soteriology it propagates).

*Parts of this chapter are based on an article cowritten with Noam Hadad (Yadgar and Hadad, "Nation-Statist Soteriology and Traditions of Defeat") and on the empirical work conducted by Hadad and presented in detail in his book *Religious Zionism: Religion, Nationalism, and Politics* (Jerusalem: Carmel, 2020). Yet the nature of the analysis and the onus of the argument in this chapter are significantly different than those of the works cited here, and I alone bear responsibility for the chapter, for the argument presented herein, and, above all, for its failings. I am grateful to Noam Hadad for allowing me to rely on these works.

The question, then, has to do with the ways in which the new traditions of the state cope with or handle older traditions that have preceded it and continue to live alongside it, and how these traditions, in turn, may react to the statist actions. More specifically, we focus here exactly on those cases where the nation-statist soteriology conflicts with narratives, symbols, and memories carried by tradition that either mark the opposite of salvation and redemption (commemorating, that is, collective defeat, catastrophe, exile), or at least undermine and complicate the state's claim, via its ideology and political culture, to the role of savior, a claim that is entailed in the ideology of the nation-state.

The confrontational, selective appropriation, or "nationalization," of the Jewish past and of foundational Jewish/Judaic notions such as messianism, exile, and redemption by the nation-statist theopolitics necessarily yields an obvious tension: this process of nationalization can never fully rewrite history and tradition, and certain elements of these, elements that can contradict important foundations of the nation-statist theopolitics, remain viable and influential. This chapter sets out to study this tension and its implications for Israeli political culture. Specifically, we are interested here in the ways in which the theopolitics of the nation-state and, especially, its soteriology—the story it tells of how it saves us from peril (captured fully in the notion of Zionist messianism discussed earlier)—engage with traditions that preceded the state and relay messages that directly contradict this politics of redemption. We will study this encounter through a retracing of the evolving Zionist and Israeli engagement with and (re)interpretation of what we may call "mnemonic" or "symbolic" loci of the catastrophe of the destruction of Jerusalem and the end of Jewish (Judean) self-rule in ancient times: the city of Jerusalem; the Western Wall and its "absent referent," the temple; and the Ninth of Av rituals commemorating the destruction of the city and its temple. The traditional rendering of these sites of memory broadcast a message of defeat and punishment by the hand of God that contradicts the nation-statist claim to redemption by way of politics and has the potential to undermine it. The chapter demonstrates how the (political) imperative of the superiority of nation-statist theopolitics suggests that so-called religious traditions are co-opted to fit in with its soteriology, with varying degrees of resistance or willing accommodation by carriers of these traditions. This co-opting may result in either the depoliticization of what the statist view would see as religion or the "theologizing" or "religionizing" of the state's own civic and secular holidays.

The following will consider, then, the ways in which Zionism generally, and Religious Zionism more specifically, have negotiated the tension entailed in their appropriation of Jewish mnemonic sites commemorating the defeat and politico-theological catastrophe of the destruction of Jerusalem and its temple, the end of Jewish (rather, Judean) self-rule, and the onset of exile in antiquity.[4]

As we will see, the message traditionally propagated by these sites—a story of sin, divine punishment, catastrophe, and a hoped-for eschatology of ultimate redemption—directly contradicts some of the most foundational elements of Zionist nationalism and the political mythology of Israeli nation-statism. We will seek to explicate this tension by also considering a relatively new addition to the nation-statist tradition, Jerusalem Day, which tends to directly contradict certain elements of the message of the traditional commemoration.

Zionist Soteriology and Jewish tradition

As we have seen, the question of Zionism's and Israeli nation-statism's relation to Jewish traditions that preceded them is far from a neglected aspect of the field of research. The predominant discourse on these issues tends to accept the secularist epistemology, presupposing the modern nation-state as secular and seeing its encounter with what the discourse (following the state) considers religion as a complicated matter, to say the least. These interventions tend to assume the nation-state as superior to religion but acknowledge that a clear break from it has not been a viable option for Zionism.[5]

More immediately relevant to the case at hand, scholars have also charted the convoluted relation between the political culture of Israeli nation-statism, on its political myths and symbols, and traditional Judaism and its symbols and myths.[6] These have tended to frame the discussion as a question of the secularization of Jewish tradition and to employ the category of civil religion to refer to the nation-statist system of myths, symbols, beliefs, and narratives.[7] In doing so, they have unwittingly reified the dichotomy of the secular versus religion, even when their own analysis has clearly challenged both the viability and the utility of this categorical distinction. By employing the concept of civil religion, they have preserved the notion that the nation-state is essentially secular, ignoring its theological claims, which are lucidly captured in its soteriology. They have also played, even if only implicitly, into the debate of whether Judaism fits within the category of religion.[8]

"Generically" speaking, soteriology narrates a movement between "two states of human existence," from "a state of deprivation (sin, corruption)" to "a state of release from that deprivation (salvation, liberation)"; it also tells of "an event that produces a change from the first state to the second."[9] Much of nationalist ideology, with its common glorification of an archaic, lost golden age of the ethnos/nation that is to be revived by the modern nation-state revolves around a soteriology in which the state plays the role of savior.[10] Probably the most important soteriology of Western modernity is the very form of the so-called secular modern nation-state itself, captured in what Cavanaugh describes as "the creation myth of the wars of religions": "The story goes that, after the Protestant Reformation divided Christendom along religious lines, Catholics and Protestants began killing each other for holding to different doctrines. The wars of religion . . . demonstrated to the West the inherent danger of public religion. The solution to the problem lay in the rise of the modern state, in which religious loyalties were marginalized and the state secured a monopoly on the means of violence."[11] This, then, is "a story of our salvation from mortal peril," where the modern sovereign nation-state is cast as savior. The lesson taught here, simply put, is Western modernity: it legitimizes—necessitates, even—the present order of things, the configuration of power where the state has a monopolistic claim to sovereignty.[12]

While the Jewish people as a collective cannot claim to have an active role in the European story of the Wars of Religion, the political Zionist rendition of Jewish nationalism, which leans heavily on the (European, Christian) notion of modern nation-statist sovereignty, is clearly indebted to the modern construction of the sovereign nation-state as savior that this myth legitimates.[13] To repeat here in summary a point made more expansively earlier, Zionism narrates a soteriology where the calamity of national exile—meaning, primarily the (political) state of lacking sovereignty—is to be redeemed by national ingathering and the establishment of a Jewish sovereign nation-state. It is this soteriology that renders Zionism a messianic and redemptive ideology.[14]

This soteriology identifies religion with exile, depicting Judaism (meaning, in this context, a narrow sense of Jewish religion, which is preoccupied with ritual and oblivious if not outright hostile to collective political action) as a collective malaise of passivity and deprivation.[15] Redemption is to be achieved by a release from this religion. It is important to note that Zionism freely and constantly employs all of these terms (e.g., exile, ingathering of exiles, redemption), whose theological or religious origins are too well established to allow us to ignore the fact that Zionism's secular political language is rooted in religious terminologies and ways of thinking (Scholem's warning of the unintended consequences of this "secularization" of the language, discussed earlier, immediately comes to mind here). This message—in effect, the replacing of religion by nation-statism, and of God by the state—is commonly held to be the core of the Zionist secularization of Judaism,[16] regardless of the fact that, given the heavily theological language of this political ideology of the state, it is hard to see the merit of the secularist terminology here.[17]

The interest of legitimizing the nation-statist configuration of power has played a role in shaping the ways in which Zionist ideology and the political culture of the State of Israel have approached elements from within the traditions carried by Jewish communities who came to compose Jewish Israeli society. This approach oscillates between rejection and adoption, reinterpretation and appropriation, disavowal and celebration. Indeed, a study of the developing and diverging ways in which various streams within Israeli political culture have approached this issue makes for one of the most illuminating narrations of Israeli political history per se.[18]

This chapter thus contributes to this political history by focusing on a case in which a message entailed in a traditional narrative and the ritual commemorating it directly contradicts the statist soteriology. Needless to say, it also speaks directly to Israel's claim to Jewishness.

The State of Israel as *Bayit Shelishi*?

Much of the tension at hand is captured symbolically in a common, highly charged political-discursive convention of referring to the State of Israel as *bayit shelishi*, literally meaning "third home/house." Thus, to give but two anecdotal but not unrepresentative examples, in David Ben-Gurion's celebration of European Jewry's contribution to the "glorious construction of *ha-bayit ha-shelishi*,"[19] and in Ari Shavit's recent polemic advocating a reaffirmation of Ben-Gurion's statism, which he simply titled *Bayit Shelishi*.[20]

This Hebrew term can be, and most commonly is, read to mean that the Israeli nation-state is the embodiment of the "Third Temple," which is the common (Jewish, Judaic) figurative meaning of *bayit shelishi*. Moreover, the literal meaning of the term—which is, it might be argued, less religiously pregnant—is not without a politico-theological charge. We will address the connotational gap opened by this difference between the literal and figurative meanings shortly. At this point, suffice it to say that common Israeli Hebrew political discourse, on its often unacknowledged theologically Jewish roots, allows, if not encourages, a reading of this term to mean that the modern nation-state of Israel is the embodiment of a resurrected temple that has for centuries symbolized Jewish collective life under divine providence.

The symbolism at play takes Zionist theopolitics by its horns: it speaks directly to the Zionist sense of the State of Israel being the reestablishment of what is traditionally seen as a divinely ordained, providential polity. This symbolism charges the political body with a sense of sacredness that is reserved, in the secularist-nationalist terminology, for the religious (i.e., apolitical, messianic, metaphysical, if not outright irrational) realm. It is clear enough why a political, national movement would seek to appropriate such a foundational element of the collective memory that preceded it. This politico-theological symbolism renders the existence of the State of Israel the fulfillment of the millennia-long (expression of) yearnings of the Jewish people, in effect making Jewish history as a whole Zionist, and the State of Israel the culmination of Jewish history itself.

Yet it is interesting to note some of the maybe unintended consequences of this likening of the political, modern, this-worldly organization to the ancient Judean political organization, which Josephus famously termed a "theocracy." First, this likening renders the Zionist proclaimed aim to make the Jewish people a "nation like all other nations" hollow. There is nothing mundane in the mythic image of the temple or the Israelite and Judean kingdoms it represents. On the contrary: the rebuilding of the temple is assumed by various Jewish traditions to be the result of a messianic revelation, an eschatology in the most basic sense of the word.

Second, this likening of the state to the temple immediately evokes (either implicitly or explicitly, as symbols often do) a sense of the precariousness of the very existence of the state. If anything, even if looked at solely secularly and historically, the fact that the two predecessors (i.e., *bayit rishon* and *bayit sheni*, the First and Second Temples, and their associated Israelite and Judean kingdoms) were ultimately destroyed looms large. Moreover, if considered in the framework of the traditional narration of the destruction of the temple (captured most fully in the Ninth of Av mourning rituals), the likening of the state to *bayit shelishi* also evokes the covenantal and hence *conditional* nature of this existence. In the biblical narration, the condition has to do with the Israelite's upholding of the covenant with God; in some rabbinical interpretations, a further stress is also put on avoiding internal strife (*sin'at ḥinam*). Modern iterations play a rather free hand when suggesting their conditionals. It is not uncommon for Israeli commentators to warn that failure to attend to this or that political matter would ultimately bring about the destruction of *bayit shelishi*. Indeed, a random internet search for the Hebrew term *bayit shelishi* renders countless references in social media, discussion groups, and news sites, all referring to matters of political contestation in contemporary Israel, most protesting and warning against what they view as the oncoming of disaster.

See, for example, how a best-selling historian, speaking for liberal, democratic, and secular Israeliness (his is supposedly decisively *not* a religious or messianic stance), and concerned with certain political developments, wonders: "Can Judaism survive the destruction of the Third Temple—the prosperous Israeli democracy—this time by the Jews themselves?"[21] Going on to compare this potential "Third Destruction" (capitalized in the original) to those that preceded it, the historian turned prophet offers a warning:

As we approach Tisha B'Av [of 5783/2023], I hope that all the questions I have posed here will remain purely theoretical. I hope that the government of Israel stops its antidemocratic power-grab, heals the national wounds, puts down the flames of Hawara [the site of an Israeli pogrom against Palestinians], and prevents a Third Destruction, whether material or spiritual. And if the government of Israel carries on with its dangerous policies, then it is the duty of all Jews, wherever they live, to resist this government in every nonviolent way we know. To do so, it is important that we realize that what is happening right now in Israel is not a fleeting political struggle, but a decisive historical event that will shape Jewish history for generations to come.[22]

It is undoubtedly a peculiar feature of Israeli political culture that the fear of a potential end of the polity is ever present in political commentaries, always looming, either in the background or the foreground, as a menacing, apocalyptic catastrophe. Maybe most famous of these warnings against the destruction of the Third Temple is the report that Moshe Dayan, then Israel's defense minister, was warning, or even lamenting, at the outbreak of the October 1973 (Yom Kippur) war, that "the temple [*bayit shelishi*] is doomed."[23] The jeremiad quoted above is also a good case in point. The concerned liberal critic is worried not just for the destruction of the state; inviting his readers to imagine a scenario where his political opponents are triumphant, he concludes that the "Third Destruction" might entail "an unprecedented kind of destruction—a spiritual destruction" and wonders (rhetorically?), "Can Judaism survive a spiritual destruction?"[24]

As Benjamin Kedar notes, referring to what he identifies as the "Masada complex" of Israeli politics (the Masada story being, in this context, a dramatic representation of the wider catastrophe of national devastation), the framing of this-worldly politics in this mythical, eschatological framework necessarily yields a problematic decision-making process, to say the least.[25]

Yet it is safe to assume that many Israelis use the term without knowingly accounting for these symbolic problematics. Myths generally allow us a layered approach to their narrations, where an implicit message may not only add to but also contradict the explicit message of the story. Particularly in our case, language also allows a degree of ambiguity that services the nationalist-statist theopolitics and the tendency of the self-perceived secular to deny its indebtedness to what it depicts as the religious. This is indeed a playing out of the danger Scholem was warning against in his letter to Rosenzweig, quoted earlier. As we have seen, the Hebrew term at hand, *bayit shelishi*, drops the word "temple" (*miqdash*) itself. In this, the term simply follows the traditional Hebrew usage of the term, where it is taken for granted that *ha-bayit* (literally, the home/house) is *beit hamiqdash* (the temple). Yet, given that *bayit* in for itself stands for important political, nation-statist values (i.e., the State of Israel being a refuge for Jews, and, more importantly, their "national home"), it is conceivable that a commentator's use of the term is meant to aim (only) at this supposedly nonreligious, yet politico-symbolically pregnant level.[26]

The tension entailed in the symbolism of Israel as the third home is further accentuated with reference to the Ninth of Av (the ritual commemorating the destruction of the temple), to the Western Wall (what has become a site of the morning ritual and a referent of the temple itself), and to the city of Jerusalem more broadly. Moreover, the Zionist endeavor to cope with this tension is indeed revealing. In this regard, Arieh Saposnik's work on Jerusalem and the Western Wall as Zionist "Sites of Redemption" is illuminating in, among other things, tracing a predominant sense of Zionist ambivalence toward the city and the site.[27] As Saposnik convincingly insists, contrary to "the standard presentation of the attitude of the Jewish national movement to the ancient city as one of all but unequivocal aversion," secular Zionism's attitude toward the city, the Western Wall, and the Temple Mount has been "a focus of considerable ambivalence."[28] This ambivalence or "duality" centers exactly on the tension between, on the one hand, Zionism's claim to Jewish history and identity, and, on the other, its aversion to what Zionism saw as the religious and exilic features of this past.[29] Furthermore, this ambivalence is fed by the shift from theology to theopolitics—that is, from the religious notion of redemption by way of God to the nationalist, secular notion of redemption by way of politics.

For self-identified secular Zionists in Ottoman (and then Mandatory) Palestine "whose familiarity with Jerusalem was much more concrete,"[30] and especially for those among them who have self-fashioned as rebels against Jewish religion and adopted an aggressively confrontational attitude toward the Jewish traditions from which they have emerged (epito-mized by Socialist Zionism, but surely exceeding its ranks), Jerusalem, the Western Wall, and the mourning rituals of the Ninth of Av presented a unique problem.[31] Granted, it was easy enough to simply ignore or ac-tively negate the religious aspects of the ritual, "its" site (i.e., the Western Wall), and the city they both symbolize and to question the religious or theological message the traditional mourning ritual professes. But the political message entailed by the site, ritual, and symbol—a message of decrying exile and the loss of self-rule—corresponded positively with certain premises of Zionist ideology, especially in the prestate era. As Saposnik puts it, for these Zionists "Jerusalem seemed in many ways to represent the twin poles of a national ignominy that lay, after all, at the very root of the Zionist impulse, on the one hand, and a sense of sanctity coupled with a vision of a future redemption that appeared to be stub-bornly attached to the city [on the other hand]."[32]

Significantly, the material, physical presence of the Western Wall in Jerusalem presented the early Zionists settlers with a unique challenge, too prominent to ignore or cast aside. Instead, they have endeavored to incorporate its sanctity inside a political-theological framework. For these Zionist activists, who were feeding also on Christian renditions of the notions of redemption and of the Holy Land, the material presence of the Western Wall, the last remaining remnant of the temple that signi-fies, above all, the ancient Judean kingdom that they have sought (sym-bolically, at the very least) to rebuild, bore obvious politico-symbolical significance.[33]

This rather immediate, contemporary political significance of the city is of a different order from that of the traditional Jewish yearning for the city of Zion and its temple. It may be relevant to remind the reader here that for most of the Jewish people, living throughout the world, for most of Jewish history, the ritual commemoration of Jerusalem and its temple does not have a material, physical locus; it is, like other Jewish rituals, to be carried in the synagogue and at home. Furthermore, while Zion has remained over centuries a focus of prayers, this has not tradi-tionally materialized into a political, this-worldly interest in Jerusalem and the Western Wall. Indeed, as Saposnik shows, it was primarily due to non- (and often anti-)Jewish orientalist interests in Palestine that the Western Wall "came to have a greater presence in both Jewish and non-

Jewish discourses and imagery."[34] This might help to explain why the Zionist appropriation of the Western Wall into a nationalist ethos was approached with "some reservation in the Diaspora."[35]

This tension between the material and the symbolic-mythical and between the theological and the theopolitical is the context in which to account for the Zionist ambivalence toward the site. Zionism did not simply do away with its theological, redemptive, or messianic charge, but strove to appropriate it, "transforming it from a center of reviled exile in the very heart of the land of would-be redemption, and hence reclaiming it from the clutches of what to many Zionists was the gravest of national desecrations, and elevating it to the centerpiece of a new national sacrality and a nationhood resanctified."[36]

In this context of the subsuming of traditional theology by the emerging political theology, the "congenital and indissoluble twinning of the 'religious' and the 'political,' the sacred and the profane, in Jerusalem's history" is highlighted.[37] And it is in this context that "Jerusalem emerges as a critical fulcrum in Zionism's attempt to appropriate political power . . . and, in the process, to redefine the sources of holiness, and the visions of redemption that they entailed, and to claim authority over them."[38]

Or, to return to the earlier suggestion that we view Zionism's relation to Judaism as one of supersessionism, Zionism's interest in Jerusalem is fed by the ideology's effort to appropriate the Jewish messianic or redemptive idea, which Jerusalem/Zion so strongly symbolizes. As Saposnik (who, as we have seen earlier, insists on assigning the notion of redemption, and not messianism, to Zionism) summarizes the point: "Fundamentally, . . . Zionism's Jerusalems—both when it set its sights on the city and when it sometimes willingly neglected it—were invariably a part of efforts to reconfigure and lay claim to a vision of redemption that were so closely associated with it."[39]

Thus, "the Wall was increasingly nationalized," as "the symbol [i.e., the site itself] and its ritualization [i.e., the Ninth of Av] were clearly both undergoing deliberate and self-conscious transformation." This politico-theological appropriation also included, then, the Ninth of Av itself, which was, according to a contemporaneous newspaper report quoted by Saposnik, newly marked in the late 1920s by "'a remarkable spectacle,' whose centerpiece was a 'solemn procession' to the Wall." Now nationalized, the Wall "had been transformed by the new ritual into a 'scene of ancient glory, now a symbol for national revival.'"[40] And so, "as Jewish-Muslim tensions mounted [at the end of the 1920's], it was a very different Wall, reflecting fundamental changes that were taking place in a nation that was now turning to it not only in prayer but increasingly in a range of civil rituals and political demonstration."[41] Considered in this context, it is not a coincidence that, at least according to Palestinian reports, the violent events of 1929, which Hillel Cohen calls "Year Zero of the Arab-Israeli Conflict," were ignited by a Zionist provocation at the site of the Western Wall.[42]

For a rebellious, self-perceived-as-secularist mindset, the Wall's material presence, its historical significance, and its politico-symbolical importance provided a motivation to act. Zionist settlers, who saw themselves as taking not only their own fate but also their nation's fate in their hands, were thus confronted with a material presence that bore symbolic meaning, with which they sometimes felt uncomfortable and sought to overcome by virtue of their political agency. As attested to by Rachel Yanait Ben-Zvi, a leading Socialist Zionist activist, when she approached the Wall, "a desire to cry out to the wall in protest against the weeping arose within me . . . to cry out against the unfortunate verdict of fate: no longer will we live in the land of destruction, we will rebuild the ruins and regenerate our land."[43] Socialist Zionists thus fashioned themselves collectively, politically, as those who would ultimately heed the mourners' cries, professing that "the house of Israel will be rebuilt with bricks, not with prayers and mourning."[44]

Yet it is interesting to note the endurance of the theological underpinning of the site and the city even for self-fashioned secularist Zionists. Thus, echoing what Gideon Katz identifies as the "volcanic" forces of Judaism threatening to undermining secular Israeli identity, Arieh Saposnik sees in the Zionist appropriation of the Western Wall the eruption of "the subterranean apocalyptic energy that Gershom Scholem identified in the Hebrew language itself—the symbolism of the Wall seemed to become increasingly compelling for Zionism in Palestine generally and for the ways in which the budding national life of the Yishuv was now presented to Jews abroad."[45]

The Ninth of Av and the Religious-Zionist Politics of Redemption

The self-professed rebellious, secularist confrontation with tradition could not sit well with a self-professed religious, Orthodox ideology—namely, Religious Zionism, to which we will now be shifting our attention. Specifically, we will focus on the Religious-Zionist negotiation of the tension between the traditionally theological message of defeat and the Zionist theopolitical message of triumph and redemption via a study of the evolving interpretation of the Ninth of Av under Israeli nation-statehood. This will be complemented by a consideration of what ultimately emerges as the appropriation and theologizing of a civic holiday: Jerusalem Day.

If the celebration and commemoration of victories is a predominant feature of nation-statist political culture, the Ninth of Av is the opposite—a commemoration of defeat.[46] A daylong ritual of mourning and fasting, the date is traditionally seen to memorialize and lament a series of defeats and catastrophes that befell the Israelites, Judeans, and the Jewish people throughout many generations. Primarily, the day marks the destruction of the Judean temple in Jerusalem in 70 CE (tradition has it that its predecessor, too, was destructed on the same day, in 586 BCE) and the exile that ensued. Importantly, this ritual carries obvious political messages, exemplifying rather brilliantly the futility of attempting to distinguish the political from the religious in Judaism or Jewish traditions. Read theologically, the ritual is meant to commemorate the divine punishment that befell the sinning people. Yet at the same time, politically, it commemorates the end of Judean (or, anachronistically, Jewish) self-rule in antiquity and the beginning of exile: the punishment from God is (among other things) also a *political* condition. The day marks the onslaught of a prolonged state of deprivation and subjugation. Traditionally, the day and its rituals also hold a message regarding the hoped-for end of this state of deprivation, an eschatological act of redemption in which the temple will be rebuilt by divine fiat, marking not only the end of exile but also, in some interpretations, the end of time itself. This eschatology fits into a wider traditional interpretation of Jewish history, where the divine punishment of exile is read to mean that only God can have the agency to redeem the people.

The relatively fast progression of politics and history rapidly underscored the Religious-Zionist dilemma. While Zionist ideology was comfortable with presenting the establishment of the State of Israel in 1948 as the achievement of redemption and as the political equivalent of building the Third Temple (in Religious-Zionist parlance, the state is, at the very least, the "*beginning* of redemption"), the failure to capture Jerusalem during the 1948 war allowed Religious Zionists to maintain the tension between the triumphant celebration of the state as redemption itself and the defeatist, mournful message of the Ninth of Av. It was the June 1967 Six Days' War, during which Israel captured Jerusalem, that presented Religious Zionists with a critical challenge in this regard: it put the two political messages—the one entailed in the traditional commemoration of the Ninth of Av, and the one professed by Zionist ideology and Israeli nation-statism—in obvious confrontation. A tradition of mourning the destruction of Jerusalem and the onset of exile conflicted with a (new) tradition celebrating Jewish sovereignty, which now included the rapidly and massively built this-worldly city of Jerusalem, as the expression of redemption itself.

In what follows, we will trace some of the main themes and developments in the ways in which Religious-Zionist spokespeople have constructed and interpreted the meaning of the Ninth of Av since 1967. We will compare these to the Religious-Zionist appropriation of Jerusalem Day. First proclaimed in May 1968, Jerusalem Day celebrates the establishment of Israeli control over East Jerusalem after the war in June 1967 (the Israeli political parlance marks this as the liberation and unification of Jerusalem). While it is an official, national holiday, Jerusalem Day has come to be identified most clearly with the Religious-Zionist camp, whose rabbinical leaders instituted the day as a religious holiday (celebrated in synagogues by recitations of a series of psalms—the Hallel—as is traditionally done on Jewish holidays), and who has led public celebrations of the holiday in parades and other ceremonies. The fact that other sectors of the Israeli public tend to be either indifferent to or critical of the holiday (which, it is important to stress, cannot be read outside of the Israeli-Palestinian conflict generally, and the symbolically charged contest over Jerusalem specifically) only further highlights the unique Religious-Zionist approach to the holiday.

My interpretation is based on Noam Hadad's comprehensive analysis of thousands of publications in Religious-Zionist platforms, focused on the public debate they offered surrounding critical events in Israeli history between 1967 and 2014.[47] The story emerging from this analysis is one of a continuous, developing framing and reframing of both the traditional and the newly declared holidays to fit within a nation-statist soteriology. In the case of the Ninth of Av, the narrative arc moves from attempts at adapting and updating the commemorative ritual so as to fit within the statist soteriology to the sidelining of the ritual by relegating it to an apolitical realm of religion and even initiatives at reforming it to comply with statist soteriology. Jerusalem Day, on the other hand, has moved along an arc of sacralization; the originally civic holiday gradually put on a theological garb.

Fitting the Ninth of Av into the Nation-Statist Soteriology

Religious-Zionist spokespeople had to confront the tension in the immediate aftermath of the June 1967 war, as Jews throughout the world prepared to mark the Ninth of Av in August of that year. Given that Religious-Zionist identity was heavily invested at the time in the (secularist, statist) dualism distinguishing nationalism from religion and seeking to uphold both by "synthesizing" the alleged separate realms, these spokespeople found themselves tasked with holding the stick from both ends: to remain loyal to the religious tradition of mourning the destruction of Jerusalem and its temple, while at the same time celebrating what they clearly saw as the newly achieved political, national liberation of the city and its rebuilding.

The attempt to negotiate the tension between a tradition of mourning (a tradition, as one writer reminded his readers, that aims to teach us of divine providence and to encourage us to contemplate the ways of God) and a political triumphalist message (in which it is human agency—the military of a secular state, at that—that achieved liberation) shaped much of the Religious-Zionist discourse on the Ninth of Av for years to come.[48] A primary solution employed in Religious-Zionist public venues consisted primarily of assigning a theopolitical meaning to the Ninth of Av itself, aiming to incorporate it within the political Zionist narrative, while preserving (separately, as it were) a tradition of religious mourning. Ultimately, this religious aspect, too, put on an increasingly Zionist, political meaning as the years progressed.

This discourse ultimately coalesced around a nationalist, theopolitical reasoning, in which what was seen as a religious argumentation was motivated by Zionist considerations. The development was gradual, and the confusion caused by the recent establishment of Israeli control over Jerusalem was palpable. Thus, for example, an editorial in *Haṣofe*, the Religious Zionists' flagship daily, betrayed a certain uneasiness with the Israeli chief rabbinate's decision not to declare the mourning rituals of the Ninth of Av obsolete following the 1967 war. Indeed, the editorial says, certain texts traditionally recited during the Ninth of Av's rituals in synagogues "include paragraphs that differ from the existing facts," but as long as the Temple Mount itself remains "desolate" (*shomem* in the original Hebrew) and the ingathering of the exiles incomplete (i.e., Jewish communities are present elsewhere than Israel), the general orientation of preserving the mourning rituals is ultimately justified.[49] Another writer later reminded his readers that although the city of Jerusalem is no longer "mournful, ruined, despised and desolate," the fact remains that in place of the temple stands "an abomination" (*shiquṣ*), and the nation is unable to "restore the crown to its glory" (i.e., to rebuild the temple itself).[50] A leading rabbi agreed that the "old mourning" for Jerusalem is no longer valid, since the city has already been rebuilt, even before the establishment of Israeli control over the eastern part of it in 1967 (Jerusalem, the western part of the city, has been declared Israel's capital city, and extensively built since 1948). Furthermore, he argued, Zionism has already achieved the national revival Jews have prayed for. Yet a "new mourning," he explained, one that focused on the fact that the temple is not rebuilt, is in place. This mourning should be expressing "our yearning for those days of the existence of our temple."[51]

Marking the first Ninth of Av following the 1967 war, *Haṣofe*'s editorial conveyed an impression that directly contradicted the mournful image of the desolate Jerusalem traditionally evoked in the synagogue rituals of the day. Reassuring its readers that "the mourners of Zion and Jerusalem find great consolation in the liberation of the city, the Temple Mount and the Western Wall from the hands of enemies," the editorial went on the reaffirm that the city of Jerusalem, unified under Israeli control, is "no longer deprived of its honor, its head is no longer lowered, and foreign legions have been expelled from it." Yet the editorial also explicated a *political* reasoning for maintaining the religious mourning rituals: the Jewish people, it asserted, acknowledges the miracle it experienced but continues to mourn the fact that "a great superpower [the USSR] re-arms the Arab armies and conspiracies are devised against Israel and Jerusalem." In this setting, the religious mourning ritual gains political value as it "strengthens the spirit, arousing the people to be worthy of achieving its missions" against such hostility.[52]

Commentators also sought to include their continuously developing assessment of political reality as part of what they presented as a religious, halakhic (i.e., in accordance with *halakha*, Jewish law) process of reasoning on the matter of preserving the mourning rituals of the Ninth of Av. In one writer's view, halakhic reasoning should acknowledge the facts that the ancient city of Jerusalem remains settled by Gentiles; "foreigners" keep on building their houses of worship in it; and, more generally, "Jerusalem is still far from what all generations have hoped to see in it as the center of learning and holiness."[53] He thus suggested that until this political reality is not fundamentally changed, the mourning rituals should remain in place. Note that such halakhic, "religious" reasoning draws the Ninth of Av toward a utopian horizon that is necessarily detached from the reality of politics: any realist assessment would have to concede that religious considerations need to be suspended (as it is unreal to expect the above conditions to be fulfilled outside of an eschatological framework), leaving the stage for the state's theopolitics to dominate.

A similar reasoning, in which a political argument is made for the continued validity of observing the religious ritual, was later expanded to include other aspects of the Israeli-Arab conflict, such as recent attacks on Israelis as well as the danger that international peace initiatives could lead to the limiting of Israeli sovereignty over the Temple Mount.[54] Echoing the rabbinic tradition that the ultimate cause of the destruction of the temple was internal strife, writers also argued that persistent political divisions further justify the maintaining of the mourning rituals.[55]

Writers repeatedly sought to instill new, contemporary (and political, if this confusing duality is of any relevance here) meaning in the mourning rituals, struggling to allow for the continued observance of the religious tradition of mourning as part of a theopolitical tradition of triumphant national revival. One editorial instructed its readers to contemplate the unfortunate fate of the State of Israel—being in a continuous state of war—when observing the Ninth of Av rituals. Commentators have mentioned time and again, as reasons for the continued mourning, that the redemption of Jerusalem is incomplete as long as the Temple Mount is held by "foreigners"; that the international community refuses to acknowledge Israeli sovereignty over East Jerusalem; that many Jews remain abroad, and they are also joined by emigrating Jewish Israelis; and that even among those Jews who do live in Israel, there is political division.[56]

As the settlement movement in the West Bank and the Gaza Strip, led by Religious Zionists, grew in size and became the focus of political controversy, its fate, too, was mentioned as cause for mourning on the Ninth of Av. Decrying the demand that Israel withdraw from territories it occupied in 1967 as manifesting disregard for the Land of the Patriarchs, one editorial explained the relevance of the Ninth of Av to contemporary Israel, drawing on a tradition that dates the biblical story of the Twelve Spies (Num. 13:1–33) to the Ninth of Av:

> The crying for generations in the Ninth of Av was instituted to mourn the urge to return to slavery and degradation, so as not to carry the heavy load of the highest freedom and its responsibility. . . . Yet that same crying unfortunately returns in our generations, too. . . . In the Ninth of Av we must remember the persistent problem that caused the destruction, the first sin, the sin of the Twelve Spies. . . . We have experienced many destructions because of the failures of the Spies. And in our days, there is a new version of spies, who slander the Land.[57]

The intensification of the political fight over Jerusalem, which has become a flashpoint of the Israeli-Palestinian conflict, only further instilled the Ninth of Av with political meaning. The fact that the enemies of the State of Israel "want Jerusalem as their capital" renders the current campaign over Jerusalem part of the story of the Ninth of Av that stretches "from ancient times to our time."[58]

Yet at the same time it became harder and harder to ignore the material, physical, and political development of the city and the strengthening of the Israeli hold over it. In some Religious-Zionist readings, this political background only further highlighted the importance of the Ninth of Av, in effect reading the religious ritual as manifesting and reinforcing a contemporaneous stance in a political conflict. One editorial proclaimed in the midst of the first Palestinian uprising (intifada) that any hesitation regarding the continued relevance of the mourning rituals is out of place, since politics proves their relevance: "The events we are witnessing make it clear that the meaning of this day continues to be valid. . . . The People of Israel is yet to settle peacefully in its land, and [enemies] try to harm us in various ways, both by direct attacks and by diplomatic maneuvers." Furthermore, Jerusalem itself is far from enjoying peace, and people refrain from going to the Western Wall for fear of attacks. There is no question, then, of the relevance of mourning on the Ninth of Av: "Jerusalem has yet to be completely redeemed, and foreigners stride the Temple Mount." The prayers of the day are hence as valid today as they ever were.[59]

Jerusalem Day and the Theologizing of a National Holiday

As the Ninth of Av was reassessed, its religious meaning reformulated against a dynamic political reality, Jerusalem Day came to embody the antithesis of the traditionally mournful Ninth of Av. Jerusalem Day allowed Religious Zionists to frame the ideologically and politically proper attitude toward the city and its symbolic referent, the nation-state: celebration instead of mourning, redemption in place of destruction, and, especially important, reaffirming sovereignty as opposed to bemoaning exile. Contrary to their predicament in relating to the Ninth of Av, Religious-Zionist spokespeople were free from the ideological tension between a traditional, religious defeatist message of destruction and exile and a political triumphalist message of liberation and rebuilding. Jerusalem Day allowed them to propagate a narrative released from a mournful tradition, celebrating the city as the epitome of national revival. Importantly, the celebration of the city in Jerusalem Day was released from the issue of the absence of the temple; the fact that the latter remains unbuilt seemed to be irrelevant. As a leading rabbi explained, it is the rebuilding of the city of Jerusalem—and not the rebuilding of the temple itself—that is the "symbol of redemption" spoken of in scripture.[60]

Released from traditional religious ambiguities, the celebration of Jerusalem Day became defiantly sectorial, even partisan, as it was mobilized also to discredit political rivals. This celebration, explained one editorial, manifests "not only our spiritual tie to Jerusalem, but also our determination—to build . . . in all parts of the city, every day and always, because Jerusalem is ours and it symbolizes the eternity of the Jewish people. . . . We will do everything to guard it, so it is not harmed by instigators and agitators, who have yet to come to terms with the city's reunification."[61] Against a backdrop of political contestation over the fate of Jerusalem in any future agreement between Israel and the Palestinians, an editorial insisted that Jerusalem's exultant national status—symbolized by Jerusalem Day and not the Ninth of Av—must be kept away from debates over the fate of the territories occupied by Israel in June 1967. "Except for a marginal minority," the editorial claimed, "the whole nation feels and believes wholeheartedly that Jerusalem, undivided, will remain forever the capital city of Israel and under Israeli sovereignty."[62] In the same spirit, it was suggested that Jerusalem Day should be used to manifest and strengthen "both internally and externally" Israeli sovereignty over the city,[63] and to facilitate a wider campaign of annexing the city's eastern suburbs.[64]

This trend gained further strength in the mid 1990s, when the Israeli government and the PLO negotiated and signed what came to be known as the Oslo Accords. The political debate at the time also revolved around a potential partition of Jerusalem as part of an Israeli-Palestinian agreement, and much of the Religious-Zionist discourse on Jerusalem Day focused on what its spokespeople saw as the danger threatening Israeli sovereignty over the city.[65]

This sense of threat also shaped the Religious-Zionist approach to the Ninth of Av, which was now dominated by nationalist political messages that pushed the religious ones aside. Viewed through the lens of a contemporary threat to Israeli sovereignty over Jerusalem, the Ninth of Av gained a renewed political relevance. In light of the looming danger, writers argued, we must remember the historical destruction of the city and mourn it in light of the impending destruction that a disloyal government is going to bring about. In effect, the danger of the Oslo Accords helped these writers tie the Ninth of Av and Jerusalem Day into a unified narrative: Jerusalem is indeed currently rebuilt under Israeli sovereignty, but any celebration of this fact is hampered by the fact that the third destruction is already on the horizon.[66]

The Repoliticization of the Ninth of Av

The first three decades following the establishment of Israeli control over Jerusalem have thus been dominated by a Religious-Zionist struggle to remain loyal to a mournful tradition and to the religious meaning of the Ninth of Av and to weave it into a Zionist political narrative by continuously attempting to instill it with new, contemporary political meaning. Yet, as the years progressed, this discourse gradually became focused on nationalist, political, and allegedly secular content, mainly concerned with reaffirming Israeli control over the territories occupied in 1967, Jerusalem first among them. Religious-Zionist thought struggled to uphold what it read as the religious nature of the Ninth of Av alongside the obvious political messages it entailed, and this religious character was increasingly being politicized, read as it was through an exclusively triumphalist Zionist ideology.

It must be stressed that Religious-Zionist spokespeople have not sought to strip away the mournful religious meaning of the Ninth of Av (what could be viewed as the secularizing of the day); instead, they sought to find a proper role for the day in the state's theopolitics, to preserve the day's status as important in the Hebrew calendar, and to transform its meaning to fit in within a modern, Religious-Zionist interpretation of Jewish history. This was taking place against a background of a general Zionist (secular) indifference to the Ninth of Av.

Gradually, as Religious-Zionist ideology itself was reassessing its commitment to a notion of synthesizing religion and nationalism, realigning along a reasserted sense of commitment to the theopolitics of the state, the struggle to uphold the Ninth of Av's religious meaning was losing steam. The Ninth of Av was rendered politically irrelevant, relegated to the status of one among other, minor days of mourning in the Jewish calendar that are no longer seen to carry explicit contemporary political meaning (e.g., the fasts of Esther and Gedaliah). During the late 1990s, the commemoration of the Ninth of Av was largely pushed to the sidelines of the main discussions on Religious-Zionist platforms.

Renewed political struggles, however, pushed the Ninth of Av back onto center stage. Thus, for example, when the Religious-Zionist camp was campaigning against what became known as the Disengagement Plan (Israel's withdrawal from the Gaza Strip and the northern West Bank in the summer of 2005), its spokespeople depicted the Ninth of Av as carrying crucial *political* meaning. The fact that the dismantling of Israeli settlements in the Gaza Strip took place immediately after the Ninth of Av was read as a premonition of sorts, encouraging writers to focus exclusively on the contemporary, Zionist, political meaning of the day and suspending its historical-traditional meaning. The historical destruction was used to depict the current Zionist tragedy in the Gaza Strip. One writer, for example, decried "the end of the state," pronounced by the Ninth of Av: "The basic premise of the state—its 'statism'—is emptied of all content. . . . This, then, is the pronouncement of these days. Not for nothing do we suffer [in this time of year]. From the chaos, a picture becomes clear: A sinking state that has reached the end of its path."[67]

Writers either implicitly or explicitly suggested parallels between the destruction of Jerusalem and the temple, and the destruction of Israeli settlements in the Gaza Strip.[68] Some even suggested that a new day of fasting and mourning to commemorate the destruction of these settlements should be established.[69] They argued that the Ninth of Av of 2005 was seeing Israeli society falling again into destruction, led into "the implosion-point of the renewed attempt to unify forces and identify a secular leadership as part of the laying of a path for the Messiah."[70]

Jerusalem Day and the Sanctification of Sovereignty

Against this background, there was little room in Religious-Zionist discourse to attend to Jerusalem Day. In retrospect, it is clear that this was but a temporary suspension of a trajectory that began earlier—namely, with the appropriation of Jerusalem Day as *the* Religious-Zionist day of celebration. While some writers, identifying the increasingly sectorial nature of Jerusalem Day, decried this development and suggested that the national character of the civic holiday should be reiterated, others have propagated a reading of the holiday that stressed its role as celebrating Religious-Zionist identity; they have used the holiday to contrast Religious Zionism with what they depicted as a diminishing secular Zionism.[71]

Reflecting the strengthening status of the Temple Mount itself and a growing political campaign in certain Religious-Zionist circles to rebuild the temple, writers also increasingly voiced the demand that Israeli sovereignty over the Temple Mount should be exercised.[72] Tellingly, this focus on the Temple Mount was also framed within a political, nationalist frame, as the exercise of Israeli sovereignty over the holiest of holy places was depicted as a matter of Zionist expediency. Most writers whose commentary focused on the Temple Mount sought neither the rebuilding of the temple nor the permission to worship on the mount, but the statist exercise of sovereignty itself. "Since we are sovereign over the Temple Mount by virtue of our very being Jews," explained one writer, "we cannot stomach a foreign rule over the mount, and we cannot stomach that Jews deprived of a sense of mastery and incapable of naturally exercising sovereignty give up on what is ours by right and by law."[73]

The Temple Mount was made into a Zionist political symbol along the lines of the nationalization of traditional Judaism itself. When rabbinical reasoning that draws upon this tradition came into conflict with the interests of the sovereign state (as interpreted by Religious-Zionist commentators, of course), the latter was assumed to be supreme. Thus, for example, in one editorial that decried the "miserable mistake" of the chief rabbinate's decision to uphold a halakhic ruling that forbids Jews from visiting the Temple Mount on the grounds of the place's sacred status; this decision, argued the editorial, is regrettable because it damages the interests of the state.[74] The conclusion is clear. "Halakhic trepidations, too, have a limit," and the time has come to prevent these from impairing sovereignty: "It is time to decide whether we relinquish our excessive halakhic trepidation or relinquish the Temple Mount."[75] The rabbis' failure to adapt their halakhic rulings to the demands of sovereignty was criticized as perpetuating the destruction of the temple, a deplorable "obsequiousness" that plays into the hands of the enemies of the state.[76] Reflecting the same logic, another writer called what he saw as the state's refusal to exercise its sovereignty over the Temple Mount a sin, and the "despicable state of the Jewish people there" its "punishment."[77] The "national honor" was deemed as necessitating that Jewish Israelis be allowed access to the site.[78] Notably, these nationalist reasonings were brought up also as part of the commemoration of the Ninth of Av, exemplifying the importation of the discourse usually developed around Jerusalem Day into what was considered to be a religious discourse.

The "Religionization" of the Ninth of Av

As mentioned earlier, the main discursive strategy adopted by Religious-Zionist writers was to attempt to instill the Ninth of Av with a renewed political meaning that in turn tended to push aside the traditional mourning of the destruction of the temple and the city. This tendency lost steam in the 1990s and was gradually replaced by a reframing of the Ninth of Av as a religious ceremony that lacks a political or actual meaning. Among other things, this was manifested in writers' focus on the destruction of the temple itself, while the mourning of the destruction and the desolation of the city was significantly played down. As one writer put it, the real meaning of the mourning during the Ninth of Av in a time when the city of Jerusalem is flourishing under Israeli sovereignty is the realization that it is a "mourning for something that will not return," that the "dead" temple will not be rebuilt.[79] Another writer reiterated that "the stages of redemption we have been blessed with" should not undermine the mourning for the absence of the temple itself: "The national body has already stepped out if its grave, the national resurrection is in its midst, but the heart, the heart is missing, and it is missing so much we do not feel its absence."[80]

Such pronouncements suggest that the tension between the triumphalist Zionist narrative and the Jewish tradition of mourning is solved—or, at the very least, negotiated—here by reformulating the tradition to fit statist theopolitics. This necessarily entails a drastic rewriting of the meaning of the ritual at hand, in effect annulling its traditional meaning and forcing it into a framework matching the ideal of nation-statist revival. As mentioned earlier, such rewriting of Jewish tradition was not novel: Socialist Zionists have long established this confrontational attitude toward Jewish tradition, aggressively rewriting the meaning of traditional symbols to fit the emerging Zionist ideology.[81] But while this attitude coheres with the Socialist-Zionist sense of rebellion against the religious Jewish past, it sits rather awkwardly with a proclaimed Religious-Zionist commitment to an Orthodox observance of this tradition.

See, for example, how one commentator described the proper role of the remembrance of the destruction of the Temple in the framework of a consciousness of renewed sovereignty. While the Temple remains unbuilt and the divine presence is absent, he said, "we must continue and mourn." Yet political reality is dramatically different: "Our blood is not freely spilled by Gentiles who seek to persecute us and annihilate us. Our daughters are not freely given to raping and abuse. We do not live in constant fear of pogroms and religious persecutions to death. The community [in Israel] remains strong, and the forces of spiritual creation in it grow stronger."[82] Therefore, according to Jewish law itself, "we must not mourn as if we still live in exile. . . . Many of those born here, in this blessed and tormented land, do not at all feel the burden of exile," which was the cause of the institution of the mourning rituals. Forcing these young generations of Israelis who enjoy the reality of Jewish sovereignty to uphold the tradition of mourning only further alienates them. The solution, then, is to "determine a framework that reflects the depth of exile we currently experience combined with the blessing of revival."[83]

Another writer was even more daring, suggesting a novel model for commemorating the Ninth of Av, by replacing its traditional meaning with a modern Zionist one. The day would be for generations marked as the time in which "we remember the horrors of the prolonged exile." Instead of the traditional day-long fasting, Jews would only fast during the night. While shorter, the fast "will not be merely symbolic," since it will be "an active night, where many people roam the streets," and public gatherings take place "in every city and in every place in Israel." These would be dedicated to reading the traditional texts bemoaning the destruction of Jerusalem, as well as to other public happenings. During the daytime, the Ninth of Av will no longer be a day of public mourning. Importantly, this "popular" reminder of the "scars" of exile in a "positive atmosphere of building and growth" will only apply to Israeli Jews. Jewish people living outside of Israel, outside of the sovereignty of Jews, would uphold, by this suggested reformulation, the traditional customs of the Ninth of Av.[84]

Conclusion

The transformation of the Ninth of Av into a religious ritual that lacks an explicit contemporary political meaning is derived from the wider ideological developments within Religious Zionism. The Western duality of (nation-statist) secular politics versus private and apolitical religion, to which Religious Zionism was historically committed, necessarily created a tension surrounding a religious ritual commemorating what was also a political catastrophe.[85]

This was further compounded by the direct confrontation between the Zionist message of national resurrection and the traditional Jewish assignation of redemption to God. This tension, like others in Religious-Zionist ideology, was resolved by a decisive reassertion of the theopolitics of the sovereign nation-state as a primary directive of this ideology, subsuming Jewish religion under the dominance of the state.[86] In this frame, Zionism and Judaism were read as synonymous, and there was no longer a need to demarcate a politically neutral sphere for religion. The radical proposals of reforming and rewriting the traditional rituals of the Ninth of Av were but an extreme expression of this trend. The forgoing of all attempts to instill the day with contemporary political meaning that would fit in with its traditional (political) message was but a less blunt (and arguably more consistent) expression of the same trend. In effect, nestled fully within the embrace of nation-statist sovereignty, Religious-Zionist commentators have given up on the endeavor to uphold the Ninth of Av as a relevant Jewish ritual. Instead, they have transformed Jerusalem Day into a major (sectorial) holiday symbolizing the reformed or updated Religious-Zionist commitments, focused as they are on sovereignty itself.

The Religious-Zionist commitment to the nation-state does not conflict with what we may call "traditional Jewish theology," nor does it merely serve or complement it. Rather, it becomes the very essence of this theology. God, who had always been the very center of Jewish theology, is either replaced in Religious-Zionist thought by the state or understood to be sacralizing the state and putting it center stage, receding to the sidelines to enable the theopolitics of the state.

The Religious-Zionist endeavor to cope with the Ninth of Av is, then, a story of the subsuming of religious traditions by the theopolitics, and especially the soteriology, of the nation-state that identifies as Jewish. Confronted with these theopolitics, tradition is either politicized or depoliticized (i.e., rendered as lacking a relevant political message) so as to make it compatible with the dominant, statist soteriology. The proclaimed Religious-Zionist commitment to an orthodox observance of this tradition only further charged this process with complexity—compared, for example, to a secular Zionist indifference to the ritual or an ultra-Orthodox, non-Zionist commitment to a traditionalist upholding of it—but did not challenge the main thrust of the story: tradition is interpreted (by some of its carriers) to fit within the theopolitics of the nation-state. Furthermore, the appropriation of Jerusalem Day as a Religious-Zionist holiday also suggests some ways in which this theopolitics might co-opt what it would see as religious tradition by introducing into this tradition political rituals and narratives that ultimately amount to a (new) religious sacralization of the state.

Lastly, I must stress that I do not wish to argue for a one-sided relationship between nation-statist theopolitics and religious tradition. Israel's own history demonstrates how political crises may lead to the resurgence of "old" interpretations of tradition to challenge statist soteriology and amend it. Thus, for example, in the enduring "myth of defeat" of the Yom Kippur (October 1973) War—an ultimately successful military campaign that is to this day remembered and commemorated as an Israeli defeat—allowing for what Charles Liebman has called the "resurface[ing] at the unconscious level" of "the contradiction between Zionist ideology" and "the threat of destruction."[87]

As noted earlier, it is my contention that the lessons of this case exceed its idiosyncrasies. There is nothing especially unique in the way that this nationalist ideology, Religious Zionism, has coped with the tension of adhering to traditional messages that are sometimes inconsistent with the ideology. The current case study tells a wider story of how nation-statist political theology negotiates, shapes, and in turn is influenced by messages entailed in traditions that it wishes to appropriate or to replace. This, in other words, is a particular instance of a universal phenomenon.

5

A Jewish Reaction to Zionist Supersessionism

Introduction

What are the possibilities—and potential limitations—of a Jewish critique of Israeli politics? (By "Jewish" I mean a critique that is committed to a loyal dialogue with Judaism as a system of thought and practice.) This question becomes urgent in face of the incessant tendency to conflate Zionism with Judaism or Jewishness. As we have seen, this conflation is vigorously promoted by Zionist ideology itself and often accepted as a truism by critics of Zionism. This chapter offers an assessment of a *Jewish* critical consideration of the politics of Zionism and its embodiment in the State of Israel, and of the meaning of Jewish politics more broadly, through an engagement with the writings of Leon Roth (1896–1963). As I suggested earlier, Roth's Jewishly informed critique of Zionism can be seen as an expression of a Jewish or even Judaic reaction to Zionist supersessionism. Thus, it allows us to consider at least one instance of Judaism "talking back" at Zionism.

The engagement with Roth, who was a British-born, Oxford-educated Zionist, immediately locates this exploration within an admittedly limited discursive and ideational space. It situates Roth's interventions—in which his commitment to British liberal democracy is joined by his religiously ethical Jewish convictions and his active agency in the Zionist enterprise in Palestine—in a rather complex relation to other, mostly Central European thinkers who also offer ethical (often critical) engagements, religious and otherwise, with Zionism, such as Hermann Cohen, Hans Kohn, Franz Rosenzweig, Hannah Arendt, Martin Buber, Yeshayahu Leibowitz, Barukh Kurzweil, and Judah Magnes.[1] Not so dissimilar from the case of what David Myers called "the lost voice of Simon Rawidowicz,"[2] or the "counter-Zionism" offered by Rabbi Binyamin (Yehoshua Radler-Feldman),[3] Roth's thought further illuminates

juxtapositions with non- and anti-Zionist, Jewishly informed oppositions to Zionism that rely on various traditions of thought, like those
offered by Joel Teitelbaum, Daniel Boyarin, and Judith Butler.[4]

Interestingly, Roth's political or ideological interventions have rarely
been studied. Therefore, while works on many of his (mostly German-
born) partners in establishing the Hebrew University furnish the shelves
of academic libraries, his voice remains forgotten, both in and outside
of Israel. Roth's own personal path—which ultimately led him to leave
the newly established State of Israel and relegated him to the sidelines of
the mainstream Jewish discourse on the state and on Zionism—instills
his point of view with a unique quality: that of someone who had joined
the Zionist enterprise with much *Jewish* hope and ultimately found the
enterprise, and the state it created, Jewishly wanting, while remaining
committed, so it appears, to the theopolitics of the nation-state. It is this
obviously limited scope of discussion that enables us to appreciate his
brand of a Jewishly informed critique of Israeli politics and the alternative understandings of Jewish politics it offers. At the same time, it
underlines the limits of such a standpoint, limits that we will consider as
the entrapment of political thought in the sovereign nation-statist frame
of the political mind.

Roth's ethical Jewish convictions direct his engaged reader rather
immediately to a unique perspective informed by a profound commitment to what is at one and the same time a universal and a particularly
Jewish duty to justice. Roth looks at Zionism and its (or the State of Israel's) rendition of Jewish politics from the outside, as it were, and finds
it wanting exactly because this politics is ultimately unethical from a
Jewish perspective. Most important is the fact that the Jewishly committed critical appreciation of Zionism/Israel leads the critic to address
the price that is exerted from Judaism itself due to actions carried by a
state that self-identifies as Jewish. Thus—maybe unwittingly, given his
original Zionist commitment—Roth encourages a critical Jewish reeval-
uation of the *Jewishness* of the state, reiterating the need to redraw the
lines demarcating the (ethical) boundaries separating Judaism from the
Jewish state.

This chapter explores the prospect that Judaism may "answer back"
to the Zionist appropriation and even critique Zionism. Specifically, the
chapter focuses on three main themes: first, the relation between Juda-

ism and Jews, questioning the "ethnicist" foundation of Zionist ideology; second, the relation between religion and politics as the two are constructed in modern European discourse, questioning the nationalist premise of the supremacy of nation-statist politics over religion; and, third, the meaning of Jewish secularism, questioning the Zionist claim to a "nonreligious" Jewish identity.

Leon Roth

Maybe the most telling fact related to Roth's intellectual and academic biography is the obvious gap between his relative obscurity and the foundational role he played in the establishment of Zionist/Israeli higher education generally, and of the study of philosophy more specifically.[5] The fact that Roth is little studied overshadows the comparative study of his thought, as the primary step—an exposition and analysis of his thought on its own terms, which is my aim here—must precede the juxtaposition of his thought with those of other, much more thoroughly studied thinkers. It is this gap, exacerbated by the fact that not a single full monograph on Roth has yet to be commercially published, that calls for a short biographical sketch before going any further.[6]

Roth personifies a unique strand of Jewish and Zionist commitments. Born in London in 1896 to a Jewish Polish merchant father and a Sheffield-born Jewish mother, Roth was one of four sons, the most famous of which was the youngest, Cecil Roth. Leon Roth received Jewish and classical education in his youth and later studied philosophy at Oxford. In 1923, he started teaching at the University of Manchester, but soon after received an invitation to join the newly forming department of philosophy in the nascent Hebrew University in Jerusalem. Judah Magnes, chancellor of the university, offered him the role of the institution's very first professor of philosophy. Roth accepted, immigrated to Palestine in 1928, and, together with Hugo Bergman, established the department and played a major role in shaping the Hebrew University at large.[7] Using his Hebrew name, Hayim Yehuda, Roth assumed the newly formed Ahad HaAm Chair in Philosophy and engaged with the legacy of Ahad HaAm in illuminating ways.[8]

Roth headed the department and, with Bergman, shaped the modern Hebrew study of philosophy in Mandatory Palestine and the newly established State of Israel. The two "determined the two trends of the study of philosophy in the department" that later came to be known as the analytical and continental traditions.[9] In its earlier stages, Roth's own work focused mostly on seventeenth-century rationalism, specifically that of Descartes and Spinoza, and on Maimonides.[10] Throughout his career, he also dealt with themes of Jewish philosophy, religion, and ethics, and it is on these themes that I will focus. In addition, Roth presided over the translation of the Western philosophical canon into Hebrew, a project that, as Neve Gordon notes, was in itself a quintessentially idealistic, Zionistically ideological undertaking.[11]

While in Mandatory Palestine, Roth would devote much of his time and attention to writing and teaching on themes of political philosophy, advocating a British interpretation of liberal democracy. As Jan Katzew highlights, while "Roth was not primarily a political philosopher," between 1945 and 1950 "he devoted his work exclusively to political philosophy. Within the five years that surrounded the birth of the State of Israel," Roth published six Hebrew monographs dealing with democracy, political philosophy, and education to prepare for democratic citizenship, joined by an English book engaging with John Stuart Mill and Walter Bagehot.[12] This turn was not coincidental:

> Roth wrote about political philosophy precisely when the State of Israel was transforming itself into a state, when the political and cultural DNA of Israel were being translated from theory to practice. Ever the educator, Leon Roth was seeking to influence the political climate in Palestine just as the political landscape of the emerging State of Israel was in formation. Roth endeavored to convince the nascent political leadership to adapt, if not adopt the democratic principles and structures in which he himself had been educated and immersed, those of Great Britain.[13]

It was only after Roth had left Israel that he wrote "the overwhelming bulk of his Jewish material," Katzew states, noting Roth's "deference to other scholars in Israel while he lived there, and his commitment to translating Judaism for those ignorant of it."[14] Importantly, the two main aspects of Roth's scholarship, Judaism and liberal democracy, were far from detached from one another. As Katzew puts it, taken together, Roth's body of work broadcasts the clear message that "a Jewish state ought to be a democratic state."[15] While obviously motivated by Zionist ideology and unmistakably committed to a politics that we may safely designate as "Jewish," Roth was far from being a "conventional" Zionist. Ultimately, he stood "aloof from Zionism in the sense in which that term has for some time now been conventionally understood."[16]

In one telling incident, while on a visit to Los Angeles as a representative of the Hebrew University in June 1947, Roth "stir[red] [the] wrath of Zionists." Answering questions at a press conference, Roth countered the main pillars of Zionist policy of the time, which was then committed to ending the British Mandate, establishing a Jewish state, and allowing unrestricted Jewish immigration to Palestine. He had spoken against the partition plan for Palestine, warning that "it will eventually lead to violence." He accepted that Jewish immigration to Palestine should be determined by the "absorptive capacity" of the land and suggested that "the [Jewish-European] refugee problem and the Palestine problem are 'two different' problems." Roth further complimented Britain for its treatment of the refugees and suggested that Canada and Australia should relax their immigration rules so as to absorb more of them. He also rebuked the "too many American yellow journalists in Palestine who are scare-mongers." In response, local Zionist leaders called Roth "an 'emissary of British Imperialism.'"[17]

While Roth clearly shared Zionist sympathies and was especially attuned to the importance of politics, "he was ultimately repelled by political Zionism."[18] What is often read as the strongest sign of his independent critical stance came when Roth left the State of Israel three years after its establishment. He returned to England but did not take another permanent job, and spent the rest of his life writing, mostly on Jewish themes, and lecturing on an occasional basis. He died in 1963 while on a visit to New Zealand.

Roth did not give a compelling, concrete account of his motivations for leaving, thereby leading to much speculation. His colleagues have suggested that personal-familial matters, institutional tensions at the Hebrew University, and ideological misgivings about the Zionist enterprise can all account for his decision to leave.[19] Clearly, given the heightened ideological atmosphere at the time, his act must have been contentious, and it has been given to ideological-political readings even if those were not his main motives. Colleagues and friends have argued that Roth was unable or unwilling to accept the ethical compromises of the Zionist struggle.[20] He specifically found it difficult to accept the atrocities carried out—and justified—in the name of Jewish nationhood. As formulated by one of his acquaintances, when confronted with these atrocities, which accompanied the struggle for statehood, Roth had experienced the "tragic experience" akin to viewing one's students "earnestly study[ing] Plato or Aristotle by day and slaughter[ing] innocent women and children at night."[21] Swimming against the rising tide of the nationalist outlook that justified these horrors as a matter of realpolitik or necessity, Roth held a "demonstrative disavowal of what was going on with the condonation or approval of most of the Jewish public in Palestine."[22]

Roth's "disappointment" with political Zionism was fed by his practical attitude to ethics. He believed that "ideas had to be relevant to modern everyday problems if their value was to be reckoned an abiding value, and, if their import was practical, they must be applied in fact." This was especially true in the case of ethics:

> This was the principal reason for his disappointment with Jewish statehood when it was ultimately realized. He has gone out to Palestine in the hope that it was to constitute a truly Jewish contribution to the polity of man. It being his experience that Jewish ethics and notions of justice where not given any marked enunciation in the national life of Israel . . . he saw no reason to remain in the country any longer. As he saw it, lip service was being offered to the ethical teaching of the bible which were at the same time being ignored in political concerns when they were inconvenient.[23]

Or, as Neve Gordon summarizes this reading, "Roth came to Israel for moral reasons and left it for moral reasons."[24]

Roth's style of writing on such topics as philosophy, Judaism, ethics, and religion, as well as on political thought, does not lend itself easily to an immediate and direct reading as a political intervention. His clearly unscripted comments at the Los Angeles press conference, as well as a handful of public letters he cosigned, which are the closest we have to a direct political intervention by Roth, leave much to be debated. Furthermore, as Raphael Loewe puts it, Roth's style is "classical in its restraint . . . which succeeds by a few masterstrokes in suggesting what it leaves unsaid."[25]

We can usefully explicate Roth's Jewishly informed critique of Zionism by focusing on three themes: the relation between Judaism and Jews, the relation between religion and politics, and the meaning of Jewish secularism. While this discussion will be informed by an engagement with Roth's wider body of work, we will be directly referencing only those works that are immediately relevant to our discussion.

A note of clarification is appropriate here. Although Zionist ideology is obviously far from uniform, as attested, for example, by the debates between Ahad HaAm and Herzl discussed earlier, I will use a generalizing language in this discussion, identifying the ultimately triumphant, state-centered political Zionism as setting the tone for this ideology as a whole and for Israeli political culture in particular. I ignore nuances in Zionist thought for the sake of drawing the background against which Roth's interventions may be better appreciated.

Judaism vs. Jews

The notion of divine election, of being a "chosen" people, is a pillar of nationalist thought, and, as we have seen, it has surely played a central role in the Zionist construction of Jewish nationalism.[26] This construction is often focused on the uniqueness of the Jewish people and on their right over the land, which is derived from their special character. As has been discussed, this nationalist construction of "chosen-ness" is comfortable with adopting the notion of divine election from Jewish tradition while denying the "agency" of God as the one who elects.[27] In other words, mainstream Zionism's is a "secular" notion of "divine" election, where the covenantal relationship entailed in this election is discarded and replaced by such abstract notions as the "genius" of the people and their "urge to life."[28]

But what does this "chosen-ness" mean? And what are its political implications? Roth's engagement with these questions—most fully developed in his last published book, *Judaism: A Portrait*, which also stands as his ultimate rebuke of the dominant Zionist interpretation of Jewish politics—is indeed illuminating. Insisting that the "doctrine" of the "chosen people" has been misunderstood by Jews and non-Jews alike and "has done much harm," Roth opens his discussion of Judaism with clarifying the meaning of "chosen-ness," warning his readers that "it is easy to claim to be of the chosen people, and to forget that the choice means duty, not privilege."[29]

Significantly, the notion of being "chosen" is phrased in the Bible as the Israelites' being a *holy* people—"that is, a people set apart with a special vocation." (Like Zionist thought in general, Roth tends to un- questionably identify the subject of modern Jewish nationalism—the contemporary Jewish people—with the biblical Israelite nation.) The rest of the Torah makes it clear that the essence of this vocation is ethi- cal conduct of private and public life. Hence, the question that looms large (at least in the context of the current, *political* reading) is how, and not whether, a betrayal of the vocation would render any discussion of *Jewish* politics simply meaningless should the politics practiced by the Jewish people express this "vocation."[30]

This very basic notion of holiness—that "election" entails duty, a commitment to a doctrine, or a teaching of a just being in the world— leads Roth to delineate an important distinction that can and should be seen as a determined judgment in a foundational tension at the very core of Zionist and Israeli politics. To understand this point, it may be helpful to consider for a moment the very notion of identifying Zionism as the *Jewish* national movement, and the State of Israel as the *Jewish* state. As we saw earlier, the debate over the meaning of this Jewish- ness or Jewish identity is a foundational feature of Israeli politics, de- termined by the tension between two conflicting readings of the matter at hand.

To recap the argument: one reading, which would prefer to see Israel as Jewish only in the sense that it is the "state of the Jews," tends to be focused almost exclusively on the demographics of majority and minor- ity groups within the state. By this reading, so long as the majority of the Israeli citizenry are identified as "Jews," the state can claim a Jewish identity for itself, regardless of questions relating to Judaism as a system of thought, ethics, and forms of life (what this reading would usually identify as "religion"). As advocates of this view often claim, whatever Jews do, politically and otherwise, in their state is by definition Jewish.

A competing reading prefers to identify Israel as a "Jewish state" in the sense that its politics corresponds with values, ideas, and ethical guidelines that emanate from within the world of Judaism. According to this reading, of which Roth's work could be considered an illuminating example, the state itself is subjected or indeed mandated to respond in principle and practice to an external *Jewish* judgment. Thus, the Jewish state or the Jews in the state could be found to act un-Jewishly.

It is through a discussion of the notion of "chosen-ness" that Roth offers his intervention in this debate, charting a clear relationship between Jews and Judaism: "Judaism is not to be considered in term of the Jews, but the Jews in terms of Judaism. Judaism is not what some or all individual Jews happen as a fact to do. It is what Jews should be doing (but often are not doing) as members of a holy people. Judaism comes first. It is not a product, but a program and the Jews are the instruments of its fulfilment."[31]

While the notion that Jews precede (and define) Judaism entails a clear sense of "ethnicity" as determining Jewish politics, the insistence that Judaism precedes the Jews pulls the rug from under such a genealogical focus: "When it is said that the Jewish people is the bearer or carrier or transmitter of Judaism, the phrase 'Jewish people' has to be understood in the widest sense. In principle, the tie constituting this people is not one of 'race' or 'blood.'" The ethical message of Judaism is universal, and anyone—regardless of "origin"—can become a carrier of this message and to abide by it; the question is one of the ideational, moral constitution of the person and of their community, and not of their accident of birth.[32]

It is not the Jews who define Judaism, then, but the reverse: Judaism precedes and defines the Jew. This necessarily entails a notion of "Jewish peoplehood" that is dramatically different from the ethnonational idea that emerged mostly in eastern Europe and came to determine Zionist and later Israeli politics. In essence, the precedence of Judaism over Jews renders the boundaries of the community that is the subject, or the collective agent of "Jewish politics," porous, allowing anyone who joins the aforesaid constitution to be a genuine part of this community: "The 'household of God' is the community of Judaism. Its root loyalty is not to a person or to an aggregate of persons but . . . to a Teaching. This Teaching is the 'Law (in Hebrew, Torah) of Moses' as it has been lived and interpreted, with ever-changing emphasis and modification, during the many long centuries of its history."[33]

Roth employs Maimonides's teaching to draw the rather radical (in its denial of the ethnic bent of the Zionist construction of Jewish ethnonationalism) lesson. Identifying the question of the voluntary or involuntary nature of the association as that which defines an association, he notes that on the Maimonidean view the community of Judaism "would seem to be, in this sense, voluntary. It is a body of persons linked by a common adherence to a determinate doctrine of the nature of God and to the determinate way of life for man which that doctrine is held to require." Drawing on Maimonides's history and sociology of religion, Roth stresses that this doctrine is "the original religion of the whole human race, it was only re-discovered by Abraham." The revelation at Mount Sinai was only the reaffirmation of this doctrine, adding to the mix the covenantal calling for Abraham's descendants as a "kingdom of priests and a holy nation." If one could be tempted (as the nationalist reading obviously is) to read this to mean "we are special, and better than others," Roth's reading of Maimonides stresses the exact opposite lesson: "This 'nation' is thus in intention infinitely expandible. Its outer limits are every single human being. . . . The two sides of the Torah, its religious truth and its moral discipline, are not secret. They are there for all to learn and live by."[34]

Furthermore, the promise entailed in the act of electing the people is *conditional*, dependent on the chosen people's adherence to the calling entailed in this holiness. Roth laments how Jews have forgotten the "if . . ." in prophetic promises: "We forget the condition. We forget that the promises must be earned. But that *is* the condition, the *sine qua non*. If we 'do not hearken', then we have no right to claim the fulfilment of the promises, far less to proclaim to the world that in us of this generation the promises are fulfilled."[35]

This leads Roth to directly discuss the political implications of the contemporaneous Zionist claim to chosen-ness. Forgetting this lesson of the prophets, Jews have come to see themselves as unconditionally deserving the benefits of the divine promise (of the Holy Land, the special privilege of the chosen). This, he says, amounts to heresy. "No doubt the politicians and diplomats will disagree," he writes. "But politicians, and even diplomats, are sometimes wrong." Indeed, the politicians' proclivity to be wrong "is one of the great, and one of the abiding, lessons which the biblical prophets have to teach us."[36] Judaism, in this scheme, becomes the judge of politics, not its enabler.

Yet, Roth insists, Judaism, the teaching that constitutes the Jews, cannot exist without a collective body practicing, interpreting, and upholding it—without, that is, a collective of Jewish people. The precedence of Judaism over the Jews, in other words, does not annul the latter. This is an important point, shifting our attention to focus squarely on politics, as it insists that a collective body—the subject of this politics—is a necessary element of Judaism. To make the point, Roth depicts the relationship between Judaism and the Jews as that between spirit and body, stressing the importance of the actual practice of "teaching" for the viability of the very notion of Jewish peoplehood. "The body of Judaism is clearly the 'Jews' or 'Jewry' or the 'Jewish people,'" and "it is agreed universally that such a body is required and exists. Judaism is not mere spirit. The 'remnant,' the 'saints,' the 'witnesses,' 'the Kingdom'—are all . . . , in Hobbes's phrase, real, not metaphorical. The way of God is a life to be lived in this world by human beings in association."[37]

This is crucial to note, since it holds Roth apart from those who suggest that Judaism could or even should be viewed as a purely intellectual and ethical spirit that can exist without a group of people living their lives as Jewish (and composing a Jewish people)—in essence, denying the relevance of Jewish politics, by focusing exclusively on a universal, apolitical notion of ethics. Roth's ethical intervention is fully committed to the particularism of the carrier of this universalist message. There is plenty in his writing to suggest that he is angry at the Jews for failing their ethical mission; nevertheless, he does not consider the option of Judaism (or the Jewish "spirit") viable without a sociopolitical body carrying this spirit.

Yet Roth rejects the notion that this "body" is somehow "biologically," "racially," "ethnically," or even "sociologically" predetermined: the political "body" of the carriers of Judaism is defined by the tradition they practice. "Ideally," he summarizes the lesson from Maimonides, "the community or 'body' of Judaism is coterminous with the whole of mankind. It is not confined to those born Jews or to those inhabiting a particular parcel of earth, except in so far as being born into a tradition, and living in an environment in which it is practiced, makes that tradition more 'natural' and therefore more easy to follow." This, then, is a *historical, traditional* (meaning, constituted by a lived, practiced tradition) sense of Jewish peoplehood, which is at the same time "metaphysical," dedicated to a metahistorical calling, "either moving nearer to or going away from, an identifiable goal."[38]

This notion of Jewish peoplehood is closely aligned with Roth's conception of Judaism, which he understands as a living, ever-developing tradition. Critically, while engaging thoroughly and continually with Judaism, Roth has not bothered to define Judaism in his work, a matter that touches the very core of his engagement with Judaism. As Katzew, who offers a detailed discussion of Roth's conception of Judaism, puts it: "Definitions limit: they 'fence in.' Roth set out to do the antithesis, to liberate Judaism from scientific precision, and relate to it as a living organism or as the subject of an artistic work."[39] Roth "harbor[ed] no scientific pretensions" in his engagement with questions of Judaism, which "retained an essential integrity throughout his life." Among other things, this phenomenological position allows for competing understandings of Judaism to coexist: "There is a tacit acknowledgement that his portrait [of Judaism] is only one of the many that are possible. It is not a definitive text about Judaism."[40]

The modern history of nationalism renders Roth's view a diatribe against the onslaught of ethnonationalism and of a quasi-racial notion of Jewishness that has come to dominate Zionism. Roth's concluding chapters of *Judaism: A Portrait* narrate the rapid reversal of roles in the relationship between Judaism and the Jews in modern Europe. Shifting his main concern "from the theoretical . . . to the practical," he offers a harsh, prophetic judgment of a political movement built around a collective self-perception of being a chosen people. Moving from theology to sociohistory, he does not mince his words, opening with a blunt summation of the narrative told by the Bible, which is to be read as a contemporary lesson:

Moses (or was it God?) knew his Jews. They were stiff-necked, corrupt, unwise, a crooked and perverse generation. They took every occasion for sinning, and they sinned every kind of sin. . . . There is no idealization of Jewry in Scripture. On the contrary, it is because the Jews were what they were that their need for Judaism was apparent. The picture given throughout is that of a violent and self-willed people whom God tried to educate without success.[41]

Religion vs. Politics

One of Zionist ideology's foundational arguments is that nationalism, as the political aspiration for establishing national statehood, is the all-encompassing, metahistorical framework of Jewish peoplehood. In this framework, which is seen as secular but carries obvious theopolitical tones, religion is seen as but a partial aspect of the nation's life, archaic and apolitical ("exilic," in the Zionist parlance). It is, in the best of cases, to be tolerated within the framework of the political. This is the background against which to consider Roth's decrying of the "politicization of Judaism" as a sin, and his redemptive suggestion that a "Judaization of our politics" is the great need of our time.[42]

As noted earlier, Roth is highly attentive to the historical nature of Judaism. As he observes, any attempt to identify the essence of Judaism is bound to be futile. Judaism cannot be discussed as a "single unit in the world," nor can it be easily compared with other "cases," since it is not clear at all to what conceptual field it belongs in the first place. Yet his "portrait" of Judaism makes it apparent that Roth takes Maimonides and his "fresh creation" of Judaism in the shape of a "unity of intellectual doctrine and moral discipline" as the ultimate benchmark for appreciating the diverse manifestations of Judaism.[43] It is the Maimonidean Judaism, Roth asserts, that "prepared Jewry in advance for what, on the European stage, was to be its greatest test."[44]

This "test" was a political one, embodied in and motivated by the granting of civil rights to Jews. Civil emancipation entailed a foundational role reversal between Jews and Judaism, and between politics and tradition: "Till now Judaism had made the Jew. From now on the Jew made Judaism. The tradition was made pliable to the political fact. . . . In the resulting struggle, the struggle to save the Jew for Judaism, it was, if anything, Judaism which was sacrificed."[45]

Roth identifies these changes as manifested most fully in the thought of Moses Mendelssohn. It was exactly the attempt to draw a clear line separating Judaism (seen as mere "religion") from politics (defined or epitomized by the "secular" nation-state)—a line Mendelssohn was demarcating in order to allow Jews to partake in the modern politics of the European nation-state—that resulted in the demise of Judaism itself.[46]

By reimagining or reinventing Judaism as a "confession" to fit within the modern (nation-statist) European political theory—on its discourse of religious tolerance and political integration—Mendelssohn instigated a process where Jews have lost Judaism: "Thus, the door was open to the Jew of English, French or German citizenship to become successively (i) the English, French, or German citizen of the Jewish confession (or 'persuasion'), (ii) the Englishman, Frenchman or German of the Jewish persuasion, and (iii) the Englishman, Frenchman or German without the Jewish persuasion."[47]

It is in this context—and only as a side note—that Roth offers a rather devastating critic of Israeli nationalism, and specifically Israel's (and, by extension, Zionism's) claim to Jewish identity. "Paradoxically," he writes, "the clearest example of this 'Mendelssohnian' development is now provided by the citizenry of the new state of Israel." The message is clear: Zionism has produced in the newly established state the Israeli *without* Judaism.[48]

Nationalism, in this reading, brings about an unwarranted reversal of the relation between religion and politics, politicizing religion. Nationalism would justify unethical behavior as expressing collective identity, or as serving the higher cause of the national interest. Roth addresses the biblical prophets as role models for resisting such politicization. Their (moral, religious, and only consequently political) power lay exactly in their refusal to be "swallowed up by nationalism." Formulated by the prophets, what would come to be considered Judaism and Jewish religion "demanded what the Israelite [meaning here: Jewish] nationalism did not give it, and often the opposite of what this nationalism gave it." This prophetic religion was the institution that "exposed the sins of the nation, and did not cover them." Buttressed by their moral-religious message, "they stood up against the kings, against the heads of the nation" and condemned the behavior of the masses as they did their leaders. "The prophets didn't accept quietly what the spirit of the nation offered them," Roth asserts. "They objected to it repeatedly." Politicization neutralizes religion: "Up until our days, religion has functioned as a conscience for nationalism. Now it cannot function as a conscience since it has been subjugated to nationalism, became part of nationalism, swallowed by nationalism."[49]

Religion was and remains that which can contest this politicization of life, meaning that "religion . . . has a political (or, if you like, an anti-political) role." Roth thus suggests that the main impetus of religion's political role—which, he says, is especially important in the immediate context of World War II and the escalating fight over Palestine—is what could be seen, paradoxically, as an *anti-political* message.[50]

Crucially, Roth made this intervention in Hebrew, in Mandatory Palestine in 1942—a context dominated by a Zionist ideology built exactly on the notion of politicizing Jewish identity, if not Judaism at large. Indeed, much of the impetus of dominant readings of modern European Jewish identity, including dominant streams within Zionist ideology, has aimed at "normalizing" the Jews, rendering them a "nation like all other nations"—that is, explicitly or implicitly, shedding the notion of the people's holiness—exactly by politicizing Jewishness—namely redefining it in terms of the politics of the sovereign nation-state. Roth is obviously writing in the context of the triumph of political Zionism over competing notions of Jewish nationalism. This background infuses his complicated treatment of the state with a flavor of heterodoxy that at the same time does not translate into an outright negation of the Zionist aspiration for sovereign nation-statehood.

Roth utilizes Judaism exactly to check the state and its politics and to offer an external judgment of these. He holds a notion of religion as directly opposed to the state, contradicting the Protestant notion of religion as an apolitical matter that is relegated to the private realm, outside of the reach of the state and away from its politics. Judaism, Roth argues, does not fit the "opinion" that "religion has nothing to do with authority," that it is "primarily a matter of feeling" and "personal." Confronted with the biblical message, this notion emerges as "unsatisfactory." This is worth noting here, because it is Roth's "thick" notion of Judaism that is incompatible with the politics of Zionism; we must remember that the state is happy with a purely spiritual, thin, and apolitical religion. Roth, in contrast, is suggesting that the moral, ethical, thick religion of the covenant is that which would counter the state.[51]

It is interesting to note that Roth addresses the modern state primarily in the context of discussing liberty and bondage, which he parallels, correspondingly, to worshiping God and submitting to idols. He does so as part of a wider discussion on the Jewish contribution to civilization, stressing that it was Jewish monotheism that enabled human liberty. "Bondage," he says, takes different forms, either spiritual or material. But "the ultimate bondage is of the mind," taking the form of submission to particulars: "Mind is bound being confined to any categories which are less than those of the whole. There are many such—stocks and stones, phrases, myths, wealth, political power. These all cramp and confine, and against them the Jewish mind has always waged war. Its God is jealous and will have none other gods besides himself. He is thus the supreme liberator."[52]

And it is in the context of this bondage of the mind—clearly un-Jewish—that the coercive power of modern state emerges in its fullest: "The last and most brutalizing of all the idols created by man" is the modern nation-state, "the all-controlling and all-interfering state." Against the totalizing rule of this state, "the last freedom comes to men from the recognition of their individual and immediate dependence on the God of the spirits of all flesh." It is *against* the modern state, then, not within or through it, that the liberating force of Judaism emerges in its fullest form. "If there is such a thing as a 'Jewish mind,' and if the Jewish mind as such has anything to contribute to mankind's common store, it may be said to consist in this sense of absolutes."[53]

Returning elsewhere to the concept of idol worship, Roth immediately turns to the state—this time couched in accompanying political concepts, all of which are but human creations—as a modern object of what the Bible sees as the ultimate sin:

> In religious language, myth is an idol. Idols are manufactured objects of worship, and the Bible mocks at the men who bow down to the work of their own hands. Yet graven images are not the only idols. They are only the more obvious ones. And they are today not the most dangerous. The dangerous idols are those we make of words, phrases like "the state," "race," "way of life," "progress," "democracy." We fall down and worship them, and, like Creon in the Greek play, are in the end broken by them. "They that make them become like them," empty, hollow, unreal.[54]

This juxtaposition of Judaism and the state fits within a larger framework, where generic "religion" proves to be, in Roth's view, the only institution to stand up to the "the great arrogance of our time, the arrogance of the state."[55] Echoing Antigone's evocation of the divine command-ment to counter the earthly rule of the king, Roth contrasts religion and politics, specifically religion and the modern state, to argue against the apparent triumph of the latter. "Political authority is essentially tempo-rary and relative," he writes, "a device to meet the changing circumstance of ever-shifting power. It is myth, not truth. When it claims to be abso-lute, it is doomed. It nullifies itself and engenders its own destruction."[56]

Granted, religion, too, limits individual liberty and seeks to dictate one's behavior, even if unlike the state its power is more "symbolic" than material. But here the major difference emerges: "The arrogance of poli-tics enslaves our humanity. The arrogance of religion creates it and gives it shape. The power of the one crushes and destroys; the authority of the other raises up."[57]

Commenting on the rabbinical treatment of the story of the Mac-cabean revolt against the Romans, Roth suggests that the suppression of the militaristic aspects of this story—aspects that, he must have been aware, have been highlighted by the Zionist reinterpretation and com-memoration of the story—betrays a wider message that bears immediate relevance to our appreciation of the modern sovereign state:

> If, as a principle of universal application, *God's* power is to be equated with his goodness, perhaps, in the rabbinic mind and as a principle of equally universal application, *man's power also* is to be equated with his goodness. Perhaps they [the rabbis] thought sincerely, apart altogether from the fear of the policeman and other considerations of the higher diplomacy, that there are virtues superior to the military. They made great use of the doctrine of the Imitation of God and constantly urge us to fol-low God in his moral attributes: "As he is merciful, be thou merciful." I am not aware of any passage in which we are urged to follow God in his *military* capacity.[58]

Roth also made note of the discrepancy between the form of the state and the various, more diverse manifestations of Jewish people-hood, suggesting that the state is not necessary for political Jewish self-expression: "State is but one of several forms of organizing society. It is indeed an important form, but not necessary, and surely not exclusive. There are several forms that match the demands of a human being, demands that are no less important than those that are fulfilled in the stat-ist organization."[59]

These comments suggest that Judaism is essentially opposed to the institution of the modern sovereign state per se. However, any discussion of Judaism and state in the current context must also consider the fact that Roth's writing on political theory, and his advocacy of British liberal democracy, strongly suggest that he aimed his critique not at the modern state in general terms, but specifically at the authoritarian, the "all controlling and all-interfering" state, suggesting a basic distinction between the two.

Yet Roth—a reader of Hobbes and a teacher of his works—could not have ignored the fact that this liberal democratic framework is itself founded on a totalizing (indeed, Hobbesian) notion of sovereignty. Ultimately, Roth, too, was unable to release the political mind from the bondage of modern sovereignty. In this regard, he seems to have been forecasting the difficulties or contradictions of liberal Zionism, although he was surely released from its debilitating secularist premises.

Ahad HaAm, the Misleading Father Figure

Roth's intellectual milieu in Mandatory Palestine generally and in the Hebrew University more particularly has celebrated Ahad HaAm as an ideological father figure of sorts. In Roth's own words, "We are all of us, in some sense and in some degree, disciples of Ahad HaAm. We all use his ideas, all speak his language."[60] This milieu, and the wider "we" Roth seems to refer to, had tended to align with Ahad HaAm's cultural or spiritual brand of Zionism. As discussed earlier, this ideological stream, when contrasted with political Zionism, viewed the national cultural reformation and rejuvenation—or spiritual resurrection of the Jewish people—as a necessary precondition for any future claim to sovereignty. While it had failed to dominate the Zionist project at large, Ahad HaAm's thought has had an enduring influence, especially with matters relating to Israel's and the Israelis' Jewish identity.[61] Throughout Israeli history, commentators have repeatedly evoked Ahad HaAm's vision as a remedy to the Israeli Jewish identity problem or crisis—namely, the apparent inability of Israeli nationalism to come to terms with its own claim to Jewish identity.

Roth's own engagement with Ahad HaAm is colored by this affinity. In his capacity as the inaugural holder of the Ahad HaAm Chair in Philosophy at the Hebrew University, Roth delivered a series of talks commemorating Ahad HaAm; he was also tasked with writing the introduction to Ahad HaAm's collected writings (in which, tellingly, as Barukh Kurzweil notes, Roth in effect "negates all of Ahad HaAm premises").[62] It is against this background that Roth's critical engagement with Ahad HaAm's thought and its heritage emerges as a challenge not only to this ideological father figure but also to Zionism, and even to Israeli Jewish identity in general. Not unlike Kurtzweil's own critical engagement with Ahad HaAm's thought and its legacy, Roth's critique can be read as an argument not just with or against the man himself, but primarily with the politico-cultural (or theopolitical) structure built upon his thought.[63]

Offering somewhat of an Oedipal release from the shadow of the father figure, Roth depicts the intellectual legacy of Ahad HaAm as out of its time and place, and Ahad HaAm the intellectual leader (as opposed to Ahad HaAm the man) as out of his philosophical and intellectual depth. It is important for Roth to put Ahad HaAm in his correct *intellectual* place, repeating in his writings that Ahad HaAm was not a philosopher, but merely used some prevalent ideas of others that were available to him. "Regretfully," he concludes, "we have to strip Ahad HaAm down."[64] This leaves Roth with "the uncomfortable impression that many of the ideas Ahad HaAm used so abundantly were ultimately unsound and ultimately incompatible with one another."[65]

Crucially, Roth finds Ahad HaAm's interventions regarding Judaism—especially on Jewish ethics—"doubtful."[66] While he sees in Ahad HaAm the "clearest recognition of the general nature of the problem" of modern Jewry, he judges Ahad HaAm as having approached the problem from the wrong angle, as it were: Ahad HaAm's commitment to modernism, specifically to the utilitarian and evolutionary thought of his time, led him astray. In Roth's terminology, this amounted to Ahad HaAm shifting the onus of discussion, along the lines of the predominant modern thought, from metaphysics to psychology. In this scheme, "religion" is turned into a subsegment of "culture," an element of "national creative power": it is (only) a historical manifestation of an essence, and it has become outdated in modernity, bound to evolve into something else.[67]

Roth judges Ahad HaAm severely for having failed to appreciate the effects of his historicizing of Judaism. For Roth, this is the origin of the Zionist/Israeli disregard for religion. It is an undermining of Judaism's ethical message more generally by rendering it a matter of "*mores*, habits of action: what men as a fact do, how men as a fact behave." Ahad HaAm fails to provide a binding reason for the continued commitment to Jewish ethics; his nationalist-mythic notion of the "national spirit" implies that "everything we do is ultimately the result of our spirit. This means that there is no deed of our deeds that cannot be justified."[68]

For Roth, who wishes to preserve an external moral perspective from which the state or national politics can still be critiqued, this is an aberration. "All common differences are swallowed up by the concept of the nation," he writes. "There is no longer sacred and profane, light and darkness, and good and evil since they are only secondary, subordinated and subjected to the 'absolutist' spirit of the nation." Religion, too, is a victim of this attitude, "enslaved to this omnipotent master."[69]

The fault lies, then, with the "ethnicist" root of Ahad HaAm's thought and that of most other Zionist ideologues: the notion that Jews, as a "nation," a "collective living organism," precede Judaism.[70] As many of Ahad HaAm's ideological adversaries argued, he could not provide a satisfactory justification for his "essentialism"—namely, his insistence that the collective "organism" of the nation should remain loyal to its past creation, since it holds the core of Jewish authenticity. His critics thus viewed themselves as free to destroy the temples of past times, and to build new ones, nourishing on any source they or the collective Jewish national body would deem fit for this purpose.[71]

One way of reading this critique is to view Roth as identifying Ahad HaAm's elitism as prohibiting the latter from seeing the dangerous implications of his (unintended?) relativism, which Roth finds to be a defining feature of Israeli Jewishness. Roth makes sure to note that Ahad HaAm himself was no relativist, but insists that Ahad HaAm failed to see how his "psychologizing" of Judaism would naturally lead to a relativistic conclusion: "On the sociological theory, and it was this which was held by Ahad HaAm, there is no and cannot be such a thing as an absolute. So, we are faced with a dilemma. If we accept his general theory, we have to abandon his moral outlook, if we accept his moral outlook, we have to abandon his general theory."[72]

The Qibya Letter: An Application of Ethics to Politics

What would it mean to Judaize politics instead of politicizing Judaism? Roth does not offer a comprehensive vision of a political program that would be Judaized, beyond, of course, his insistence that politics should be subjected to the judgment of what he presents as Jewish ethics. It seems to me that a good way to appreciate what this would mean in practice is reflected in his intervention on the debate surrounding the Qibya massacre.[73] Roth was either signatory or cosignatory to several other letters protesting Zionist or Israeli atrocities, such as a public letter decrying the Sharafat massacre in 1951,[74] and a letter to prime minister David Ben Gurion protesting the Israeli decision in 1949 to settle Jewish immigrants in Deir Yassin, the locus of another massacre.[75] His intervention, especially given the politico-discursive context in which it came, distills an explication of what it would mean for the state to be subjected to an external, Jewish judgment.[76] Specifically, it gives a very concrete sense of the price exerted from Judaism itself by the realpolitik of the running of a state viewed as Jewish (i.e., the price exerted from Judaism by its politicization; in this, the letter is not unreminiscent of Ahad HaAm's famous letter to *Haaretz* from 1 September 1922, protesting a "revenge killing" of a Palestinian Arab boy by Jews).

On the night of 14–15 October 1953, a newly established commando group of the Israeli military set out on a "reprisal operation" in the then Jordanian West Bank. This operation was a reaction to the killing of a mother and her two children in the Israeli town of Yahud by a Palestinian Fedayeen unit that crossed the border into Israel near the village of Qibya (Yahud was established in 1948 on the ruins of the Palestinian village Al-Yahudiya/Al Abbasiyya, which neighbored Qibya). The Fedayeen's attack was a link in a series of similar acts that threatened the fragile Israeli sense of security. The Israeli soldiers killed sixty-nine civilians, two-thirds of them women and children, and destroyed forty-five houses in the village.[77]

The Qibya massacre brought about a storm of international condemnation and protest, unprecedented in the state's short history. Importantly, many of those condemning it were spokespeople for Jewish communities outside of Israel. The debate that took place over Jewish platforms outlined what would later become the familiar lines of critique and apologetics concerning the State of Israel. The Israeli *has-bara* was loyally formulated by Rabbi Abraham Cohen, president of the Board of Deputies of British Jews and the Rabbi of Birmingham. Cohen summarized his defense of Israel in three "propositions": (1) in principle, "reprisals are morally wrong," but (2) those who have themselves carried such actions in the past cannot condemn others for doing the same, and (3) "no individual, Jew or Gentile, is entitled to condemn the Israelis who felt impelled to take such drastic action at Qibya, unless he can conscientiously assert: 'If I were living in that area and my own or my neighbor's wife and children had been murdered by Arab infiltrees [*sic*], I would oppose any suggestion to retaliate.'" Cohen further suggested that those Jews who condemn Israel but do not meet this condition are "probably moved not so much by moral indignation as by self-interest on the plea . . . 'What will the Gentiles say?'" The bottom line of the president of the Board of Deputies was accordingly unequivocal: "Many of the judges, both governments and individuals, who condemned [the Israelis] so unsparingly should have maintained a decent silence after searching their conscience."[78]

Roth's letter was formulated as a direct reaction to Cohen's "propositions," identifying the issue at stake not as a political or communal matter, but as an ethical one. He suggests that Cohen, in exempting Israelis from responsibility and directing his judgment toward the gentiles, failed to consider other important factors of what is at stake: "There is, for example, the religion, or the system of thought, called Judaism. And there are, too, the non-Israeli Jews considered either in themselves or in so far as they represent, or profess, Judaism." The issue, then, is specifically Jewish, as in having to do with Judaism: "The problem is whether either Judaism or Jewry can acquiesce in this 'incident.'" A historical view would suggest an almost immediate rejection of such an operation, "the type of action which we have been accustomed to say that Judaism taught the world to condemn and from which Jewry itself has so often suffered."[79]

For Roth, the abrogation of *Jewish* principles and values for the sake of the interests of the ("Jewish") state may simply be too dear a price to pay. If Israelis and Jews condone such actions, he rhetorically asks,

> shall we still be able to say that we demand one law for all and that we do not do to others what we do not wish others to do to us? That the *lex*

talionis is not Jewish; that we abhor the spilling of blood, even of animals; that we are commanded in the Pentateuch to care for the non-Jew ("love the stranger"), as was noted by the rabbis . . . thirty-six times? Shall we still be able to say that institution of properly constituted courts or the investigation of crime is one of the fundamental moral requirements of Judaism; that the Torah bans private revenge and insists on due process of law; that fathers should not be killed for the sins of children nor children for the sins of fathers, but each man should suffer for his own acts; that responsibility before both God and man is in Jewish eyes personal? [80]

Ultimately, the main victim of the abrogation of these Jewish foundations are the Israeli Jews themselves. Roth does not mince his words when making this point:

The real tragedy is of course for the Israelis. And it does not lie in the political deterioration of their borders. It lies in the moral deterioration of their souls. What manner of men are these who could contrive this action, or what persons could carry it out? And what manner of men are those who, arrogantly dismissing the moral issue, bemuse themselves and us with their *realpolitik*? Where terrorism is used as an instrument of policy the worst consequences fall on those who use it. [81]

The supremacy of (Jewish) ethics over (Israeli or Jewish) politics dictates that this politics is to be judged "from the outside," as it were, a judgment that is not bound by the logic or the interest of the state, but is determined by a universal message, which is necessarily "external" to the politics of the state: "It is surely a truism that the very meaning of morality is the correction of feeling by judgement. Judgement to be judgement must be external to the facts." [82]

Roth confirms that Jewishly (i.e., ethically), there cannot be even a "half-hearted approval" of the Israeli attack on Qibya. He does not hesitate to compare this attack to war atrocities carried out by the Nazis in Lidice and Oradour, equally and unequivocally condemning them all. Furthermore, Roth's commitment to the universality of Jewish ethics dictates that a Jewishly moral judgment is not the exclusive prerogative of Jews alone. Gentiles, too, can employ a Jewish ethical perspective to judge the politics of the Jewish state. He asks: "Can we cry out against honest and liberal-minded men, even of other religions and types of thought, who on the grounds taught by Judaism recognize an Israeli action for what it is?"[83]

Conclusion

Roth clearly expected the Zionist enterprise in Palestine to be guided by a Jewish ethical calling and to yield a sociopolitical reality that is committed to this ethics—and, in this regard, would be anything but "normal" (as in the Zionist yearning to normalize the Jews and to make them a "nation like all other nations"). His moral message is clear, even if implicit: a people committed to their holiness must be guided by a higher ethical directive. Yet, for Zionism, this may be revealed to be a non- or even an anti-political horizon, and Roth has not bothered to offer a clear explication of what a commitment to the notion of the nation's "holiness" may lead to politically. A narrative arc that begins with the idea of holiness or sacredness as emerging from the Creator and goes on to discuss the qualities manifested by this sacredness ends with a rather cryptic note regarding the holiness of the people, the land, and the language.

It may be argued that Roth ultimately failed to form a coherent, systematic, and, in the final analysis, influential political voice because he was indebted to the notion of modern sovereignty. In this, he may be exemplifying the problematic nature of any attempt to think outside of and to speak against a dominant order of the world. As mentioned earlier, Roth pivoted toward political philosophy and, implicitly, to politico-philosophical, liberal-democratic advocacy in the pivotal moment when the Zionist community in Palestine was becoming a sovereign state. This led him to a detailed engagement with liberal democratic tradition and theory and, in a sense, *away* from Jewish matters as in a discourse on and of Judaism and from within Judaism.[84] He did make a point of reading certain elements in Jewish tradition or history (e.g., Maimonides's rationalism) as fitting into the democratic form. But this was not so much an engagement with Judaism as it was a reading of Judaism so as to *make it* fit in with liberal democracy.

This is crucial, since his interventions hold potential for a critical Jewish appreciation of Zionist Israeli nation-statehood, taking part in a conversation carried by such thinkers as those mentioned in this chapter's introduction. Yet Roth himself seems, at this moment of heightened attention to politico-philosophical matters and from within the soon-to-be-state, to relegate Judaism to the side and to focus on liberal democracy based on the English precedent as the blueprint for the Zionist polity. It is as if he agreed, in the most pivotal of political moments, that considerations of Judaism are secondary to politics.

In light of this, what is even more striking is the fact that Roth offers what could be considered his most systematic Jewish critique of certain tendencies within political Zionism (even if he does not always explicate the point), only after having left Israel. It is as if the prophet had to first leave the confines of the political framework (of which he was a subject since immigrating to Palestine) to be able to formalize a Jewish critique of political Zionism and the State of Israel.

In this regard, Roth may be pointing, again, to the problematics of formulating a Jewish critique from within the Zionist discourse, or the nation-statist discourse more generally. In other words, he is showing the precariousness of a position of "exile within sovereignty."[85] Or, to paraphrase Mahmoud Mamdani and Raif Zreik, he is putting in question the possibility of a Jewish person to still arrive at (or remain in) Palestine as an immigrant instead of a settler.[86] Can such a person—committed to Judaism and taking part in the Zionist or Israeli enterprise—hold on to a view of Judaism that contradicts the nationalist politicization of Judaism à la Zionist ideology? Roth's own tragic arc suggests a negative answer: the nationalization of Judaism seems to be stronger than the Jewish person himself.

Conclusion

Reclaiming "Tribalism"

Widely predicted to be bygone phenomena of the nineteenth and twentieth centuries, nationalism and nation-statism have proven to be resilient, persistent, and resurgent. Yet the academic field dedicated to the study of nationalism seems to have moved away from discussing these phenomena, with scholars and pundits alike increasingly preferring to frame their discussion of the maladies of nationalism as dealing with a novel or renewed case of populism.[1] It is, however, in one of the field's recent outliers—a later and direct intervention on nationalism, Sivamohan Valluvan's *The Clamour of Nationalism*—that we find a refreshingly forceful reminder of what nationalism is ultimately about: exclusion as much as inclusion. It is about Othering.

Writing under the shadow of the "2016 moment" (i.e., Brexit in the UK, and Trump's Make America Great Again movement in the United States), and, with many similar European trends in mind, Valluvan identifies the West as being caught in a third historical nationalist moment. The first such moment in this scheme is the mid-nineteenth-century's "Spring of Nations," and the second is marked by the early twentieth-century's era of protectionist mercantilism, closely tied to the fading of imperial powers. This third moment represents a development of nationalism as well as a reassertion of its basic premise: a reaffirmation of the "us" group (or, rather, its very creation) by way of negating those who do not belong. As Valluvan puts it, "Nationalism, as opposed to being a claim premised primarily on active belonging, is principally a wager of non-belonging, an assertion of the nation's 'constitutive outside.'" The sense of national identity "is less a question of being moved by desires about who we are and more a question of being agitated by concerns about who we definitely are not."[2]

While mainly focused on the UK and Europe, Valluvan—here building on Hannah Arendt's work—closely attends to the ways in which
Zionist nationalism and its embodiment in Israeli nation-statism manifest this same basic fact of nationalism. Moreover, Zionism and Israeli
nation-statism exemplify a chain of Othering and exclusion, where a
group that has been marked as a national Other adopts the nation-statist
imperative to escape its predicament, only to be marking another group
as its national Other: "Having been rendered a minority or 'subject race'
that has to rely on the whim and munificence of the ruling national
majority, the only worthwhile political goal that remains is to realize
a nation-state for oneself. The exclusionary chauvinism of nationalism
was in turn rendered manifestly immanent, insofar as those who resist
their marginalisation were obliged ultimately to commit themselves to
their own chain of nation-making essentialisms and exclusions."[3]

Valluvan further reads the 2018 Nation-State Law (discussed in chapter 1) as the ultimate expression of this logic. This Israeli Basic Law's
roots are firmly planted in the European nation-statist logic of exclusion:

> The enduring place of antisemitism for European nation-making projects
> resulted in the consolidation of dreams among many Jews for another
> nation-state elsewhere. And it is, of course, equally well documented that
> the actual pursuit and realisation of that elsewhere, that promised home-
> land, has itself been so constitutively reliant upon a variety of radically
> exclusionary principles and practices. This wider realisation of a confes-
> sionally Jewish state—one that trades on the "erasure" of the Palestinians
> already there—reached its logical apogee in the recent promulgation in
> Israel of the "nation-state law," legislation that further underscored the
> overt ethnic supremacism of the state's existence, explicitly clarifying that
> "only Jews have the right of self-determination in Israel."[4]

Crucially, as Valluvan is quick to note, the lesson here is not really, or
only, about Israel, but primarily about nation-statism: "Israel . . . is not necessarily exceptional; it is to my mind only a particularly stark and visceral
instantiation of how historical exclusion at the hand of one set of nation-
state logics can itself often precipitate new nation-state exclusions."[5]

This, indeed, was the point with which this volume opened. While focused exclusively on the Israeli case, this book should be read as saying

something about the general "form" of nationalism and nation-statism that Zionism and Israel embody. The tendency to single out Israel—a trend shared by both advocates and detractors of the state—is easily understood, almost trivial: no other state in the world claims to be either Jewish or the nation-state of the Jewish people. Yet, if we pay closer attention to the ways in which the building blocks of Zionist ideology and Israeli nation-statism have been shaped in the image of a European, post-Reformation, nationalist epistemology, we can quite easily see this local Jewish idiosyncrasy dissolving, and the more general, global lesson emerging. Maybe most important of all in this regard is the way in which Judaism itself has been read, interpreted, and remade to fit in the European, modern sovereign-state-oriented (and, ultimately, Christian) notion of "nation"—so much so that Didi Herman titled her article dealing with these matters "Christian Israel."[6]

But is there a way out of this nation-statist bind? My aim in this book has been primarily interpretive, and the attentive reader will have realized that my analysis, whether critical of its subject matter or not, does not pretend to hold a solution or even determined answers to the questions that guided my intervention. I pretend to have an answer neither to the local, Zionist, Israeli, or Jewish questions at hand, nor to the global issues they embody—namely, the dominance of the politics of nationalism and nation-statism.

Yet this local case can suggest—from within its idiosyncrasies— avenues for further exploration of the more general, global form. Specifically, I would suggest that we focus on nationalism's and nation-statism's harsh, often abusive treatment of the multivocality and multiplicity of traditions that preceded it and that are carried by those who are rendered members of the national in-group. That is to say: among many other things, a Jewish critical perspective on Zionist ideology and Israeli nation-statism suggests that an inversion of our critical gaze from matters of the exclusionary nature of nationalism (as done convincingly and comprehensively by Valluvan, for example) to the matter of the ways in which nation-statism homogenizes the in-group can open avenues for thinking beyond the nationalist order of the world. In other words, what Valluvan calls "nation-making essentialisms" deserve attention not only from the outside, as it were (i.e., the consideration of the ways in which the in-group is built by demarcating its "constitutive outside"), but also from the inside: the erasure of the multivocality of the traditions nationalized by the state.[7]

The Jewish case lends itself rather naturally to such a point of view. Jewish communities have been historically dispersed geographically, and are diverse and heterogenous in terms of language, culture, tradition, practice, and belief. To put it simply, Jews have been *Jewishly* diverse; the very meaning of their Jewishness, their very being-in-the-world as Jewish people, took on varying, differing, sometimes competing and conflicting shapes. Thus, to give but one, admittedly banal example, returning to the Passover seder discussed earlier, while we may generalize and say that the seder ritual is a pillar of Jewish tradition, the practical, material, auditory, culinary, textual, and even halakhic aspects of this ritual are far from uniform in the Jewish world. Jews have been celebrating the seder is such diverse ways, drawing upon differing intrinsic and extrinsic resources and influences, that an outside observer will be forgiven if failing to see that some of these divergent ceremonies of eating and reading a text on a certain spring night are in actuality variations on the same tradition. The same can be said of much of what ultimately makes up the Jewish being-in-the-world.

Put simply, there is no one Jewish tradition, and what Zionism has addressed (rather, rendered) as the "Jewish people" has been a diverse and heterogenous collection of communities, traditions, and histories. This diversity or heterogeneity has obviously posed a problem for a homogenizing nation-building project. Proponents of Israeli nation-statism—what in Israeli Hebrew is often termed, following Ben-Gurion's cue, *mamlakhtiyut*—have been explicit in identifying Jewish heterogeneity as a threat to statism and to the nation-state itself.[8]

To deal with the threat, the Israeli state has employed a "melting pot" policy that aimed to do away with Jewish diversity. Importantly, this project was shaped by orientalist tendencies, which, as Amnon Raz-Krakotzkin has shown, have also informed the Zionist negation of exile and erasure of the Jewish past.[9] The two aspects of the nation-statist project—the Othering of the "not us" and the creation-through-melting of the "unified us"—were closely related to the Zionist supersessionist attitude toward Judaism. In Aziza Khazzoom's phrasing, this has resulted in a "great chain of orientalism." Modern Jewish history, she writes, "can be conceptualized as a series of orientalizations": the first object of the

orientalist gaze was Judaism itself, as "Jews came to view Jewish tradition as oriental, developed intense commitments to westernizations as a
form of self improvement, and became threatened by elements of Jewish
culture that represented the Jewish past." This fed the Othering of those
Jewish communities who were perceived as lacking in Westernization.
As a result, "when a putatively less western group threatened the westernization project of another," it was Othered and excluded.[10]

A recent articulation of this statist theopolitics can be found, by way
of example, in Ari Shavit's polemic of a Ben Gurion–inspired reaffirmation of Israeli nation-statism, albeit now rhetorically more attentive to
the diversity of Israeli society. Seeking to revitalize the Ben-Gurionist
deification of the state, Shavit narrates a story of the rise and decline of
mamlakhtiyut. According to Shavit, Ben-Gurion's homogenizing project was motivated by a "deep anxiety" regarding the "Jewish people's
proclivity to sectarianism, tribalism, and anarchy," which he identified
as the outcome of exile. It thus emerges that "Ben Gurion's idea of statism," the foundation of Israeli nation-statehood, "emanated from horror," the horror of heterogeneity: "He claimed that the greatest threat to
Jewish national existence is the inability of Jews to function as a national
unit. . . . More than he feared the hatred of Jews in Europe, and more
than he feared the Arab resistance in the Land of Israel, he feared the
Jews' historical pattern of behavior—towards themselves and towards
their state. He feared the Jewish attraction to individualism, to sectarianism, to tribalism, to rebelliousness, and to fanaticism."[11]

Statism, explains Shavit, was the remedy Ben-Gurion devised for this
Jewish malady. It is illuminating to read Shavit's rendition of this foundation of nation-statism also because of its unreconstructed commitment to the political theology of the state. For Ben-Gurion, he explains,
the establishment of the nation-state of Israel has been the "real core of
the Zionist enterprise." All other Zionist imperatives are but "deriva-
tives of the central national enterprise: the transformation of a divided
people that has a proclivity to sectarianism, into one, united nation by
subordinating it to a powerful statist mechanism and to a deep statist
ethos."[12]

Ben-Gurion's success at imposing this statism, premised on "the melting pot, which was aimed at dissolving earlier identities and creating
an Israeli identity, uniform and new," was what enabled the flourish-

ing of the State of Israel, which Shavit identifies as "the Israeli miracle that astonished the world." Yet this project, he admits, "also had a dark side" to it: "In order to form the new Israeli identity, it [statism] erased the traditional identity of many of the immigrants to Israel. In order to empower the young state, it crushed a large number of communities, to which many of the immigrants belonged. It did not treat with respect Judaism and the immense cultural assets that were created in exile. Since it was oriented toward the future, it had a distinct tendency to negate the past."[13] This has resulted, Shavit admits, in "discrimination, silencing, and racism" toward those who did not fit the Zionist, Ashkenazi, and secular mold of the melting pot, such as Mizrahi, ultra-Orthodox, and Religious-Zionist Jews, as well as those whom Shavit calls "Israel's Arabs." As a result, "racism, misogyny and homophobia" became widespread.[14]

Shavit reads Israeli history since 1973 as a series of rebellions by these discriminated groups against the statist dominance. His own polemic, calling for a "new statism" that will somehow enshrine the state while "respecting every tribe, every minority, and every individual," full of inconsistencies as it is, is beside the point of my discussion here. What should be highlighted in this context is what goes unnoticed in Shavit's assessment of statism, as in many other, powerful critiques of the Israeli melting-pot project: that the nation constructed by the state, the product of this melting and reshaping project, is defined as "Jewish," not as "Israeli"; the Israeli nation-building project is aimed at building a Jewish, not Israeli (or otherwise) nation. Moreover, the state is determined that the nation represented in and by its sovereignty is the Jewish people at large, including Jews who are residents and citizens of other nation-states, while actively denying the very existence and viability of an "Israeli" nation.[15]

Needless to say, the State of Israel has been playing a central and influential role in shaping the very meaning of Jewishness and Judaism. As we have seen, advocates of Israeli statism indeed celebrate this fact and bemoan the persistence of the view that Jewish identity is about more than feeling an affiliation with the State of Israel. And it is exactly this basic linkage between Judaism, or Jewish traditions, and what the statist mindset derogatorily calls "tribalism" that offers us an appreciation of the possibilities of talking back at nation-statism.

What the Jewish-Israeli case suggests is that it is a rehabilitation of "tribalism"—as in communal identities fed by and carrying varying traditions—that may be the way out of the nationalist bind. I am using "tribalism" here (a dangerous term, no doubt) rather loosely, to highlight the universally parochial nature of our communal identities: we are all (hence the universal) members of such traditional or local (either geographically or culturally; hence the parochial), communities or identity groups. I am, in other words, referring to tribalism as subjectivity, not as an ontological formation. This distinction is taken from Paul James, who explains that, "as a subjectivity and ideology, tribalism refers to the accumulation of practices and meanings of identity, practically assumed or self-consciously effected, that either take the social frame as given (as subjectivity) or as politicized in some commonsensical way (as ideology)."[16]

It is, in this regard, a telling fact that one of the very few venues in Israel today where one might experience expressions, faded as they may be, of these vastly rich and diverse cultures that have been melted into the nation-statist pot are synagogues. Go to an Iraqi synagogue, and with a bit of luck you will be able to hear Hebrew pronounced in a starkly different way than the modern dialect propagated by the state as proper Hebrew; go to a Syrian synagogue, and with luck you may experience a Jewish soundscape that is quintessentially Arab; go to a Moroccan one if you wish to hear Judaism sung in a North African soundscape; needless to say, these will be vastly different from what you may encounter in a variety of Ashkenazi synagogues, both in Israel and outside of it. Any sense one may have of a unified, uniform national language, liturgy, ritual, or practice would be immediately put in question.

The very fact that this *Jewish* variety exists and persists works to undermine, even if only implicitly, the nation-statist homogenizing force. It is no coincidence that one of the first, and ultimately failed, missions taken by the newly formed Ministry of Religions in the nascent State of Israel was the devising and propagation of a liturgical and architectural uniformity in Israeli synagogues (not surprisingly, the uniform model was shaped in the image of the Ashkenazi tradition carried by the dominant ethnoclass).[17]

It should also come as no surprise that this Jewish variety was eagerly preserved in other historical contexts, which were not dominated by the nation-statist drive. Such, for example, is the setting for what Raz-Krakotzkin has offered as a Jewish political theology that stands contra Zionism as an alternative model for Jewish collectivity: sixteenth-century Safed. The backdrop to what Raz-Krakotzkin names a Mishnaic consciousness (versus the Millenarian biblical consciousness of Zionism) was distinctly Jewishly diverse. At its peak, the Jewish population of Safed consisted of no less than sixteen distinct groups, organized mostly around places of origin, as well as along lines of lingual identity and traditions of Jewish practice and liturgy.[18]

Moreover, this Jewish diversity was positively interpreted—celebrated, even—as manifesting the variety of ways to reach the Divine. Thus, for example, Isaac Luria is said to have "recognized the validity of the different liturgical traditions among Jews from various regions and cultures."[19] He is reported to have said on the differences in liturgical and practical tradition among "Ashkenazim and Sephardim, Catalans and Italians, *et cetera*," that "there are twelve gates above, corresponding to the twelve tribes [of Israel], and the prayers of every individual ascend by way of one of these gates. . . . Surely these gates are not identical, each is different than the other, and so are the prayers varied. Therefore, each and every one should hold on to his custom of prayer, since who knows to what tribe he belongs, and his prayer does not ascend but through this gate."[20]

Indeed, it is exactly the persistence of an ethnic (for lack of a better term) diversity in the Jewish/Judaic world, a diversity that often angers those wishing to see a united Jewish nation, that suggests the virtue of tribalism in resisting the homogenizing impetus of nationalism. The plurality, diversity, and heterogeneity of Jewish traditions—that which statism feared and wished to dissolve—holds the potential for Judaism, lived through these diverging traditions, to talk back at Zionist supersessionism and the nation-statism it theologizes.

To draw the global lesson from the local case at hand: remembering that nation-statism is not only about the exclusion of the national Other but also about the creation and homogenizing of the national self by way of erasing differences that are by definition "traditional" (i.e., they nourish on traditions that precede the nation-statist impetus) allows us to see the value of these parochial, local, communal, ethnic, religious traditions in resisting nationalism.

Tribalism has, of course, been the focus of much worry and criticism; commentators often depict it as the opposite of rational (secular) democratic politics. They often use the word "tribal" in a derogatory manner, suggesting something of a politically correct version of "primitive," to denote an irrational, visceral, and instinctual parochialism for which there is no place in the rational public sphere of the corporate society upon which modern, democratic nation-statist politics relies.[21]

Yet the picture is obviously more nuanced than that. Tribalism does indeed pose, as Michael Walzer phrased it, an ethically and politically "difficult problem." This problem deals exactly with the tension between, on the one hand, a democratic notion of recognition and open political participation, and, on the other, the fear of social disintegration and infighting. Writing in the wake of the collapse of the Soviet Union and the ensuing emergence of the previously repressed "local and particular," the "ethnic, religious and national identities," Walzer is critical of the attempt at a "containment" of these identities without giving them proper recognition.[22]

Granted, the dangers are apparent: tribalism can be easily given to manipulation by (nationalist) "demagogues [who] exploit the hopes for national revival, linguistic autonomy, the free development of schools and media," or it can be used by "other demagogues [who] exploit the fears of the minorities, defending ancient irredentisms and looking (like the Serbs in Croatia) for outside help."[23] But if one is truly committed to a democratic notion of mass political participation, one has to acknowledge that people are embodied in their traditions: "Bring the 'people' into political life and they will arrive, marching in tribal ranks and orders, carrying with them their own languages, historic memories, customs, beliefs, and commitments. And once they have been summoned, once they have arrived, it isn't possible to do them justice within the old political order."[24]

Walzer seems to acknowledge that nation-statism tends to crush and deny this diversity, and he cannot find a moral justification for this erasure, even if the political prudence of homogenizing the state's population into a cohesive nation is obvious. Ultimately, he writes, "there doesn't seem to be any humane or decent way to disentangle the tribes, and at the same time the entanglements are felt to be dangerous. . . . The problem, then as now, is that justice, whatever it requires, doesn't seem to permit the kinds of coercion that would be necessary to 'hold their noses together.' So we have to think about divorce, despite its difficulties."[25]

Confusingly, as Paul James critically remarks, Walzer identifies tribalism with nationalism.[26] It is apparent—and Walzer's critics were quick to note this—that he merely uses "tribalism" to denote a sense of nationalist, if not always nation-statist, unity.[27] But the merit of his discussion of the problem of attending to particularistic diversity is nevertheless illuminating. Relying on Karl Deutsch's work, Walzer sees democracy as "the 'facilitator' of tribalism."[28]

An exhaustive discussion of tribalism is obviously beyond the scope of the current work. Without dismissing the concerns raised in various treatments of tribalism, I wish to suggest that tribalism can be also seen to manifest a virtue of diversity and heterogeneity that is often crushed by nation-statism. This traditional diversity or heterogeneity also bears direct relevance to the matter of the exclusionary impetus of nationalism. Thus, in the Zionist Israeli case, this Jewish diversity has worked to challenge and even subvert the foundational national distinction of "Jew vs. Arab." While it may have been rather straightforward and fairly simple (ethical considerations notwithstanding) for an originally Eastern European, Yiddish-speaking Jewish community to view Muslim, Christian, and other Arabs in Ottoman and Mandatory Palestine and later in Israel as their ultimate Others (as dictated by the foundational Othering of Zionist Israeli nation-statism), the same cannot be said of Jewish people arriving at Israel from Arab and Muslim lands. Both sides of the newly created national divide—both Palestinian Arabs and Israelis originating in Muslim and Arab lands—have at times insisted on rejecting the nationalist divisions imposed by the nation-statist logic and highlighted what they share more than what separated them. Importantly, this has not amounted to a naive sense of unity or identification; differences remained and were even highlighted. But these differences were not read as dictating a political, statist order, such as a hierarchy of the privilege to collective rights.[29]

It comes as no surprise that spokespeople for nation-statism—advocates of the political theology of the nation-state—are now increasingly wishing to mobilize this Jewish diversity, which has proved persistent even in the face of the fiercest of nationalizing enterprises, to the service of the state. Such is Shavit's polemic, where a proposal for a "new statism" is premised upon recognition of diversity. Similarly, as noted earlier, other recent polemics seek to celebrate Mizrahi tradition-ism while reading it as quintessentially nation-statist, in effect rendering this traditionism a service to the state.[30] Clearly, the relationship at hand is not unidirectional. Just as traditions may speak back at the nation-state, so the state does not remain mute.

But it is also clear that the dominant nation-statist voice tends to out-right delegitimize non-statist traditions as local and parochial, hence divisive on a national scale. Indeed, this is the context in which the ad-jective "tribal" is assigned to such traditions and identities as a deroga-tion, suggesting that these traditions are primitive and, ultimately, so divisive as to necessarily lead to anarchy. The "tribal" is here contrasted with the "rational," which nation-statist politics allegedly embody.

Nevertheless, if we do not fall into the nation-statist-interested frame of reference, it is easy to see that advocating for non-nation-statist tradi-tions does not amount to a call for anarchy. Alasdair MacIntyre's force-ful intervention in *After Virtue* can function here as an illuminating guide. As MacIntyre insists, his critique of the modern state should not be confused with an advocacy of anarchism. As he puts it, the "neces-sary distancing of the moral self from the governments of modern states must not be confused with any anarchist critique of the state. Nothing in my argument suggests, let alone implies, any good grounds for rejecting certain forms of government as necessary and legitimate; what the argu-ment does entail is that the modern state is not such a form of govern-ment."[31] The fact that the tradition of the virtues he is speaking for "also involves a rejection of the modern political order" does not amount to an apolitical or anti-political stance. There are many tasks that demand the functioning of a government: from vindicating the rule of law ("so far as it is possible in a modern state") to exercising generosity. But we must also acknowledge that the politics of the nation-state "expresses in its institutional forms a systematic rejection" of the tradition.[32]

MacIntyre is referring here, of course, to the tradition of virtues, on which his work focuses, but it is not hard to see how the Israeli case teaches us also of the nation-statist rejection of other forms, pre- and non-statist, of tradition. Here, again, Amnon Raz-Krakotzkin's reconstruction of the Safedi model of Jewish political theology proves highly informative and suggestive. It allows us to see how a "Mishnaic consciousness" challenges foundational premises of the nation-statist political theology, highlighting exactly the diversity of Jewish experience and the affinities it enables between Jewish and other communities (such as the case of sites of pilgrimage that are shared by Jews, Muslims and Christians alike).[33] Similarly, Daniel Boyarin's reclamation of a non-statist Jewish collectivity via the notion of *Judaïtude* clearly redirects us to the multivocality and diversity of Jewish histories and tradition as the precondition for such collectivity.[34]

The very last lines of MacIntyre's *After Virtue* can also function as a guide for considering possible venues out of the nation-statist bind. Cautioning against drawing "too precise" historical parallels, MacIntyre nevertheless suggests a contemporary lesson that can be learned from "the epoch in which the Roman empire declined into the Dark Ages." He tells us that "a crucial turning point" in this history took place when "men and women of good will" were no longer preoccupied with the very survival of the empire. They "ceased to identify the continuation of civility and moral community with the maintenance of that imperium. What they set themselves to achieve instead—often not recognizing fully what they were doing—was the construction of new forms of community within which the moral life could be sustained so that both morality and civility might survive the coming ages of barbarism and darkness."[35]

Arguing that modern politics—the politics of the modern nation-state—has ushered in another such epoch of moral decline, MacIntyre draws the lesson:

> What matters at this stage is the construction of local forms of community within which civility and the intellectual and moral life can be sustained through the new dark ages which are already upon us. And if the tradition of the virtues was able to survive the horrors of the last dark ages, we are not entirely without grounds for hope. This time however the barbarians are not waiting beyond the frontiers; they have already been governing us for quite some time. And it is our lack of consciousness of this that constitutes part of our predicament.[36]

It is indeed difficult to imagine a reality outside of the dominance of the nation-state. And it might just be that the "parochial" and "tribal" hold the potential to do just that.

ACKNOWLEDGMENTS

Many of the arguments in this book are the result of a continuous conversation I have held (in both literal and figurative senses) with Brian Klug and his writings. Brian and I have come to see that we are often addressing the same set of problems, motivated by a similar Jewish concern, amounting to a project that Brian has so insightfully termed "unasking the Jewish question." Furthermore, we often find ourselves in agreement regarding the judgment of these issues and the manner in which we would have wanted to see them addressed. I am grateful for the opportunity to hold these conversations with Brian and would be forever indebted to him for the ways in which they have informed my work.

Working with Jennifer Hammer at NYU Press has been a delight, and I am grateful for the attention, care, and sound advice she has given me. Thanks also to Veronica Knutson, Valerie Zaborski, and Emily Shelton.

Chapter 1 is an expanded version of: Yaacov Yadgar, "'Jewish' Politics or the Politics of 'Jews'? On Israeli Nation-Statehood," *ReOrient* 6, no. 1 (2020): 20–46.

Chapter 3 is based on Yaacov Yadgar, "Nostalgia and Political Analysis: A Perspective from the Israeli Case," *Politics*, 18 May 2022, https://doi.org/10.1177/02633957221098028.

Chapter 5 is based on Yaacov Yadgar, "'The Great Sin of Today Is the "Politicization" of Our Judaism, the Great Need, the "Judaization" of Our Politics'": Leon Roth and the Possibilities of a Jewish Critique of Zionist Politics," *Journal of Modern Jewish Studies* 22, no. 4 (2023): 412–37.

NOTES

INTRODUCTION

1 Cavanaugh, *Theopolitical Imagination*, 2.

2 Sells, "Saudi Nationalism, Wahhabi Da'wā, and Western Power," 275.

3 Valluvan, *Clamour of Nationalism*.

4 I should also note at the outset that while I do speak, throughout this book, about how nationalism, the state, or nation-statism "do" things, I do not mean to assign to them an independent agency akin to human agents. Rather, as Mark Bevir and R. A. W. Rhodes explain, the state can be seen as "a series of contingent and un-stable cultural practices, which in turn consists of the political activity of specific human agents." It is those practices on which I focus, and less so on the activity of those specific human agents. Bevir and Rhodes, *State as Cultural Practice*, 1.

5 Freeden, "Is Nationalism a Distinct Ideology?," 748.

6 Yadgar, *Israel's Jewish Identity Crisis*; Yadgar, *Sovereign Jews*.

7 Hazony, *Virtue of Nationalism*. See also Schneider, "Nationalists of the World, Unite!"; Schneider, "Light among the Nations"; and Schneider and Hotam, "Dangerous Minds."

8 See, for example, Brubaker, "Religion and Nationalism."

9 Devji, *Muslim Zion*.

10 Essa, *Hostile Homelands*.

11 Dalsheim, *Israel Has a Jewish Problem*; Yadgar, *Israel's Jewish Identity Crisis*.

12 For example, Raz-Krakotzkin, *Mishna Consciousness, Biblical Consciousness*; Raz-Krakotzkin, "Exile, History"; Raz-Krakotzkin, "Religion and National-ism"; Boyarin, *No-State Solution*; Rabkin, *Threat from Within*; Rabkin, *What Is Modern Israel?*; Boyarin and Boyarin, *Powers of Diaspora*; Boyarin, *Palestine and Jewish History*; Boyarin, "Hegel's Zionism?"; Klug, *Being Jewish and Doing Justice*.

13 Dalsheim, *Israel Has a Jewish Problem*, 6.

14 Said, "Zionism from the Standpoint of Its Victims."

1. THE JEWISH STATE VERSUS THE JEWS' STATE

1 For a comprehensive genealogical and cultural study of the terms "Jew" and "Ju-daism," see Baker, *Jew*; and Boyarin, *Judaism*.

2 Boyarin, *Judaism*, 40.

3 MacIntyre, *Whose Justice?*, 12.

4 Mine is a much less sophisticated and less attentive usage of the terms here than that of Deutscher's *Non-Jewish Jew*.

5 This can be said to be the immediate, literal translation of Herzl's *Der Judenstaat*. However, the German ease with using a noun where English speakers would use an adjective also renders "The Jewish State" a perfectly acceptable translation of the same title. I am grateful to Kathrin Gowers for her help in clarifying this.

6 For a consideration of non-European readings of Jewish peoplehood and politics, which sometimes stand as oppositional alternatives to this dominant European Zionist framework, feeding on Jewish experiences in Arab and Muslim-dominated cultures and countries, see Behar and Benite, *Modern Middle Eastern Jewish Thought*; and Evri, *Return to Al-Andalus*.

7 See, for example, Cohn and Dirks, "Beyond the Fringe"; and Dirlik, "Rethinking Colonialism."

8 Boyarin, *No-State Solution*.

9 Hallaq, *Impossible State*.

10 Cavanaugh, *Myth of Religious Violence*.

11 See Julie Cooper's review of the field of Jewish political thought, which highlights this field's crippling commitment to the idea of the modern state: "Turn to Tradition."

12 Diasporic readings of Jewish politics, such as those by Boyarin and Boyarin *Powers of Diaspora*; Boyarin, *No-State Solution*; and Butler, *Parting Ways* stand out as examples of a Jewishly informed critique that is not bound by the logic of the state. Santiago Slabodsky's *Decolonial Judaism* offers an illuminating reading of decolonial Jewish thought that has been informed by a dialogue with systems of thought developed in the Global South. See also Myers's analysis in *Between Jew and Arab* of Simon Rawidowicz's Jewish critique of Israel. See also Graubart, *Jewish Self-Determination beyond Zionism*. Khaled Furani has developed a similar critique of the modern nation-state, which nourishes on Muslim horizons, and especially the notion of *khalifa* ("Khalifah and the Modern Sovereign").

13 Dabashi, *Theology of Discontent*, xvi.

14 Brubaker, "Religion and Nationalism."

15 Schmitt, *Political Theology*; Kahn, *Political Theology*.

16 Editorial, "Jewish Coercion Administration."

17 Ram, *Iranophobia*.

18 Alpher, "Ḥoq Hamarkolim Mokhiaḥ Shehaḥilonim Sovlim Mirigshei Neḥitut."

19 For a comprehensive presentation of the "religionization" argument, see Peled and Peled, *Religionization of Israeli Society*. For a critical assessment of this discourse see Yadgar, *Israel's Jewish Identity Crisis*, chap. 3.

20 Yehoshua, "Hapetil Hakaful."

21 Halkin, "What Ahad Ha'am Saw."

22 Ahad HaAm, "Yalquṭ Qaṭan." The essay is reprinted in Ahad HaAm, *Collected Writings*, 313–20. Page numbers here refer to this later reprint. The essay is also reprinted, with a wealth of corresponding documents, in Goldshtein, *Ahad Ha'am and Herzl*.

23 Halkin, "What Ahad Ha'am Saw."

24 Goldshtein, *Ahad Ha'am and Herzl*.

25 Conforti, "East and West in Jewish Nationalism"; Conforti, *Shaping a Nation*, chap. 4.

26 Shimoni, *Zionist Ideology*, 270.

27 Plamenatz, "Two Types of Nationalism."

28 Shimoni, *Zionist Ideology*, chap. 7.

29 Ahad HaAm, *Collected Writings*, 316, 317, 319.

30 Ahad HaAm, 316.

31 Ahad HaAm, 317, 318.

32 Ahad HaAm, 317.

33 Ahad HaAm, 316, 317.

34 For a thoughtful consideration of the relevance of Ahad HaAm's thought to contemporary Jewish politics see Brian Klug's introduction in Ahad HaAm, *Words of Fire*.

35 Ahad HaAm, *Collected Writings*, 319.

36 Goldshtein, *Ahad Ha'am and Herzl*.

37 The "Uganda plan" was a proposal to establish a Jewish polity, under British colonial rule, in Eastern Africa instead of Palestine, causing a great rift within the Zionist movement. See Laqueur, *A History of Zionism*, chap. 3; Shimoni, *Zionist Ideology*, chap. 7; and Alroey, *Zionism without Zion*.

38 Herzl, *Congress Addresses*, 36.

39 Nordau's essay was published simultaneously in both German—Max Nordau, "Achad-HaAm über 'Altneuland,'" *Die Welt* 13, no. 3 (1903), 11—and Hebrew newspapers, in installments, translated by N. Sokolov, *Haṣefira* 13, no. 3–17, no. 3 (1903): 51–55, and *Haṣofe* 20, no. 3 (1903): 75. It is reprinted in Nordau's collected writings: *Zionist Writings*, 2:110–19. Also available in Goldshtein, *Ahad Ha'am and Herzl*, 75–83.

40 Nordau, *Zionist Writings*, 2:112.

41 Herzl, *Zionist Writings*, 1:44–58.

42 Penslar, *Theodor Herzl*, 109.

43 Penslar, 110.

44 Herzl, *Zionist Writings*, 1:51–52.

45 Herzl, 1:57.

46 For an explication of liberalism's commitment to nationalism, see Valluvan, *Clamour of Nationalism*.

47 Shumsky, *Beyond the Nation-State*, 71, 73.

48 Shumsky, 71, 73.

49 Ahad HaAm, *'Al Parashat Derakhim*, 5690, 3:56.

50 Ahad HaAm, 3:56.

51 Lapidot, *Jews out of the Question*.

52 Sartre, *Anti-Semite and Jew*, 91. See Lapidot, *Jews out of the Question*, 70–84.

53 As Jonathan Boyarin notes, more than thirty years later, in an interview with Benny Levy, Sartre highlighted his indebtedness to a Hegelian view of history in analyzing Jewish history. The fascinating exchange merits reproduction:

SARTRE: When I said that there is not any Jewish history, I was thinking of history in a well-defined form: the history of Germany, the history of America, of the United States. That is, the history of a sovereign, political reality with a homeland and with other similar states. When one should have thought of history as being something else, if one meant that there is a Jewish history. It was necessary to conceive of Jewish history not only as a dissemination of Jews throughout the world, but also as the unity of the diaspora, the unity of the dispersed Jews . . .

LEVY: In other words, the history that Hegel put on our landscape wanted to get rid of the Jew, and it is the Jew who will allow us to get out of this history that Hegel wanted to impose on us.

SARTRE: Absolutely. Quoted in Boyarin, "Hegel's Zionism?," 141.

54 Shumsky, *Beyond the Nation-State*, 70.

55 I have discussed this matter in detail in Yadgar, *Sovereign Jews*, 65–160.

56 '*Al Parashat Derakhim*, 5690, 1:79–90.

57 Don-Yehiya, "Secularization"; Zeira, *Qeru'im Anu*.

58 Glickson, *Aḥad Ha'am*, 176.

59 Yadgar, *Israel's Jewish Identity Crisis*.

60 See Zvi Zameret's convincing argument regarding the central role of Ahad HaAm's vision in shaping the Israeli "secular" education system. Zameret, "Ahad Ha'am."

61 See, for example, A. B. Yehoshua's triumphant secular discussion of the question "Who is a Jew?" where the author suggests that the exploration of the question must begin with the Halakhic definition, "because at base it provides most of the data essential for the rest of the discussion." Yehoshua, "Mihu Yehudi." See my discussion in Yadgar, *Israel's Jewish Identity Crisis*, chap. 1.

62 Yadgar, *Israel's Jewish Identity Crisis*, chap. 2.

63 knesset.gov.il. I have analyzed the Basic Law in detail in Yadgar, chap. 2. The following discussion builds upon my analysis there.

64 Barak, "Constitutional Revolution"; Barak, "Constitutionalization of the Israeli Legal System."

65 Falah, "Israeli 'Judaization' Policy in Galilee"; Yiftachel and Rumley, "Impact of Israel's Judaization Policy."

66 Barak is here quoting another ruling: Justice D. Levin in EA 2/88 *Ben-Shalom v. the Twelfth Knesset's Central Elections Committee* [8], 231.

67 Barak, *Aadel Ka'adan v. Israel Lands Administration*, 19–20. An unofficial English translation of the ruling is available at the Cardozo Law collection of opinions of the Supreme Court of Israel: versa.cardozo.yu.edu.

68 Barak, "Values of the State of Israel." Much of the same arguments are made in his Ka'adan decision: Barak, *Aadel Ka'adan v. Israel Lands Administration*.

69 "Bagaṣ Qa'dan," Wikipedia (Hebrew), he.wikipedia.org (accessed 28 February 2024).

70 Editorial, "Basic Law."

71 Helman and Arbel, "Doresh 'igun." I have previously erroneously identified the IZS's 2009 draft proposal as the original draft of the bill (Yadgar, *Israel's Jewish Identity Crisis*, 84). In fact, the bill has originated in 2004 by the Israel Policy Center. This center has since stopped working (some of its core members went on to establish the Kohelet Forum, which has attracted much attention following initiatives at "overhauling" Israel's Judicial system). See Slymovics, "U.S. Billionaires"; and Sadeh and Shomrim, "Kohelet Tentacles." An archive of the center's website is available online, suggesting that it promoted both this Basic Law and a reform to the judicial appointments procedure already in 2004; the first full draft of the bill I was able to extract from this archive is a 2006 second rendition. web.archive.org.

72 Helman and Arbel, "Doresh "'igun," 6.

73 Quoted in Bender, Ayreh, "Berov Shel 62 Tomkhim Mol 55 Mitnagdim. Ḥoq haleóm Ushar Baknesset." *Maariv*, 19 July 2018.

74 Editorial, "A State for Some of Its Citizens. *Haaretz*, 11 March 2019.

75 For example, Avraham, "Hamemshala Taṣbi'ah 'al 'Ḥoq haṢiyonut'"; and Lipkin, "Ḥoq haṢiyonut." At the time of writing the fate of this proposed resolution remains unclear.

76 Quoted in Horovitz, "Far-Right Minister Pushes Decree."

77 Lis, "Far-Right Israeli Minister Wants Cabinet Vote."

78 Lis, "Judicial Coup's Next Step."

79 See my analysis of this debate in Yadgar, *Israel's Jewish Identity Crisis*, chap. 2.

2. ZIONISM AS SUPERSESSIONISM

1 Hertzberg, *Zionist Idea*, 15.

2 Hertzberg, 21.

3 Midgley, *Utopias, Dolphins, and Computers*, 1996.

4 Midgley, 2.

5 Midgley, 2.

6 MacIntyre, *Tasks of Philosophy*, 3–23.

7 The term "Judaism" itself is not without its problems, a point to which I will return later. At this point suffice is to say that I use it here to mean an expansive system of thought, ethics, practices, texts, traditions, and so on.

8 Avineri, *Varieties*, 21.

9 Avineri, *Making of Modern Zionism*, 13.

10 Avineri, 13.

11 Avineri, 222.

12 Shimoni, *Zionist Ideology*, chap. 7.

13 Salmon, "Dat veleumiyut," 115.

14 Salmon, 118.

15 Boyarin, "Hegel's Zionism?"; Raz-Krakotzkin, "Secularism."

16 Avineri, "Zionism and the Jewish Religious Tradition," 2.

17 Raz-Krakotzkin, "Religion and Nationalism"; Herman, "Christian Israel"; Yadgar, *Sovereign Jews*.

18 For a critical consideration of this filial reading of supersessionism, see Jackson, *Mordecai Would Not Bow Down*, 124.
19 Crome, *Christian Zionism and English National Identity*, 3.
20 Soulen, *God of Israel and Christian Theology*, 4–5.
21 Soulen, 5.
22 Jackson, *Mordecai Would Not Bow Down*, 121.
23 Jackson, 124.
24 Jackson, 130.
25 Jackson, 121.
26 Jackson, 124.
27 Soulen, *God of Israel and Christian Theology*, x.
28 Jackson, *Mordecai Would Not Bow Down*, 126–30.
29 Donaldson, "Supersessionism and Early Christian Self-Definition," 6.
30 Novak, "Supersessionism Hard and Soft," 27.
31 Novak, 30.
32 Crome, *Christian Zionism and English National Identity*, 3–4, n4.
33 As one recent engagement with this practice summarizes the matter at hand: "These 'seders,' organized by and for Christians, borrow from Jewish Passover traditions for the purpose of Christian teaching and celebration. Typically they make reference to the most well-known Passover meal in history—the Last Supper. You can find a wide range of guides and instructions online, each offering their own ritual and spin." Greenfield, "Offended by Christian Seders?" See Moyaert, "Christianizing Judaism?," 147–50.
34 Klug, "Appropriating Judaism?," 4.
35 Cynamon-Murphy, "Why Christians Should Not Host." An ultimately critical engagement with negative Jewish reactions to the news of Christian seders reports of
   A torrent of online outrage from Jewish voices. A viral tweet critiquing one Christian woman's seder photos gained national news attention with its acerbic remark: "I think I just had a rage blackout." Further didactic responses followed and were widely shared, like: "Hebrew school teacher here, and I'd like to offer my services to Christians wanting to lead a Passover Seder! Just follow these 4 easy steps: 1) Don't 2) F*cking 3) Do 4) It." Greenfield, "Offended by Christian Seders?"
36 Novak, "Supersessionism Hard and Soft," 28.
37 Focusing primarily on its British and American variations: for example, Crome, *Christian Zionism and English National Identity*; Goldman, *God's Country*; Lewis, *Origins of Christian Zionism*; McDermott, *New Christian Zionism*; McDermott, *Israel Matters*; Sturm, "Christian Zionism as Religious Nationalism"; Sturm, "Religion as Nationalism."
38 Crome, *Christian Zionism and English National Identity*, 3.
39 Smith, *Chosen Peoples*.
40 D'Costa, "New Zionism," 58.
41 Crome, *Christian Zionism and English National Identity*, 195.

42 McDermott, *New Christian Zionism*, 12.

43 McDermott, 12.

44 McDermott, 13.

45 McDermott, 12.

46 Klug, "Appropriating Judaism?," 6.

47 Goldman, *Zeal for Zion*, 8.

48 Klug, "Appropriating Judaism?," 6.

49 Raz-Krakotzkin, "Secularism," 291.

50 See also Raz-Krakotzkin, *Mishna Consciousness*; Raz-Krakotzkin, "Religion and Nationalism."

51 Klug, "Appropriating Judaism?," 7–8.

52 Raz-Krakotzkin, "Religion and Nationalism," 38.

53 Avineri, *Making of Modern Zionism*, 217; in an updated, 2017 epilogue to his book Avineri is warning that the revolution is nevertheless "interrupted."

54 Syrkin, *Writings*, 169–70.

55 Klug, "Appropriating Judaism?," 10. See also Boyarin, "Christian Invention of Judaism"; and Boyarin, *Judaism*.

56 Hertzberg, *Zionist Idea*, 15.

57 Yedidya, "Between Messianism and Zionism."

58 Hertzberg, *Zionist Idea*, 15.

59 Hertzberg, 16.

60 Berdyczewski, *Maamarim*, 2:23.

61 Syrkin, *Writings*, 68–69.

62 Syrkin, 169–70.

63 Hertzberg, *Zionist Idea*, 21.

64 Syrkin, *Writings*, 169–70.

65 Brenner, *Ketavim*, 4: 1296.

66 Klatzkin, *Teḥumim*, 64.

67 Hertzberg, *Zionist Idea*, 16.

68 Yadgar, *Sovereign Jews*.

69 Hertzberg, *Zionist Idea*, 16.

70 Hertzberg, 16.

71 Hertzberg, 16–17.

72 Myers, "History as Ideology"; Ram, "Zionist Historiography."

73 Hertzberg, *Zionist Idea*, 17.

74 Hertzberg, 17–18.

75 Hertzberg, 17–18.

76 Hertzberg, 18.

77 Saposnik, *Zionism's Redemptions*, 3.

78 Saposnik, 4.

79 Saposnik, 8.

80 Saposnik, 10.

81 Zerubavel, *Recovered Roots*, 7, 26.

82 Saposnik, *Zionism's Redemptions*, 10.
83 See also Saposnik's critique of Zerubavel's argument (168).
84 Nora, "Between Memory and History," 16.
85 Zerubavel, *Recovered Roots*, 7.
86 Zerubavel, 43; the Eliade quote is from Eliade, *Myth and Reality*, 51.
87 Raz-Krakotzkin, "Exile, History"; Don-Yehiya, "Negation of Galut."
88 Peled, *"The New Man" of the Zionist Revolution*, 13.
89 Almog, *Sabra*; Shapira, *New Jews, Old Jews*.
90 Kurzweil, "New Canaanites in Israel"; Diamond, *Homeland or Holy Land?*; Shavit, *New Hebrew Nation*; Porath, *Life of Uriel Shelah*; Vaters, "Hebrew from Samaria."
91 Zerubavel, *Recovered Roots*, 26; the Berdyczewski quote is from Berdyczewski, *Ba-Derekh*, 2, 20.
92 Raz-Krakotzkin, "Secularism," 293.
93 Raz-Krakotzkin, 176.
94 Myers, "Between Supersessionism and Atavism," 264.
95 Donaldson, "Supersessionism and Early Christian Self-Definition," 6.
96 Raz-Krakotzkin, "Secularism"; Boyarin, "Hegel's Zionism?"
97 Ginzburg, "History and/or Memory."
98 Raz-Krakotzkin, "Secularism," 276.
99 Raz-Krakotzkin, 279, 287, 288.
100 Raz-Krakotzkin, 289–90.
101 Avineri, "Hegel and the Emergence of Zionism."
102 Boyarin, "Hegel's Zionism?," 141.
103 Boyarin, 138.
104 Boyarin, 143.
105 Boyarin, 138–39.
106 Boyarin, 143.
107 Boyarin, 137.
108 Boyarin, 147.
109 Hertzberg, *Zionist Idea*, 18.
110 Hertzberg, 19.
111 Hertzberg, 19.
112 Hertzberg, 19.
113 Hertzberg, 19.
114 Hertzberg, 20; for an extensive discussion of Ahad HaAm's so-called secularization of Judaism, see Yadgar, *Sovereign Jews*, chap. 5.
115 Hertzberg, *Zionist Idea*, 20.
116 Hertzberg, 20.
117 Saposnik, *Zionism's Redemptions*, 7, 20.
118 Hertzberg, *Zionist Idea*, 20.
119 Avineri, *Making of Modern Zionism*, 219, 221, 222.
120 Shain, *Israeli Century*.
121 Shain, 1.

122 Yadgar, *Sovereign Jews*, chap. 8.

123 The full Hebrew presentation of Yehoshua's argument is found in Yehoshua, *Homeland Grasp*, 60–67. Published in English as Yehoshua, 'The Meaning of Homeland.'

124 Runesson, "Particularistic Judaism and Universalistic Christianity?"

125 Quoted in Blumenfeld, "A. B. Yehoshua."

126 Yehoshua, "Mihu Yisre'eli."

127 Boyarin, "Hegel's Zionism?," 151.

128 Yehoshua, *For Normality*, 132.

129 Raz-Krakotzkin, "Exile Pt. 1," 32.

130 Yehoshua, "Hapetil Hakaful."

131 Liebman and Don-Yehiya, *Civil Religion in Israel*, chaps. 2 and 4.

132 Lilker, *Kibbutz Judaism*; Tsur, "Pesach in the Land of Israel"; Don-Yehiya and Liebman, "Symbol System of Zionist-Socialism"; Yadgar, *Sovereign Jews*, 144–50.

133 Liebman and Don-Yehiya, *Civil Religion in Israel*, chap. 4; Kedar, "Ben-Gurion's Mamlakhtiyut"; Kedar, *Mamlakhtiyut*.

134 Yadgar and Hadad, "Post-Secular Interpretation of Religious Nationalism"; Yadgar and Hadad, "Nation-Statist Soteriology and Traditions of Defeat."

135 Katz, "Fear from Judaism in Israeli Culture," 207.

136 Sheleg, *Jewish Renaissance in Israeli Society*. See also Azulay and Tabory, "House of Prayer for All Nations"; and Werczberger and Azulay, "Jewish Renewal Movement."

137 Dalsheim, *Israel Has a Jewish Problem*.

138 Katz, "Fear from Judaism in Israeli Culture," 191–92.

139 Katz, 191.

140 Dalsheim, *Israel Has a Jewish Problem*.

141 Katz, "Fear from Judaism in Israeli Culture," 192–93.

142 Katz, 192n1.

143 Katz, 193.

144 Derrida, *Specters of Marx*.

145 For example, Krummel, *Crafting Jewishness in Medieval England*, 1–21.

146 Lincoln and Lincoln, "Toward a Critical Hauntology," 194.

147 Lincoln and Lincoln, 194; Gordon, *Ghostly Matters*.

148 There is a growing field of literature on hauntology, and it would be futile to try and cover this matter in sufficient detail here. For an overview see, in addition to the works cited above, the articles curated in *Ethos* 47 no. 4 (December 2019); and Rahimi, *Hauntology of Everyday Life*.

149 Gerhard (Gershom) Scholem to Franz Rosenzweig, 7 Tevehth 5678 (26 December 1926); trans. Martin Goldner, printed in Cutter, "Ghostly Hebrew," 417–18, who also offers a detailed analysis of the letter. See also Derrida's reading of the letter in Derrida, *Acts of Religion*, 191–226; and Herzog, "'Monolingualism' or the Language of God."

150 Katz, "Fear from Judaism in Israeli Culture," 206.

151 Klug, "Appropriating Judaism?," 13.
152 Novak, "Supersessionism Hard and Soft," 28.
153 Novak, 28.
154 Novak, 28.
155 Rabkin, *Threat from Within*.
156 Kaplan, "Rabbi Joel Teitelbaum."
157 Weiss, *Judaism*, 1.
158 Weiss, 7.
159 "Neturei Karta Message to Visitors."
160 Weiss, *Judaism*, 6–9.
161 Butler, *Parting Ways*, 2.
162 Butler, 1–2.
163 Adam, "Zionism and Judaism," 279.
164 Adam, 281, 282.
165 Leibowitz, *Judaism, Human Values*; Myers, *Between Jew and Arab*; Gordon, "Jewish Voice for Co-Existence"; Diamond, *Barukh Kurzweil and Modern Hebrew Literature*.
166 Roth, "Right Is Might."
167 Chetrit, "Shas and the 'New Mizrahim.'"
168 See Rabkin, *Threat from Within*.

3. ISRAELI NOSTALGIA

1 Margalit, "Nostalgia," 271–75.
2 Margalit, 274.
3 Yadgar, *Secularism and Religion*; Yadgar, "Post-Secular Look at Tradition"; Yadgar, "Masortiyut."
4 Ben Haim, *Second Israel*; Toubul, *Sephardic Masorti Zionism*.
5 Bruyneel, *Settler Memory*.
6 Baron, "Newer Emphases in Jewish History," 240.
7 Avineri, *Varieties*, 18.
8 See Bottici, *Philosophy of Political Myth*; Smith, *Myths and Memories of the Nation*; Bouchard, *Social Myths and Collective Imaginaries*; Flood, *Political Myth*; Hosking and Schopflin, *Myths and Nationhood*; and Nicholls, *Myth and the Human Sciences*.
9 For example, Hofstadter, *American Political Tradition*; Schlesinger, "New Conservatism"; and Lasch, "Politics of Nostalgia."
10 The electoral successes of Brexit and its advocates in the UK and Donald Trump's "Make America Great Again" are exemplary in this regard. See Campanella and Dassu, *Anglo Nostalgia*; Campanella and Dassu, "Brexit and Nostalgia"; and Mitchell, *Imperial Nostalgia*.
11 Hofstadter, *American Political Tradition*, 1.
12 Cassin, *Nostalgia*, 30.
13 Boym, *Future of Nostalgia*, xvi.

14 Taylor, "Interpretation and the Sciences of Man"; Bauman, *Hermeneutics and Social Science*; Rabinow and Sullivan, *Interpretive Social Science*; Bernstein, *Beyond Objectivism and Relativism*.

15 Stewart, "Nostalgia—A Polemic," 227.

16 Boym, *Future of Nostalgia*, xvii.

17 Stewart, "Nostalgia—A Polemic," 228.

18 Stewart, 228.

19 Stewart, 228.

20 Greene, "Feminist Fiction," 298.

21 Tannock, "Nostalgia Critique"; Kenny, "Back to the Populist Future."

22 Kenny, 256.

23 Stewart, "Nostalgia—A Polemic," 228.

24 Levy, "Anti-Netanyahu Camp."

25 Levy, "Anti-Netanyahu Camp."

26 Boym, *Future of Nostalgia*, xiii.

27 Rotbard, *White City, Black City*, 68.

28 Rotbard, 68.

29 Zerubavel, "'Mythological Sabra' and Jewish Past," 122.

30 Rotbard, *White City, Black City*, 69.

31 Seroussi, "Nostalgic Zionist Soundscapes," 40.

32 Rotbard, *White City, Black City*, 64–69.

33 Seroussi, "Nostalgic Zionist Soundscapes," 40–41.

34 Mehager, "Why '67 and Not '48?"

35 Noy, "Ḥamishim Gevanim."

36 Zubaida and Nurielli, "Ha'ir Halevana."

37 Zubaida, "I Am (Not) Israeli," 57–59.

38 Seroussi, "Nostalgic Zionist Soundscapes," 36.

39 Moss, Nathans, and Tsurumi, *From Europe's East*.

40 Quoted in Boym, *Future of Nostalgia*, 3.

41 Kotef, *Colonizing Self*.

42 Zreik, "When Does a Settler Become a Native?"; Mamdani, *Neither Settler Nor Native*; Evri and Kotef, "When Does a Native Become a Settler?"

43 Boym, *Future of Nostalgia*, 12.

44 Boym, xvi.

45 Boym, xiv.

46 Roth, *Plot against America*; Neelakantan, "Philip Roth's Nostalgia"; Stoffer, "Dying to Belong."

47 Gross, *Beyond the Synagogue*.

48 Gross, 75–76.

49 Gross, *Beyond the Synagogue*.

50 Boym, *Future of Nostalgia*, xiv.

51 Seroussi, "Nostalgic Zionist Soundscapes," 35.

52 Zerubavel, *Recovered Roots*.

53 Smith, "'Golden Age' and National Renewal"; Smith, *Myths and Memories of the Nation.*

54 Anderson, *Imagined Communities.*

55 Hobsbawm, "Introduction."

56 Hosking and Schopflin, *Myths and Nationhood.*

57 Muro, "Nationalism and Nostalgia," 573.

58 Boym, *Future of Nostalgia*, xviii.

59 Boym, 41.

60 Boym, xviii.

61 Boym, xviii.

62 Boym, xvi–xvii.

63 Boym, 55.

64 Chetrit, "Shas and the 'New Mizrahim'"; Yadgar, "SHAS as a Struggle to Create a New Field."

65 Gadamer, *Truth and Method*; MacIntyre, *After Virtue*, 88–108; Taylor, "Interpretation and the Sciences of Man."

66 Midgley, *Utopias, Dolphins, and Computers*, 1996, 17.

67 It may be not out of place to remind the reader that, by this measure, Americans have a far better access to material representations and "presences" of their past two or even three centuries. And, as Rachel Gross's study shows, Jewish Americans, too, can claim historical sites—old synagogues, in this case—as loci of nostalgia. See Gross, *Beyond the Synagogue.*

4. REDEMPTION POLITICS

1 Cavanaugh, *Theopolitical Imagination*, 2. See also Milbank, *Theology and Social Theory*; McAllister and Napolitano, "Political Theology/Theopolitics"; and Brody, "Is Theopolitics an Antipolitics?"

2 Bottici, *Philosophy of Political Myth*; Bouchard, *Social Myths and Collective Imaginaries*; Nicholls, *Myth and the Human Sciences*; Anderson, *Imagined Communities*; Hobsbawm and Ranger, *Invention of Tradition.*

3 Cavanaugh, *Myth of Religious Violence.*

4 Schwartz, *Religious Zionism*; Inbari, *Messianic Religious Zionism*; Don-Yehiya, "Messianism and Politics"; Hellinger, Hershkowitz, and Susser, *Religious Zionism and the Settlement Project*; Sagi and Schwartz, *Religious Zionism and the Six-Day War*; Katsman, "Hyphen Cannot Hold"; Hadad, *Religious Zionism*; Yadgar and Hadad, "Post-Secular Interpretation of Religious Nationalism."

5 For example: Almog, Reinharz, and Shapira, *Zionism and Religion*; Salmon, *Religion and Zionism.* For a critical appreciation of the secularist discourse on study of Israeli nation-statehood see Yadgar, *Sovereign Jews*; Yadgar, *Israel's Jewish Identity Crisis*; and Herman, "Christian Israel."

6 Handelman and Katz, "State Ceremonies of Israel"; Handelman, *Nationalism and the Israeli State*; Don-Yehiya, "Secularization"; Don-Yehiya and Liebman, "Symbol System of Zionist-Socialism"; Liebman and Don-Yehiya, *Civil Religion in Israel*;

Liebman and Don-Yehiya, "Reconciling Traditional Culture and Political Needs"; Zerubavel, *Recovered Roots*; Shoham, *Israel Celebrates Jewish Holidays*.

7 Following, of course, Rousseau, and, more immediately, Bellah, "Civil Religion in America"; and Bellah and Hammond, *Varieties of Civil Religion*.

8 Batnitzky, *How Judaism Became a Religion*; Boyarin, "Christian Invention of Judaism"; Boyarin, *Judaism*; Magid, "Is Judaism a Religion?"

9 Root, "Narrative Structure of Soteriology," 145.

10 Smith, "'Golden Age' and National Renewal."

11 Cavanaugh, *Myth of Religious Violence*, 123.

12 Cavanaugh, 123–24.

13 Herman, "Christian Israel"; Yadgar, *Sovereign Jews*.

14 Hertzberg, *Zionist Idea*, 14–100; Saposnik, *Zionism's Redemptions*.

15 Don-Yehiya, "Negation of Galut"; Raz-Krakotzkin, "Exile, History."

16 Shimoni, *Zionist Ideology*, chap. 7; Avineri, "Zionism and the Jewish Religious Tradition."

17 Raz-Krakotzkin, "Religion and Nationalism"; Raz-Krakotzkin, "Secularism."

18 Liebman and Don-Yehiya, *Civil Religion in Israel*.

19 Quoted in Cohen, *Enemies, A Love Story*, 15.

20 The full Hebrew title of the book is *Bayit Shelishi: Mi'am Shevatim Le'am* [From a nation of tribes to a people]. The English title chosen by the publisher for this book does away with this charged term: Shavit, *A New Israeli Republic*.

21 The article was published simultaneously in *Haaretz*'s Hebrew and English editions. The Hebrew edition has *bayit shelishi* (i.e., without the word "Temple") whereas the English edition, which I am quoting here, uses "Third Temple." Harari, "Can Judaism Survive?'

22 Harari.

23 Manor, *Yigal Allon*, 125.

24 Harari, "Can Judaism Survive?"

25 Kedar, "Masada."

26 Kotef, *Colonizing Self*, 2–3, 17.

27 Saposnik, "Wailing Walls and Iron Walls"; Saposnik, *Zionism's Redemptions*, chap. 6 and p. 136.

28 Saposnik, 137, 136.

29 Saposnik, 137.

30 Saposnik, 137.

31 Liebman and Don-Yehiya, *Civil Religion in Israel*, chap. 2.

32 Saposnik, *Zionism's Redemptions*, 137.

33 Raz-Krakotzkin, "Religion and Nationalism in the Jewish and Zionist Context."

34 Saposnik, *Zionism's Redemptions*, 142.

35 Saposnik, 154.

36 Saposnik, 139.

37 Saposnik, 138.

38 Saposnik, 139.

39 Saposnik, 139.

40 Saposnik, 149.

41 Saposnik, 148–49.

42 Cohen, *Year Zero of the Arab-Israeli Conflict*, 1.

43 Quoted in Liebman and Don-Yehiya, *Civil Religion in Israel*, 54.

44 Quoted in Liebman and Don-Yehiya, 54. See also Saposnik, "Wailing Walls and Iron Walls."

45 Katz, "Fear from Judaism in Israeli Culture"; Saposnik, *Zionism's Redemptions*, 152.

46 This is not to suggest that national traditions necessarily shy away from marking defeats, sometimes even celebrating them as ultimate triumphs. See Kapferer, *Legends of People, Myths of State*; and Liebman, "Myth of Defeat."

47 Hadad, *Religious Zionism*. See also Yadgar and Hadad, "Post-Secular Interpretation of Religious Nationalism."

48 Auerbach, "Ḥazon Veneḥama Beyamenu."

49 *Haṣofe*, 11 August 1967.

50 Dichovsky, "Tishʻa Beʼav Birʼi Hahalakha."

51 Goren, "Meʼevel Lenaḥama."

52 *Haṣofe*, 15 August 1967.

53 Katz, "Avlei Ṣion Veyerushalayim."

54 *Haṣofe*, 4 August 1968; 11 August 1970.

55 *Haṣofe*, 1 August 1971.

56 *Haṣofe*, 24 July 1977; 2 August 1979; 7 August 1984; 31 July 1990.

57 *Haṣofe*, 19 July 1983.

58 *Haṣofe*, 27 August 1993.

59 *Haṣofe*, 10 August 1989.

60 Goren, "Binyan Yerushalyim Kesemel Hageʼula."

61 *Haṣofe*, 23 May 1990.

62 *Haṣofe*, 11 May 1983.

63 *Haṣofe*, 12 May 1991.

64 *Haṣofe*, 15 May 1988.

65 For example, *Haṣofe*, 19 May 1993; 28 May 1995.

66 *Haṣofe*, 17 July 1995; 6 August 1995.

67 Eitam, "Habesora Shbetokh Haḥurban."

68 Felix, "Al Ma Avda Haʼareṣ."

69 Qaniʼel, "Ṣom Gush Qaṭif."

70 Ḥevroni, "Koḥo Shel Hamanhig."

71 Sherlo, "Yom Yerushalayim."

72 Chen, *Speedily in Our Days*; Chen, "Visiting the Temple Mount"; Persico, "End Point of Zionism."

73 Eldad, "Har Habayit Leyadenu."

74 *Haṣofe*, 11 May 2007.

75 Segal, "Laʻalot El Hahar."

76   Meidad, "Kolo Biydey Ha'aravim."
77   Eliṣor, "Habayit Hashelishi."
78   Khalfa, "Zeqifut Haqoma Hale'umit."
79   Me'ir, "Avlut 'al Ma Shelo Yashuv."
80   Elyashiv, "Halev Ḥaser Akh Einenu Margishim."
81   Don-Yehiya and Liebman, "Symbol System of Zionist-Socialism."
82   Berkovitch, "Avlut Mishtana."
83   Berkovitch.
84   Sorek, "Im Lo Tirṣo."
85   Yadgar and Hadad, "Post-Secular Interpretation of Religious Nationalism."
86   See also Inbari, *Messianic Religious Zionism*; Inbari, "Prophetic Disappointment and Ideological Change."
87   Liebman, "Myth of Defeat," 413. See also Macleod, *Defeat and Memory*.

5. A JEWISH REACTION TO ZIONIST SUPERSESSIONISM

1   It would be futile to try and properly cite here an ever-growing body of literature on most of these thinkers (Barukh Kurzweil stands out as the least studied among them). For some of the latest works, see Vatter, *Living Law*; Barak-Gorodetsky, *Judah Magnes*; Meir, "Rosenzweig and the Cohen-Buber Dispute"; Fiebig, "From Scepticism to Tolerance"; Gordon, *Toward Nationalism's End*; and Diamond, *Barukh Kurzweil and Modern Hebrew Literature*.
2   Myers, *Between Jew and Arab*.
3   Tzoreff, "Political Theology of the Feminine Jew"; Tzoreff, "Galician Yeshiva-Boḥur and Two Cities"; Tzoreff, *R. Binyamin, Binationalism and Counter-Zionism*.
4   Boyarin, *No-State Solution*; Butler, *Parting Ways*; Kaplan, "Rabbi Joel Teitelbaum"; Rabkin, *Threat from Within*.
5   As David Heyd commented recently, most teachers and students of philosophy in Israel would have never heard of Roth. See Heyd, "Leon Roth's Utopian Vision."
6   The closest to a book-length consideration of Roth we currently have is Jan Katzew's unpublished dissertation: Katzew, "Leon Roth—His Life and Work." See also Batnitzky, "Tale of Two Leo(n)s"; Heyd, "Leon Roth's Utopian Vision"; Katzew, "Completing Creation through Education"; Katzew, "Leon Roth's Judaism"; Gordon and Motzkin, "Between Universalism and Particularism"; Gordon, "Zionism, Translation"; Gordon, "Jewish Voice for Co-Existence"; Harvey, "Leon Roth on Hebrew, English, and Arabic"; Harvey, "After Qibya"; Harvey, "The Religious-Political Paradox"; Schvarcz, "Democracy and Judaism"; Schvarcz and Brodsky, "Love, Freedom, and Bondage"; and Roswald, "Leon Roth."
7   Gordon and Motzkin, "Between Universalism and Particularism."
8   Ahad HaAm, who was a father figure to the Hebrew University in general, and to many of its founding members, including Roth, in particular, died a year earlier. Zipperstein, *Elusive Prophet*; Goldstein, *Ahad Ha'am*.
9   Heyd, "Leon Roth's Utopian Vision," 100.

10 For lack of space, I will not reference all of Roth's works here. For a comprehensive list of his publications see Loewe, *Studies in Rationalism, Judaism & Universalism*, 323–36. Many of the books and articles by (and also on) Roth are available on the Leon Roth Foundation's website (leonroth.org). See also Heyd, 100–101; and Gordon and Motzkin, "Between Universalism and Particularism."

11 Gordon, "Jewish Voice for Co-Existence." Heyd further notes that Roth, who came from a comfortable background and had his income secured by his family, donated his university salary to the translation project. Heyd, 100.

12 Katzew, "Jewish State," 1.

13 Katzew, 1.

14 Katzew, "Leon Roth's Judaism," 93.

15 Katzew, "Jewish State," 1.

16 Loewe, "Memoir," 3.

17 "Prof. L. Roth Stirs Wrath of Zionists," *B'nai B'rith Messenger*, 6 June 1947.

18 Loewe, "Memoir," 3.

19 For a detailed consideration of Roth's potential motivations to leave, see Schvarcz, "Democracy and Judaism"; and Schvarcz, Ma Sheyakholti Latet Nattati.

20 Loewe, "Memoir," 5.

21 Schmidt, "Herbert Samuel's Moral Philosophy," 268.

22 Loewe, "Preface," xi.

23 Loewe, "Memoir," 8–9.

24 Gordon, "Jewish Voice for Co-Existence," 150.

25 Loewe, "Memoir," 8.

26 Smith, *Chosen Peoples*; Gurkan, *Jews as a Chosen People*, chaps. 7, 10; Abulof, "Roles of Religion"; Saposnik, *Zionism's Redemptions*.

27 Raz-Krakotzkin, "There Is No God."

28 Raz-Krakotzkin, "Religion and Nationalism"; Yadgar, *Sovereign Jews*.

29 Roth, *Judaism*, 16.

30 Roth, 16.

31 Roth, 16.

32 Roth, 16.

33 Roth, 17.

34 Roth, 99.

35 Roth, *Is There a Jewish Philosophy?*, 78.

36 Roth, 78–79.

37 Roth, *Judaism*, 99.

38 Roth, 100.

39 Katzew, "Leon Roth's Judaism," 91.

40 Katzew, 92–93.

41 Roth, *Judaism*, 203.

42 Roth, *Is There a Jewish Philosophy?*, 168.

43 Roth, *Judaism*, 215, 214.

44 Roth, 216.
45 Roth, 217.
46 Roth, 220.
47 Roth, 221.
48 Roth, 221.
49 Roth, "Mekom Hadat Bevinyan Haʾareṣ," 75.
50 Roth, 75–76.
51 Roth, *Is There a Jewish Philosophy?*, 123.
52 Roth, 72.
53 Roth, 72.
54 Roth, 126.
55 Roth, 104.
56 Roth, 121.
57 Roth, 104.
58 Roth, 142.
59 Roth, "Mediniyut Ufolitika Betorat Aplaton," 10.
60 Roth, *Is There a Jewish Philosophy?*, 156.
61 Zameret, "Ahad Haʾam."
62 Kurzweil, *Our New Literature*, 193.
63 Kurzweil, 190–224.
64 Roth, *Is There a Jewish Philosophy?*, 157.
65 Roth, 167.
66 Roth, 167.
67 Roth, *Judaism* , 223.
68 Roth, 225.
69 Roth, "Mekom Hadat Bevinyan Haʾareṣ," 74.
70 Shimoni, *Zionist Ideology*, 15.
71 Yadgar, *Sovereign Jews*, chap. 5.
72 Roth, *Judaism*, 226.
73 Roth, "Right Is Might."
74 Norman Bentwich, D. W. Senator, Leon Roth, and Leon Simon, "Readers' Letters: The Sharafat Incident." On the massacre, see Morris, *Palestinian Refugee Problem Revisited*, 206–7.
75 Martin Buber, Ernest Simon, W. D. Senator, and H. Y. Roth to Ben Gurion, 6 June 1949, State Archives, Prime Minister's Office, Absorption of Immigrants in Agriculture, 7133 5559/C. See also Segev, *1949*; and Epstein, "For the Sake of Freedom." For a detailed consideration of somewhat of a less complimentary public letter of Roth ("Disorder in Palestine," *Times*, 5 June 1936), see Dubnov, "Most Vicious Lies."
76 For a consideration of the context, and an evaluation of the letter in comparison to Yeshayahu Leibowitz's famous letter protesting the same massacre, see Harvey, "After Qibya."
77 Shlaim, *Iron Wall*, 95–96.

78 Cohen, "Right Is Might."
79 Roth, "Right Is Might," 21.
80 Roth, 21.
81 Roth, 21.
82 Roth, 21.
83 Roth, 21.
84 Heyd, "Leon Roth's Utopian Vision.".
85 Raz-Krakotzkin, "Exile, History."
86 Mamdani, *Neither Settler nor Native*, 19; Zreik, "When Does a Settler Become a Native?"

CONCLUSION
1 Valluvan, *Clamour of Nationalism*, chap. 2.
2 Valluvan, 36.
3 Valluvan, 44.
4 Valluvan, 45.
5 Valluvan, 45.
6 Herman, "Christian Israel." See also Raz-Krakotzkin, "Religion and Nationalism"; and Yadgar, *Sovereign Jews*.
7 Valluvan, *Clamour of Nationalism*, 44.
8 Liebman and Don-Yehiya, *Civil Religion in Israel*; Kedar, *Mamlachtiyut*.
9 Raz-Krakotzkin, "Secularism"; Raz-Krakotzkin, "Exile, History."
10 Khazzoom, "Great Chain of Orientalism," 482.
11 Shavit, *A New Israeli Republic*, loc. 5%.
12 Shavit, loc. 5%.
13 Shavit, loc. 6%.
14 Shavit, loc. 7%.
15 Yadgar, *Sovereign Jews*, 163–86.
16 James, *Globalism, Nationalism, Tribalism*, 326.
17 Borabek, "Ministry of Religious Affairs."
18 Raz-Krakotzkin, *Mishna Consciousness, Biblical Consciousness*; Altshuler, *Life of Rabbi Yoseph Karo*, 258.
19 Fine, *Physician of the Soul*, 235.
20 Hayyim Vital, *Peri 'Etz Hayyim*, Sha'ar Hatefila, introduction. I am consulting here the partial translation of this quote in Fine, 235.
21 One such recent work, for example, is Christopher Beem's polemic for democracy—written, again, in the shadow of the Trumpian turn of American politics. Beem treats tribalism as a dangerous "vice" that threatens the virtues of democracy. Tribalism, he explains, emanates from an "instinctual" need to distinguish friend from foe, but it clearly undermines the sense of corporate society required for democracy to function. Beem, *Seven Democratic Virtues*.
22 Walzer, "New Tribalism," 146.

23 Walzer.

24 Walzer, 163–64.

25 Walzer, 165.

26 James, *Globalism, Nationalism, Tribalism*, 9.

27 Rule, "Tribalism and the State." Walzer himself seems to be of two minds as to the nation-statist implications of tribalism. Seeing "tribal identities [as] neither total nor final," he concludes that "tribal politics can and does take many forms." In reply to James Rule, he seems to be supportive of the insistence of Jews, Armenians, Kurds, and Palestinians that their "tribal" identity is to be safeguarded by a nation-state, while deciding that "Scots, Catalans, Copts, and Druse, for example, probably don't need states of their own. But they, too, will ask for some sort of political accommodation in the postimperial world." Walzer, "Michael Walzer Replies," 524.

28 Walzer, 523.

29 Cohen, *Enemies, A Love Story*.

30 Ben Haim, *Second Israel*; Toubul, *Sephardic masorti Zionism*.

31 MacIntyre, *After Virtue*, 254.

32 MacIntyre, 254–55.

33 Raz-Krakotzkin, *Mishna Consciousness*.

34 Boyarin, *No-State Solution*.

35 MacIntyre, *After Virtue*, 263.

36 MacIntyre, 263.

BIBLIOGRAPHY

Abulof, Uriel. "The Roles of Religion in National Legitimation: Judaism and Zionism's Elusive Quest for Legitimacy." *Journal for the Scientific Study of Religion* 53, no. 3 (2014): 515–33.

Adam, Yehudi. "Zionism and Judaism." *Judaism* 29, no. 3 (Summer 1980): 279–85.

Ahad HaAm. *Kol Kitvey Ahad HaAm (Collected Writings)*. Tel-Aviv and Jerusalem: Dvir, 5707.

———. Words of Fire: *Selected Essays of Ahad HaAm*. Devon: Notting Hill, 2015.

———. "Yalquṭ Qaṭan—Altneuland." *Hashiloaḥ* 10, no. 6 (December 1902): 566–78.

———. *'Al Parashat Derakhim*. Vol. 1–3. Berlin: Judischer Verlag, 5690.

Almog, Oz. *The Sabra: The Creation of the New Jew*. Berkeley: University of California Press, 2000.

Almog, Samuel, Jehuda Reinharz, and Anita Shapira, eds. *Zionism and Religion*. Hanover, NH: University Press of New England, 1998.

Alpher, Rogel. "Ḥoq Hamarkolim Mokhiaḥ Shehahilonim Sovlim Mirigshei Neḥitut." *Haaretz*, 9 January 2018.

Alroey, Gur. *Zionism without Zion: The Jewish Territorial Organization and Its Conflict with the Zionist Organization*. Detroit, MI: Wayne State University Press, 2016.

Altshuler, Mor. *The Life of Rabbi Yoseph Karo*. Tel Aviv: Haim Robin Tel Aviv University Press, 2016.

Anderson, Benedict. *Imagined Communities: Reflections on the Origin and Spread of Nationalism*. London: Verso, 1998.

Auerbach, Simḥa Bunem. "Ḥazon Veneḥama Beyamenu." *Haṣofe*, 9 August 1968.

Avineri, Shlomo. "Hegel and the Emergence of Zionism." *Hegel Bulletin* 3, no. 2 (1982): 12–18.

———. *The Making of Modern Zionism: Intellectual Origins of the Jewish State*. New York: Basic Books, 1981.

———. *Varieties of Zionist Thought*. Tel Aviv: Am Oved, 1980.

———. "Zionism and the Jewish Religious Tradition: The Dialectics of Redemption and Secularization." In *Zionism and Religion*, edited by Shlomo Almog, Jehuda Reinharz, and Anita Shapira, 1–12. Hanover, NH: University Press of New England, 1998.

Avraham, Yaron. "Hamemshala Taṣbi'ah 'al 'Ḥoq haṢiyonut.'" N12, 28 May 2023. www.mako.co.il.

Azulay, Naama, and Ephraim Tabory. "'A House of Prayer for All Nations': Unorthodox Prayer Houses for Nonreligious Israeli Jews." *Sociological Papers* 13 (2008): 22–41.

Baker, Cynthia M. *Jew.* New Brunswick, NJ: Rutgers University Press, 2017.

Barak, Aharon. *Aadel Ka'adan v. Israel Lands Administration.* No. 6698/95, High Court of Justice, 8 March 2000.

———. "The Constitutionalization of the Israeli Legal System as a Result of the Basic Laws and Its Effect on Procedural and Substantive Criminal Law." *Israel Law Review* 31, nos. 1–3 (1997): 3–23.

———. "A Constitutional Revolution: Israel's Basic Laws." *Constitutional Forum* 4, no. 3 (1993): 83–84.

———. "The Values of the State of Israel as a Jewish and Democratic State." *Baacademia* 24 (December 2012): 58–66.

Barak-Gorodetsky, David. *Judah Magnes: The Prophetic Politics of a Religious Binationalist.* Translated by Merav Datan. Philadelphia: Jewish Publication Society, 2021.

Baron, Salo. "Newer Emphases in Jewish History." *Jewish Social Studies* 25, no. 4 (1963): 245–58.

"Basic Law: Apartheid in Israel." *Haaretz*, 30 May 2013.

Batnitzky, Leora. *How Judaism Became a Religion: An Introduction to Modern Jewish Thought.* Princeton, NJ: Princeton University Press, 2011.

———. "A Tale of Two Leo(n)s: Leon Roth, Leo Strauss, and the Place of Jewish Thought in the Western Canon." *Modern Judaism* 40, no. 1 (2020): 4–16.

Bauman, Zygmunt. *Hermeneutics and Social Science: Approaches to Understanding.* London: Hutchinson, 1978.

Beem, Christopher. *The Seven Democratic Virtues: What You Can Do to Overcome Tribalism and Save Our Democracy.* University Park: Penn State University Press, 2022.

Behar, Moshe, and Zvi Ben-Dor Benite. *Modern Middle Eastern Jewish Thought: Writings on Identity, Politics, and Culture, 1893–1958.* Waltham, MA: Brandeis University Press, 2013.

Bellah, Robert N. "Civil Religion in America." *Daedalus* 96 (1967): 1–21.

Bellah, Robert N., and Phillip E. Hammond. *Varieties of Civil Religion.* San Francisco: Harper & Row, 1980.

Bender, Aryeh. "Berov Shel 62 Tomkhim Mol 55 Mitnagdim: Ḥoq Hale'om Ushar Baknesset." *Maariv*, 19 July 2018.

Ben Haim, Avishay. *Second Israel: The Sweet Vision, The Bitter Oppression.* Rishon LeZion: Miskal—Yedioth Ahronoth Books & Chemed Books, 2022.

Bentwich, Norman, D. W. Senator, Leon Roth, and Leon Simon. "Readers' Letters: The Sharafat Incident." *Jerusalem Post*, 12 February 1951.

Berdyczewski, Micha Yosef. *Ba-Derekh.* Lipsia: Shtiebel, 1922.

———. *Ma'amarim.* Vol. 2. Lipsia: Shtiebel, 5682.

Berkovitch, Dov. "Avlut Mishtana." *Makor Rishon*, 5 August 2011.

Bernstein, Richard J. *Beyond Objectivism and Relativism: Science, Hermeneutics, and Praxis.* Oxford: B. Blackwell, 1983.

Bevir, Mark, and R. A. W. Rhodes. *The State as Cultural Practice*. Oxford: Oxford University Press, 2010.

Blumenfeld, Revital. "A. B. Yehoshua: Hashoah Hie Kishalon Shel Ha'am Hayehudi." *Haaretz*, 18 March 2012.

Borabek, David. "The Ministry of Religious Affairs and the Formation of Religion in the State of Israel, 1948–1958." PhD diss., Ben-Gurion University of the Negev, 2023.

Bottici, Chiara. *A Philosophy of Political Myth*. Cambridge: Cambridge University Press, 2007.

Bouchard, Gerard. *Social Myths and Collective Imaginaries*. Translated by Howard Scott. Toronto: University of Toronto Press, 2017.

Boyarin, Daniel. "The Christian Invention of Judaism: The Theodosian Empire and the Rabbinic Refusal of Religion." *Representations* 85, no. 1 (1 February 2004): 21–57.

——. *Judaism: The Genealogy of a Modern Notion*. New Brunswick, NJ: Rutgers University Press, 2018.

——. *The No-State Solution: A Jewish Manifesto*. New Haven, CT: Yale University Press, 2023.

Boyarin, Jonathan. "Hegel's Zionism?" In *Remapping Memory: The Politics of TimeSpace*, edited by Jonathan Boyarin, 137–60. Minneapolis: University of Minnesota Press, 1994.

——. *Palestine and Jewish History: Criticism at the Borders of Ethnography*. Minneapolis: University of Minnesota Press, 1996.

Boyarin, Jonathan, and Daniel Boyarin. *Powers of Diaspora: Two Essays on The Relevance of Jewish Culture*. Minneapolis: University of Minnesota Press, 2002.

Boym, Svetlana. *The Future of Nostalgia*. New York: Basic Books, 2002.

Brenner, Yosef Ḥayim. *Ketavim*. Tel Aviv: Sifriyat Po'alim & Haqibutz Hameuḥad, 5738.

Brody, Samuel Hayim. "Is Theopolitics an Antipolitics?" In *Dialogue as a Trans-Disciplinary Concept: Martin Buber's Philosophy of Dialogue and Its Contemporary Reception*, edited by Paul Mendes-Flohr, 61–88. Berlin: De Gruyter, 2015.

Brubaker, Rogers. "Religion and Nationalism: Four Approaches." *Nations and Nationalism* 18, no. 1 (2012): 2–20.

Bruyneel, Kevin. *Settler Memory: The Disavowal of Indigeneity and the Politics of Race in the United States*. Chapel Hill: University of North Carolina Press, 2021.

Butler, Judith. *Parting Ways: Jewishness and the Critique of Zionism*. New York: Columbia University Press, 2012.

Campanella, Edoardo, and Marta Dassu. *Anglo Nostalgia: The Politics of Emotion in a Fractured West*. Oxford: Oxford University Press, 2019.

——. "Brexit and Nostalgia." *Survival* 61, no. 3 (4 May 2019): 103–11.

Cassin, Barbara. *Nostalgia: When Are We Ever at Home?* Translated by Pascale-Anne Brault. New York: Fordham University Press, 2016.

Cavanaugh, William T. *The Myth of Religious Violence: Secular Ideology and the Roots of Modern Conflict*. New York: Oxford University Press, USA, 2009.

——. *Theopolitical Imagination: Christian Practices of Space and Time*. London: Bloomsbury/T&T Clark, 2003.

Chen, Sarina. *"Speedily in Our Days . . .": The Temple Mount Activists and the National-Religious Society in Israel.* Sede Boqer: Ben Gurion Research Institute for the Study of Israel and Zionism, 2017.

———. "Visiting the Temple Mount—Taboo or Mitzvah." *Modern Judaism: A Journal of Jewish Ideas and Experience* 34, no. 1 (1 February 2014): 27–41.

Chetrit, Sami Shalom. "Shas and the 'New Mizrahim': Back to Back in Parallel Axles: Criticism of and Alternative to European Zionism." *Israel Studies Forum* 17, no. 2 (2002): 107–13.

Cohen, A. "Right Is Might: Dr. Cohen's Propositions." *Jewish Chronicle*, 20 November 1953.

Cohen, Hillel. *Enemies, A Love Story: Mizrahi Jews, Palestinian Arabs, and Ashkenazi Jews from the Rise of Zionism to Present.* Jerusalem: Ivrit, 2022.

———. *Year Zero of the Arab-Israeli Conflict, 1929.* Translated by Haim Watzman. Waltham, MA: Brandeis University Press, 2015.

Cohn, Bernard S., and Nicholas B. Dirks. "Beyond the Fringe: The Nation State, Colonialism, and the Technologies of Power." *Journal of Historical Sociology* 1, no. 2 (1988): 224–29.

Conforti, Yitzhak. "East and West in Jewish Nationalism: Conflicting Types in the Zionist Vision." *Nations and Nationalism* 16, no. 2 (2010): 201–19.

———. *Shaping a Nation: The Cultural Origins of Zionism, 1882–1948.* Jerusalem: Yad Yitzhak Ben Zvi, 2019.

Cooper, Julie E. "The Turn to Tradition in the Study of Jewish Politics." *Annual Review of Political Science* 19 (2016): 67–87.

Crome, Andrew. *Christian Zionism and English National Identity, 1600–1850.* New York: Palgrave Macmillan, 2018.

Cutter, William. "Ghostly Hebrew, Ghastly Speech: Scholem to Rosenzweig, 1926." *Prooftexts*, 10 (1990): 413–33.

Cynamon-Murphy, Rebecca. "Why Christians Should Not Host Their Own Passover Seders." Religion Dispatches, 11 April 2014. https://religiondispatches.org/why-christians-should-not-host-their-own-passover-seders/.

Dabashi, Hamid. *Theology of Discontent: The Ideological Foundation of the Islamic Revolution in Iran.* New York: Transaction, 2006.

Dalsheim, Joyce. *Israel Has a Jewish Problem: Self-Determination as Self-Elimination.* Oxford: Oxford University Press, 2019.

D'Costa, Gavin. "A New Zionism." *First Things*, no. 284 (1 June 2018): 57–61.

Derrida, Jacques. *Acts of Religion.* Edited by Gil Anidjar. New York: Routledge, 2002.

———. *Specters of Marx: The State of the Debt, the Work of Mourning, and the New International.* Translated by Peggy Kamuf. New York: Routledge, 2006.

Deutscher, Isaac. *The Non-Jewish Jew: And Other Essays.* London: Verso, 2017.

Devji, Faisal. *Muslim Zion: Pakistan as a Political Idea.* Cambridge, MA: Harvard University Press, 2013.

Diamond, James S. *Barukh Kurzweil and Modern Hebrew Literature.* Chico, CA: Scholars Press, 1983.

———. *Homeland or Holy Land? The "Canaanite" Critique of Israel.* Bloomington: Indiana University Press, 1986.

Dichovsky, Shelomo. "Tish'a Be'av Bir'i Hahalakha." *Haṣofe*, 20 July 1972.

Dirlik, Arif. "Rethinking Colonialism: Globalization, Postcolonialism, and the Nation." *Interventions* 4, no. 3 (1 January 2002): 428–48.

Donaldson, Terence. "Supersessionism and Early Christian Self-Definition." *JJMJS* 3 (2016): 1–32.

Don-Yehiya, Eliezer. "Messianism and Politics: The Ideological Transformation of Religious Zionism." *Israel Studies* 19, no. 2 (2014): 239.

———. "The Negation of Galut in Religious Zionism." *Modern Judaism* 12, no. 2 (1992): 129–55.

———. "Secularization, Negation, and Accommodation of Conceptions of Traditional Judaism and Its Terms in Socialist Zionism." *Kivunim* 8 (1980): 29–46.

Don-Yehiya, Eliezer, and Charles S. Liebman. "The Symbol System of Zionist-Socialism: An Aspect of Israeli Civil Religion." *Modern Judaism* 1, no. 2 (1 September 1981): 121–48.

Dubnov, Arie. "The Most Vicious Lies as Told in Silence." Siha Mekomit, 20 March 2021. www.mekomit.co.il.

Eitam, Noa. "Habesora Shbetokh Haḥurban." *Makor Rishon*, 12 August 2005.

Eldad, Aryeh. "Har Habayit Leyadenu." *Basheva'*, 27 May 2014.

Eliade, Mircea. *Myth and Reality.* Translated by Willard R. Trask. New York: Harper & Row, 1963.

Eliṣor, Uri. "Habayit Hashelishi." *Makor Rishon*, 12 July 2013.

Elyashiv, Natanel. "Halev Ḥaser Akh Einenu Margishim." *Makor Rishon*, 1 August 2014.

Epstein, Alek. "For the Sake of Freedom: The Role of the Jerusalem Academic Community in the Development of Critical Discourse during the Crucial Years of State-Building." *Cathedra* 106 (December 2002): 139–76.

Essa, Azad. *Hostile Homelands: The New Alliance Between India and Israel.* London: Pluto, 2022.

Evri, Yuval. *The Return to Al-Andalus: Disputes over Sephardic Culture and Identity between Arabic and Hebrew.* Jerusalem: Magnes, 2020.

Evri, Yuval, and Hagar Kotef. "When Does a Native Become a Settler? (With Apologies to Zreik and Mamdani)." *Constellations* (2020): 1–16.

Falah, Ghazi. "Israeli 'Judaization' Policy in Galilee." *Journal of Palestine Studies* 20, no. 4 (1991): 69–85.

Felix, Menaḥem. "Al Ma Avda Ha'areṣ." *Me'at Min Ha'or*, Av 5765.

Fiebig, Anne. "From Scepticism to Tolerance of 'the Other': The Example of Yeshayahu Leibowitz." In *Yearbook of the Maimonides Centre for Advanced Studies, 2019*, edited by Yoav Meyrav, 243–64. Berlin: De Gruyter, 2020.

Fine, Lawrence. *Physician of the Soul, Healer of the Cosmos: Isaac Luria and His Kabbalistic Fellowship.* Stanford, CA: Stanford University Press, 2003.

Flood, Christopher. *Political Myth.* London: Routledge, 2001.

Freeden, Michael. "Is Nationalism a Distinct Ideology?" *Political Studies* 46, no. 4 (1998): 748–65.

Furani, Khaled. "Khalifah and the Modern Sovereign: Revisiting a Qur'anic Ideal from within the Palestinian Condition." *Journal of Religion* 102, no. 4 (October 2022): 482–506.

Gadamer, Hans-Georg. *Truth and Method.* Translated by J. Winsheimer and D. G. Marshall. 2nd ed. New York: Crossroad, 1989.

Ginzburg, Carlo. "History and/or Memory: On the Principle of Accommodation." In *Thinking Impossibilities: The Intellectual Legacy of Amos Funkenstein*, edited by Robert S. Westman and Davie Biale, 193–206. Toronto: University of Toronto Press, 2008.

Glickson, Moshe. *Aḥad Ha'am: Ḥayaw ufa'olo.* Jerusalem: Haaretz, 1926.

Goldman, Samuel. *God's Country: Christian Zionism in America.* Philadelphia: University of Pennsylvania Press, 2018.

Goldman, Shalom L. *Zeal for Zion: Christians, Jews, and the Idea of the Promised Land.* Chapel Hill: University of North Carolina Press, 2010.

Goldstein, Joseph. *Ahad Ha'am and Herzl: The Struggle for Political and Cultural Nature of Zionism in the Shade of Altneuland Affair.* "Kuntresim": Texts and Studies 99. Jerusalem: Hebrew University of Jerusalem, Ben-Zion Dinur Center for Research in Jewish History, 2011.

———. *Ahad Ha'am: The Prophet of Zionism.* Brighton: Sussex Academic Press, 2004.

Gordon, Adi. *Toward Nationalism's End: An Intellectual Biography of Hans Kohn.* Waltham, MA: Brandeis University Press, 2017.

Gordon, Avery. *Ghostly Matters: Haunting and the Sociological Imagination.* Minneapolis: University of Minnesota Press, 2008.

Gordon, Neve. "A Jewish Voice for Co-Existence." *Global Dialogue*, no. 3 (Autumn 2001): 149–52.

———. "Zionism, Translation, and the Politics of Erasure." *Political Studies* 50, no. 4 (September 2002): 811–28.

Gordon, Neve, and Gabriel Gideon Hillel Motzkin. "Between Universalism and Particularism: The Origins of the Philosophy Department at Hebrew University and the Zionist Project." *Jewish Social Studies* 9, no. 2 (2003): 99–122.

Goren, Shelomo. "Binyan Yerushalyim Kesemel Hage'ula." *Haṣofe*, 6 May 1983.

———. "Me'evel Lenaḥama." *Haṣofe*, 22 July 1983.

Graubart, Jonathan. *Jewish Self-Determination beyond Zionism: Lessons from Hannah Arendt and Other Pariahs.* Philadelphia, PA: Temple University Press, 2023.

Greene, Gayle. "Feminist Fiction and the Uses of Memory." *Signs* 16, no. 2 (1991): 290–321.

Greenfield, Ben. "Offended by Christian Seders? Don't Have One." Jewish Telegraphic Agency, 2 April 2021. www.jta.org.

Gross, Rachel B. *Beyond the Synagogue: Jewish Nostalgia as Religious Practice.* New York: New York University Press, 2021.

Gurkan, S. Leyla. *The Jews as a Chosen People: Tradition and Transformation.* London: Routledge, 2008.

Hadad, Noam. *Religious Zionism: Religion, Nationalism, and Politics.* Jerusalem: Carmel, 2020.

Halkin, Hillel. "What Ahad Ha'am Saw and Herzl Missed—and Vice Versa." Mosaic, 5 October 2016. mosaicmagazine.com.

Hallaq, Wael B. *The Impossible State: Islam, Politics, and Modernity's Moral Predicament.* Columbia University Press, 2012.

Handelman, Don. *Nationalism and the Israeli State: Bureaucratic Logic in Public Events.* New York: Routledge, 2020.

Handelman, Don, and Elihu Katz. "State Ceremonies of Israel: Remembrance Day and Independence Day." In *Israeli Judaism: The Sociology of Religion in Israel,* edited by Shlomo Deshen, Charles S. Liebman, and Moshe Shokeid, 75–86. New Brunswick, NJ: Transaction, 1995.

Harari, Yoval Noah. "Can Judaism Survive a Messianic Dictatorship in Israel?" *Haaretz,* 13 July 2023.

Harvey, Warren Zev. "After Qibya: Yeshayahu Leibowitz, Ḥayim Yehuda Roth, and Neḥama Leibowitz." In *Yeshayahu Leibowitz: Between Conservatism and Radicalism—Reflections on His Philosophy,* edited by Aviezer Ravitzky, 354–65. Jerusalem: Van Leer Jeruslaem Institute, Hakibbutz Hameuchad, 2007.

———. "Leon Roth on Hebrew, English, and Arabic." *Iyyun: The Jerusalem Philosophical Quarterly* 62 (2013): 332–38.

———. "The Religious-Political Paradox according to Leon Roth." In *Religion and State in Twentieth-Century Jewish Thought,* edited by Aviezer Ravitzky, 357–66. Jerusalem: Israel Democracy Institute, 2005.

Hazony, Yoram. *The Virtue of Nationalism.* New York: Basic Books, 2018.

Hellinger, Moshe, Isaac Hershkowitz, and Bernard Susser. *Religious Zionism and the Settlement Project: Ideology, Politics, and Civil Disobedience.* Albany: State University of New York Press, 2018.

Helman, Dubi, and Adi Arbel. "Doresh 'igun." Institute for Zionist Strategies, July 2009. http://izs.org.il .

Herman, Didi. "Christian Israel." In *Reimagining the State: Theoretical Challenges and Transformative Possibilities,* edited by Davina Cooper, Nikita Dhawan, and Janet Newman, 114–32. London: Routledge, 2019.

Hertzberg, Arthur. *The Zionist Idea: A Historical Analysis and Reader.* Garden City, NY: Doubleday, 1959.

Herzl, Theodor. *The Congress Addresses of Theodor Herzl.* Translated by Nellie Straus. New York: Federation of American Zionists, 1917.

———. *Zionist Writings: Essays and Addresses.* Translated by Harry Zohn. Vol. 1. 2 vols. New York: Herzl, 1973.

Herzog, Annabel. "'Monolingualism' or the Language of God: Scholem and Derrida on Hebrew and Politics." *Modern Judaism: A Journal of Jewish Ideas and Experience* 29, no. 2 (1 May 2009): 226–38.

Ḥevroni, Ido. "Koḥo Shel Hamanhig." *Makor Rishon,* 12 August 2005.

Heyd, David. "Leon Roth's Utopian Vision of a Liberal State." *Iyyun: The Jerusalem Philosophical Quarterly* 68 (2020): 99–112.

Hobsbawm, Eric J. "Introduction: Inventing Traditions." In *The Invention of Tradition*, edited by Eric J. Hobsbawm and Terence O. Ranger, 1–14. Cambridge: Cambridge University Press, 1983.

Hobsbawm, Eric J., and Terence O. Ranger, eds. *The Invention of Tradition*. Cambridge: Cambridge University Press, 1992.

Hofstadter, Richard. *The American Political Tradition: And the Men Who Made It*. New York: Knopf, 1948.

Horovitz, Michael. "Far-Right Minister Pushes Decree to Make Zionism a 'Guiding Value' in Gov't Decisions." *Times of Israel*, 27 April 2023.

Hosking, Geoffrey A., and George Schopflin. *Myths and Nationhood*. New York: Routledge, 1997.

Inbari, Motti. *Messianic Religious Zionism Confronts Israeli Territorial Compromises*. Cambridge: Cambridge University Press, 2012.

———. "Prophetic Disappointment and Ideological Change among Israeli Settlers' Rabbis: The Case of Rabbis Yehuda Amital and Shmuel Tal." *Religions* 12, no. 11 (November 2021): 1017.

Jackson, Timothy P. *Mordecai Would Not Bow Down: Anti-Semitism, the Holocaust, and Christian Supersessionism*. New York: Oxford University Press, 2021.

James, Paul. *Globalism, Nationalism, Tribalism: Bringing Theory Back In*. London: Sage, 2006.

"The Jewish Coercion Administration." *Haaretz*, 22 May 2013.

Kahn, Paul W. *Political Theology: Four New Chapters on the Concept of Sovereignty*. New York: Columbia University Press, 2011.

Kapferer, Bruce. *Legends of People, Myths of State: Violence, Intolerance, and Political Culture in Sri Lanka and Australia*. Washington, DC: Smithsonian Institution, 1988.

Kaplan, Zvi Jonathan. "Rabbi Joel Teitelbaum, Zionism, and Hungarian Ultra-Orthodoxy." *Modern Judaism* 24, no. 2 (2004): 165–78.

Katsman, Hayim. "The Hyphen Cannot Hold: Contemporary Trends in Religious-Zionism." *Israel Studies Review* 35, no. 2 (1 September 2020): 154–74.

Katz, Dov. "Avlei Şion Veyerushalayim." *Haşofe*, 19 July 1974.

Katz, Gideon. "The Fear from Judaism in Israeli Culture." *Iyunim* 35 (2021): 191–210.

Katzew, Jan. "A Jewish State Ought to Be a Democratic State." Paper presented at the Leon Roth Conference, Jerusalem, 2019.

———. "Completing Creation through Education." *International Journal of Education and Social Science* 4, no. 6 (June 2017): 5–12.

———. "Leon Roth—His Life and Work: The Place of Ethics in Jewish Education." PhD diss., Hebrew University, 1997.

———. "Leon Roth's Judaism: A (Self) Portrait." In *Homo Homini: Essays in Jewish Philosophy Presented by His Students to Professor Warren Zev Harvey*, edited by Shemu'el Vigodah, Ari Ackerman, Esther Eisenmann, and Aviram Ravitsky, 91–126. Jerusalem: Magnes, 2016.

Kedar, Benjamin. "Masada: The Myth and the Complex." *Jerusalem Quarterly* 24 (1982): 57–63.

Kedar, Nir. "Ben-Gurion's Mamlakhtiyut: Etymological and Theoretical Roots." *Israel Studies* 7, no. 3 (2002): 117–33.

———. *Mamlakhtiyut: Ben-Gurion's Civilian Conception*. Sede Boqer: Ben-Gurion University Press, 2009.

Kenny, Michael. "Back to the Populist Future? Understanding Nostalgia in Contemporary Ideological Discourse." *Journal of Political Ideologies* 22, no. 3 (2017): 256–73.

Khalfa, Zebulon. "Zeqifut Haqoma Hale'umit." *Kipa*, 3 August 2014. https://www.kipa.co.il.

Khazzoom, Aziza. "The Great Chain of Orientalism: Jewish Identity, Stigma Management, and Ethnic Exclusion in Israel." *American Sociological Review* 68, no. 4 (August 2003): 481.

Klatzkin, Jacob. *Tehumim: Ketavim (Spheres: Essays)*. Berlin: Dvir, 1925.

Klug, Brian. "Appropriating Judaism? Christian Seders, Christian Zionists and Other Cases." Presented at the Religion and Cultures of Exclusion/Inclusion lecture series, Oxford Centre for Religion and Culture, Regent's Park College, University of Oxford, 26 April 2021.

———. *Being Jewish and Doing Justice: Bringing Argument to Life*. Edgware: Vallentine Mitchell, 2011.

Kotef, Hagar. *The Colonizing Self: Or, Home and Homelessness in Israel/Palestine*. Durham, NC: Duke University Press, 2020.

Krummel, Miriamne Ara. *Crafting Jewishness in Medieval England: Legally Absent, Virtually Present*. New York: Palgrave Macmillan, 2011.

Kurzweil, Barukh. "The New Canaanites in Israel." *Judaism* 2 (1953): 3–15.

———. *Our New Literature: Continuation of Revolution?* Tel Aviv: Schocken, 1971.

Lapidot, Elad. *Jews out of the Question: A Critique of Anti-Anti-Semitism*. Albany: State University of New York Press, 2020.

Laqueur, Walter. *A History of Zionism*. New York: Schocken, 1989.

Lasch, Christopher. "The Politics of Nostalgia: Losing History in the Midst of Ideology." *Harper's*, 1 November 1984.

Leibowitz, Yeshayahu. *Judaism, Human Values, and the Jewish State*. Edited by Eliezer Goldman. Translated by Yoram Navon, Zvi Jacobson, Gershon Levi, and Raphael Levy. Cambridge, MA: Harvard University Press, 1995.

Levy, Gideon. "The Anti-Netanyahu Camp Is Longing for a Country That Never Was." *Haaretz*, 8 September 2019.

Lewis, Donald M. *The Origins of Christian Zionism: Lord Shaftesbury and Evangelical Support for a Jewish Homeland*. Cambridge: Cambridge University Press, 2014.

Liebman, Charles S. "The Myth of Defeat: The Memory of the Yom Kippur War in Israeli Society." *Middle Eastern Studies* 29, no. 3 (1993): 399–418.

Liebman, Charles S., and Eliezer Don-Yehiya. *Civil Religion in Israel: Traditional Judaism and Political Culture in the Jewish State*. Berkeley: University of California Press, 1983.

———. "The Dilemma of Reconciling Traditional Culture and Political Needs: Civil Religion in Israel." *Comparative Politics* 16, no. 1 (1983): 53–66.

Lilker, Shalom. *Kibbutz Judaism: A New Tradition in the Making*. Darby: Norwood, 1982.

Lincoln, Martha, and Bruce Lincoln. "Toward a Critical Hauntology: Bare Afterlife and the Ghosts of Ba Chúc." *Comparative Studies in Society and History* 57, no. 1 (January 2015): 191–220.

Lipkin, Sapir. "Ḥoq haṢiyonut." N12, 29 May 2023. www.mako.co.il.

Lis, Jonathan. "Far-Right Israeli Minister Wants Cabinet Vote on 'Zionism as Guiding Value' in Government Decisions." *Haaretz*, 27 April 2023.

———. "Judicial Coup's Next Step: Israel's Nation-State Law as Policy." *Haaretz*, 28 May 2023.

Loewe, Raphael. "Memoir." In *Studies in Rationalism, Judaism, and Universalism: In Memory of Leon Roth*, edited by Raphael Loewe, 1–11. New York: Routledge & Kegan Paul, 1966.

———. "Preface." In *Studies in Rationalism, Judaism & Universalism: In Memory of Leon Roth*, edited by Raphael Loewe, ix–xiii. New York: Routledge & Kegan Paul, 1966.

Loewe, Raphael, ed. *Studies in Rationalism, Judaism, and Universalism: In Memory of Leon Roth*. London: Routledge, 1966.

MacIntyre, Alasdair. *After Virtue: A Study in Moral Theory*. 3rd ed. Notre Dame, IN: University of Notre Dame Press, 2007.

———. *The Tasks of Philosophy: Volume 1: Selected Essays*. Cambridge: Cambridge University Press, 2006.

———. *Whose Justice? Which Rationality?* Notre Dame, IN: University of Notre Dame Press, 1988.

Macleod, Jenny, ed. *Defeat and Memory: Cultural Histories of Military Defeat in the Modern Era*. New York: Palgrave Macmillan, 2008.

Magid, Shaul. "Is Judaism a Religion and Why Should We Care?" In *What Is Religion?*, edited by Aaron W. Hughes and Russell T. McCutcheon, 85–89. Oxford: Oxford University Press, 2021.

Mamdani, Mahmood. *Neither Settler nor Native: The Making and Unmaking of Permanent Minorities*. Cambridge, MA: Harvard University Press, 2020.

Manor, Udi. *Yigal Allon: A Neglected Political Legacy, 1949–1980*. Brighton: Sussex Academic Press, 2017.

Margalit, Avishai. "Nostalgia." *Psychoanalytic Dialogues* 21, no. 3 (1 May 2011): 271–80.

McAllister, Carlota, and Valentina Napolitano. "Political Theology/Theopolitics: The Thresholds and Vulnerabilities of Sovereignty." *Annual Review of Anthropology* 50, no. 1 (2021): 109–24.

McDermott, Gerald R. *Israel Matters: Why Christians Must Think Differently about the People and the Land*. Grand Rapids, MI: Brazos, 2017.

McDermott, Gerald R., ed. *The New Christian Zionism: Fresh Perspectives on Israel and the Land*. Downers Grove, IL: IVP Academic, 2016.

Mehager, Tom. "Why '67 and Not '48? Because of the 'Loot' That Was Distributed to Ashkenazim." *Haaretz*, 9 May 2021.

Meidad, Yisrael. "Kolo Biydey Ha'aravim." *Makor Rishon*, 27 July 2012.

Meir, Ephraim. "Rosenzweig and the Cohen-Buber Dispute on Zionism." *Archivio Di Filosofia* 88, no. 1 (2020): 83–96.

Me'ir, Yiṣḥaq. "Avlut 'al Ma Shelo Yashuv." *Makor Rishon*, 27 July 2009.

Midgley, Mary. *Utopias, Dolphins and Computers: Problems in Philosophical Plumbing*. London: Routledge, 1996.

Milbank, John. *Theology and Social Theory: Beyond Secular Reason*. Oxford: Blackwell, 2006.

Mitchell, Peter. *Imperial Nostalgia: How the British Conquered Themselves*. Manchester: Manchester University Press, 2021.

Morris, Benny. *The Birth of the Palestinian Refugee Problem Revisited*. 2nd ed. Cambridge: Cambridge University Press, 2004.

Moss, Kenneth B., Benjamin Nathans, and Taro Tsurumi, eds. *From Europe's East to the Middle East: Israel's Russian and Polish Lineages*. Philadelphia: University of Pennsylvania Press, 2021.

Moyaert, Marianne. "Christianizing Judaism? On the Problem of Christian Seder Meal." In *Is There a Judeo-Christian Tradition?*, edited by Emmanuel Nathan and Anya Topolski, 137–64. Boston: De Gruyter, 2016.

Muro, Diego. "Nationalism and Nostalgia: The Case of Radical Basque Nationalism." *Nations and Nationalism* 11, no. 4 (2005): 571–89.

Myers, David N. "History as Ideology: The Case of Ben Zion Dinur, Zionist Historian 'Par Excellence.'" *Modern Judaism* 8, no. 2 (1988): 167–93.

———. *Between Jew and Arab: The Lost Voice of Simon Rawidowicz*. Waltham, MA: Brandeis University Press, 2009.

———. "Between Supersessionism and Atavism: Toward a Neo-Secular View of Religion." In *Secularism in Question: Jews and Judaism in Modern Times*, edited by Ari Joskowicz and Ethan Katz, 261–76. Philadelphia: University of Pennsylvania Press, 2015.

Neelakantan, Gurumurthy. "Philip Roth's Nostalgia for the Yiddishkayt and the New Deal Idealisms in *The Plot against America*." *Philip Roth Studies* 4, no. 2 (2008): 125–36.

"Neturei Karta Message to Visitors." Neturei Karta International. Accessed 24 January 2022. www.nkusa.org.

Nicholls, Angus. *Myth and the Human Sciences*. New York: Routledge, 2016.

Nora, Pierre. "Between Memory and History: Les Lieux de Mémoire." *Representations*, no. 26 (1989): 7–24.

Nordau, Max. *Zionist Writings: In Four Books*. Edited by B. Netanyahu. Translated by Y. Yeivin and H. Goldberg. Vol. 2. 4 vols. Jerusalem: Hasifriya Haṣiyonit, 1960.

Novak, David. "Supersessionism Hard and Soft." *First Things*, no. 290 (1 February 2019): 27–32.

Noy, Amos. "Ḥamishim Gevanim Shel Lavan." Hanizu.wordpress, 20 May 2020.

Peled, Rina. *"The New Man" of the Zionist Revolution: Hashomer Haza'ir and his European Roots*. Tel Aviv: Am Oved, 2002.

Peled, Yoav, and Horit Herman Peled. *The Religionization of Israeli Society*. London: Routledge, 2018.

Penslar, Derek. *Theodor Herzl: The Charismatic Leader*. New Haven, CT: Yale University Press, 2020.

Persico, Tomer. "The End Point of Zionism: Ethnocentrism and the Temple Mount." *Israel Studies Review* 32, no. 1 (1 June 2017): 104–22.

Plamenatz, John. "Two Types of Nationalism." In *Nationalism: The Nature and Evolution of an Idea*, edited by Eugene Kamenka, 29–31. London: Edward Arnold, 1976.

Porath, Yehoshua. *The Life of Uriel Shelah*. Tel Aviv: Maḥbarot Lesifrut, 1989.

"Prof. L. Roth Stirs Wrath of Zionists." *B'nai B'rith Messenger*, 6 June 1947.

Qaniʾel, Sehlomo. "Ṣom Gush Qaṭif." *Nequda*, August 2004.

Rabinow, Paul, and William M Sullivan, eds. *Interpretive Social Science: A Second Look*. Berkeley: University of California Press, 1987.

Rabkin, Yakov M. *A Threat from Within: A Century of Jewish Opposition to Zionism*. Translated by Fred A. Reed. New York: Zed, 2006.

———. *What Is Modern Israel?* London: Pluto, 2016.

Rahimi, Sadeq. *The Hauntology of Everyday Life*. Cham: Palgrave Pivot, 2021.

Ram, Haggai. *Iranophobia: The Logic of an Israeli Obsession*. Stanford, CA: Stanford University Press, 2009.

Ram, Uri. "Zionist Historiography and the Invention of Modern Jewish Nationhood: The Case of Ben Zion Dinur." *History and Memory* 7, no. 1 (1995): 91–124.

Raz-Krakotzkin, Amnon. "Exile, History, and the Nationalization of Jewish Memory: Some Reflections on the Zionist Notion of History and Return." *Journal of Levantine Studies* 3, no. 2 (2013): 37–70.

———. "Exile within Sovereignty: Toward a Critique of the 'Negation of Exile' in Israeli Culture. Part 1." *Teorya uviqoret (Theory and Criticism)* 4 (1993): 23–55.

———. *Mishna Consciousness, Biblical Consciousness: Safed and Zionist Culture*. Tel-Aviv: Van leer Institute Press & Hakibbutz Hameuchad, 2022.

———. "Religion and Nationalism in the Jewish and Zionist Context." In *When Politics Are Sacralized: Comparative Perspectives on Religious Claims and Nationalism*, edited by Nadim N. Rouhana and Nadera Shalhoub-Kevorkian, 33–53. Cambridge: Cambridge University Press, 2021.

———. "Secularism, the Christian Ambivalence toward the Jews, and the Notion of Exile." In *Secularism in Question: Jews and Judaism in Modern Times*, edited by Ari Joskowicz and Ethan Katz, 276–98. Philadelphia: University of Pennsylvania Press, 2015.

———. "There Is No God, but He Promised Us the Land." *Mitaʿam* 2 (2005): 71–76.

Root, Michael. "The Narrative Structure of Soteriology." *Modern Theology* 2, no. 2 (1986): 145–58.

Roswald, Mordecai. "Leon Roth: A Philosopher-Teacher." *Modern Age* 48 (2006): 337–46.

Rotbard, Sharon. *White City, Black City*. Tel Aviv: Babel, 2005.

Roth, Hayim Yehuda. "Mediniyut ufolitika betorat aplaton." In *Eshkolot*, edited by Moshe Shuva and Yehoshua Gutmann, 1:3–10. Jerusalem: Magnes, 5714.

———. "Mekom Hadat Bevinyan Ha'areṣ." *Gilyonot* 13, no. 2 (1942): 74–79.

Roth, Leon. "Disorder in Palestine." *Times*, 5 June 1936.

———. *Is There a Jewish Philosophy? Rethinking Fundamentals*. London: Littman Library of Jewish Civilization, 1999.

———. *Judaism: A Portrait*. London: Faber & Faber, 1960.

———. "Right Is Might: Professor Roth on the Moral Issue." *Jewish Chronicle*, 4 December 1953.

Roth, Philip. *The Plot against America*. London: Jonathan Cape, 2004.

Rule, James B. "Tribalism and the State: A Reply to Michael Walzer." *Dissent* 39, no. 4 (1992): 519–23.

Runesson, Anders. "Particularistic Judaism and Universalistic Christianity? Some Critical Remarks on Terminology and Theology." *Studia Theologica: Nordic Journal of Theology* 54, no. 1 (July 2000): 55–75.

Sadeh, Shuki, and Shomrim. "The Kohelet Tentacles: Inside the Web Surrounding the Right-Wing Think Tank." *Haaretz*, 12 February 2023.

Sagi, Avi, and Dov Schwartz. *Religious Zionism and the Six Day War: From Realism to Messianism*. Translated by Batya Stein. New York: Routledge, 2018.

Said, Edward W. "Zionism from the Standpoint of Its Victims." *Social Text* 1 (1979): 7–58.

Salmon, Yosef. "Religion and Nationalism in the Early Zionist Movement." In *Jewish Nationalism and Politics: New Perspectives*, edited by Jehuda Reinharz, Yosef Salmon, and Gideon Shimoni, 115–40. Boston: Zalman Shazar Center for Jewish History & the Tuaber Institute, Brandeis University, 1996.

———. *Religion and Zionism: First Encounters*. Jerusalem: Magnes, 2002.

Saposnik, Arieh. "Wailing Walls and Iron Walls: The Western Wall as Sacred Symbol in Zionist National Iconography." *American Historical Review* 120, no. 5 (1 December 2015): 1653–81.

———. *Zionism's Redemptions: Images of the Past and Visions of the Future in Jewish Nationalism*. Cambridge: Cambridge University Press, 2021.

Sartre, Jean-Paul. *Anti-Semite and Jew*. Translated by George Joseph Becker. New York: Schocken, 1948.

Schlesinger, Arthur. "The New Conservatism: Politics of Nostalgia." *Reporter*, 16 June 1955.

Schmidt, Helmut D. "Herbert Samuel's Moral Philosophy." In *Studies in Rationalism, Judaism, and Universalism: In Memory of Leon Roth*, edited by Raphael Loewe, 255–72. New York: Routledge & Kegan Paul, 1966.

Schmitt, Carl. *Political Theology: Four Chapters on the Concept of Sovereignty*. Edited by George Schwab. Chicago: University of Chicago Press, 2006.

Schneider, Suzanne. "Light among the Nations." Jewish Currents, 28 September 2023. jewishcurrents.org.

———. "Nationalists of the World, Unite!" *Foreign Policy*, 8 January 2019.

Schneider, Suzanne, and Yotam Hotam. "Dangerous Minds." *New Statesman*, 29 April 2023 (online only). www.newstatesman.com.

Schvarcz, Benjamin. "Democracy and Judaism in Leon Roth's Actions and Thought." *Bifraṭ Uvikhlala* 3 (December 2017): 139–66.

———. "Ma Sheyakholti Latet Nattati." *Haaretz*, 26 November 2019.

Schvarcz, Benjamin, and Edward Brodsky. "Love, Freedom, and Bondage in the Writings of Leon Roth." *University of Toronto Journal of Jewish Thought* 3 (2013): 1–20.

Schwartz, Dov. *Religious Zionism: History and Ideology*. Translated by Batya Stein. Boston: Academic Studies Press, 2008.

Segal, Arnon. "La'alot El Hahar." *Nequda*, May 2005.

Segev, Tom. *1949: The First Israelis*. New York: Free Press, 2018.

Sells, Michael A. "Saudi Nationalism, Wahhabi Da'wā, and Western Power." In *When Politics Are Sacralized: Comparative Perspectives on Religious Claims and Nationalism*, edited by Nadera Shalhoub-Kevorkian and Nadim N. Rouhana, 275–306. Cambridge: Cambridge University Press, 2021.

Seroussi, Edwin. "Nostalgic Zionist Soundscapes: The Future of the Israeli Nation's Sonic Past." *Israel Studies* 19, no. 2 (2014): 35–50.

Shain, Yossi. *The Israeli Century: How the Zionist Revolution Changed History and Reinvented Judaism*. Translated by Levy and Hope. New York: Wicked Son, 2021.

Shapira, Anita. *New Jews, Old Jews*. Tel-Aviv: Am-Oved, 1997.

Shavit, Ari. *A New Israeli Republic*. Rishon LeZion: Miskal–Yedioth Ahronoth Books & Chemed Books, 2021.

Shavit, Jacob. *The New Hebrew Nation: A Study in Israeli Heresy and Fantasy*. London: Frank Cass, 1987.

Sheleg, Yair. *The Jewish Renaissance in Israeli Society: The Emergence of a New Jew*. Jerusalem: Israel Democracy Institute, 2010.

Sherlo, Yuval. "Yom Yerushalayim." *Shabaton*, Iyar 5765.

Shimoni, Gideon. *The Zionist Ideology*. Hanover, NH: University Press of New England, 1995.

Shlaim, Avi. *The Iron Wall: Israel and the Arab World*. London: Penguin, 2014.

Shoham, Hizky. *Israel Celebrates Jewish Holidays and Civic Culture in Israel*. Translated by Lenn Scharm. Leiden: Brill, 2017.

Shumsky, Dmitry. *Beyond the Nation-State: The Zionist Political Imagination from Pinsker to Ben-Gurion*. New Haven, CT: Yale University Press, 2018.

Slabodsky, Santiago. *Decolonial Judaism: Triumphal Failures of Barbaric Thinking*. New York: Palgrave Macmillan, 2015.

Slymovics, Nettanel. "The U.S. Billionaires Secretly Funding the Right-Wing Effort to Reshape Israel." *Haaretz*, 11 March 2021.

Smith, Anthony D. *Chosen Peoples: Sacred Sources of National Identity*. Oxford: Oxford University Press, 2004.

———. "The 'Golden Age' and National Renewal." In *Myth and Nationhood*, edited by Geoffrey Hosking and George Schopflin, 36–59. London: Hurst, 1997.

———. *Myths and Memories of the Nation*. Oxford: Oxford University Press, 1999.

Sorek, Yoav. "Im Lo Tirṣo . . ." *Makor Rishon*, 16 July 2010.

Soulen, R. Kendall. *The God of Israel and Christian Theology*. Minneapolis, MN: Augsburg Fortress, 1996.

"A State for Some of Its Citizens." *Haaretz*, 11 March 2019.

Stewart, Kathleen. "Nostalgia: A Polemic." *Cultural Anthropology* 3, no. 3 (1988): 227–41.

Stoffer, Heidi. "Dying to Belong: Violence and Nostalgia in Paradise and *The Plot against America*." *Modern Horizons*, November 2011, 1–7.

Sturm, Tristan. "Christian Zionism as Religious Nationalism Par Excellence." *Brown Journal of World Affairs* 24, no. 1 (2018 2017): 7–22.

———. "Religion as Nationalism: The Religious Nationalism of American Christian Zionists." *National Identities* 20, no. 3 (27 May 2018): 299–319.

Syrkin, Nahman. *Kitvei Nahman Syrkin (Writings)*. Edited by Berl Katznelson and Yehouda Kaufman. Tel Aviv: Dvir, 1939.

Tannock, Stuart. "Nostalgia Critique." *Cultural Studies* 9, no. 3 (1 October 1995): 453–64.

Taylor, Charles. "Interpretation and the Sciences of Man." *Review of Metaphysics* 25, no. 1 (September 1971): 3–51.

Toubul, Ophir, ed. *Sephardic masorti Zionism*. Rishon LeTsiyon: Yedioth Ahronoth, 2021.

Tsur, Muky. "Pesach in the Land of Israel: Kibbutz Haggadot." *Israel Studies* 12, no. 2 (2007): 74–103.

Tzoreff, Avi-Ram. "A Galician Yeshiva-Boḥur and Two Cities: Hameʿorerʾs Minority Report." *Prooftexts* 39, no. 3 (2022): 307–40.

———. "The Political Theology of the Feminine Jew and Anticolonial Criticism in the Writings of Yehoshua Radler-Feldman (R. Binyamin) during WWI." *Jewish Quarterly Review* 111, no. 1 (2021): 105–29.

———. *R. Binyamin, Binationalism, and Counter-Zionism*. Jerusalem: Zalman Shazar Center for Jewish History, 2023.

Valluvan, Sivamohan. *The Clamour of Nationalism: Race and Nation in Twenty-First-Century Britain*. Manchester: Manchester University Press, 2019.

Vaters, Roman. "'A Hebrew from Samaria, Not a Jew from Yavneh': Adya Gur Horon (1907–1972) and the Articulation of Hebrew Nationalism." PhD diss., University of Manchester, 2015.

Vatter, Miguel. *Living Law: Jewish Political Theology from Hermann Cohen to Hannah Arendt*. New York: Oxford University Press, 2021.

Walzer, Michael. "Michael Walzer Replies." *Dissent* 39, no. 4 (1992): 523–24.

———. "The New Tribalism: Notes on a Difficult Problem." *Dissent* 39, no. 2 (1992): 164–71.

Weiss, Yisroel. *Judaism: An Alternative to Zionism*. Wembley: Islamic Human Rights Commission, 2001.

Werczberger, Rachel, and Naʾama Azulay. "The Jewish Renewal Movement in Israeli Secular Society." *Contemporary Jewry* 31, no. 2 (2011): 107–28.

Yadgar, Yaacov. *Israel's Jewish Identity Crisis: State and Politics in the Middle East*. Cambridge: Cambridge University Press, 2020.

———. "Masortiyut." *Mafte'ah* 5 (2012): 143–64.

———. "A Post-Secular Look at Tradition: Toward a Definition of Traditionism." *Telos* 156 (2011): 77–98.

———. *Secularism and Religion in Jewish-Israeli Politics: Traditionists and Modernity*. London: Routledge, 2011.

———. "SHAS as a Struggle to Create a New Field: A Bourdieuan Perspective of an Israeli Phenomenon." *Sociology of Religion* 64, no. 2 (20 June 2003): 223–46.

———. *Sovereign Jews: Israel, Zionism, and Judaism*. Albany: State University of New York Press, 2017.

Yadgar, Yaacov, and Noam Hadad. "Nation-Statist Soteriology and Traditions of Defeat: Religious Zionism, the Ninth of Av, and Jerusalem Day." *Politics and Religion* 15, no. 3 (2022): 506–25.

———. "A Post-Secular Interpretation of Religious Nationalism: The Case of Religious Zionism." *Journal of Political Ideologies* 28, no. 2 (4 May 2023): 238–55.

Yedidya, Asaf. "Between Messianism and Zionism: The Religious Proto-Zionists: Transforming from Theurgic-Symbolic Messianism to Zionist Activism." *Religions* 13, no. 1 (January 2022): 52.

Yehoshua, A. B. *For Normality: Five Essays on the Questions of Zionism*. Jerusalem: Schocken, 1980.

———. "Hapetil Hakaful Shel Hayisre'elim." *Haaretz*, 29 September 1988.

———. *Homeland Grasp*. Edited by Avner Holtzman. Tel Aviv: Haqibutz Hameuḥad, 2008.

———. "The Meaning of Homeland." In *The A. B. Yehoshua Controversy: An Israel-Diaspora Dialogue on Jewishness, Israeliness, and Identity*, 7–13. New York: Dorothy and Julius Koppelman Institute on American Jewish-Israeli Relations, American Jewish Committee, 2006.

———. "Mihu Yehudi." *Haaretz*, 9 May 2013.

———. "Mihu Yisre'eli." *Haaretz*, 13 September 2013.

Yiftachel, Oren, and Dennis Rumley. "On the Impact of Israel's Judaization Policy in the Galilee." *Political Geography Quarterly* 10, no. 3 (1 July 1991): 286–96.

Zameret, Zvi. "Ahad Ha'am and the Shaping of Secular Education." *Iyunim Bitkumat Israel* 16 (2006): 171–94.

Zeira, Moti. *Qeru'im Anu: Zikqatah Shel Hahityashvut Ha'ovedet Bishenot Ha'esrim El Hatarbut Hayehudit*. Jerusalem: Yad Yitzhak Ben Zvi, 2002.

Zerubavel, Yael. "The 'Mythological Sabra' and Jewish Past: Trauma, Memory, and Contested Identities." *Israel Studies* 7, no. 2 (2002): 115–44.

———. *Recovered Roots: Collective Memory and the Making of Israeli National Tradition*. Chicago: University of Chicago Press, 1995.

Zipperstein, Steven J. *Elusive Prophet: Aḥad Ha'am and the Origins of Zionism*. Berkeley: University of California Press, 1993.

Zreik, Raef. "When Does a Settler Become a Native?" *Constellations* 23, no. 3 (2016): 351–64.

Zubaida, Hani. "I Am (Not) Israeli." In *Contemplating Israeliness: Eighteen Proposals*, edited by Tamar Hermann and Ofer Shiff, 55–64. Tel-Aviv: Lamda, Open University Press & the Ben Gurion Centre for the Study of Israel and Zionism, University of Ben Gurion, 2020.

Zubaida, Hani, and Benny Nurielli. "Ha'ir Halevana: Haneo-Mapainiqim 'Menaqim' Et Tel Aviv." *Haaretz*, 1 June 2020.

INDEX

Abraham, 137

absorptive capacity, immigration and, 132

Adam, Yehudi, 74

After Virtue (MacIntyre), 163, 164

agency, 25, 167n4

Ahad HaAm, 19–24, 29, 30, 70; on antisemitism, 27–28; on authenticity, 26;
on chosenness, 63; Hebrew University
relation to, 130, 145–46, 182n8; Jewish
politics relation to, 32; Roth, L., relation to, 145–47

algia (longing), 88, 96, 98–99

Alkalai, Yehuda, 53

Altneuland (Herzl), 19, 20; Europe relation
to, 23–24; Gentiles in, 22

anarchy, 163

ancestry, 8–9

Antigone, 144

antisemitism, 59, 66, 154; identity relation
to, 27–28; "Jew" relation to, 24–25, 26;
in postexilic history, 55; supersessionism relation to, 45–46, 50

anti-Zionism, 74; of ultra-Orthodox Jews,
73

"apartheid," 36

apocalyptic catastrophe, 108

appropriation, 40, 46–47, 129–30; Christianity and, 52, 53; by Christian Zionism,
51–52; of Jerusalem Day, 114–15, 122,
127; of Passover seder, 67; by Religious
Zionism, 103; supersessionism and, 69;
by theopolitics, 102; of traditions, 44,
71; of Western Wall, 111–12

Arab-Israeli war, 15, 112

archaeological sites, 99–100

Arendt, Hannah, 154

Ashkenazi ethnoclass, 81; "melting-pot"
policy and, 158; nostalgia of, 6, 77–79,
80, 84, 86–87, 90–94, 99–100; synagogue uniformity and, 159; Zionism,
relation to, 95

Australia, 132

authenticity, 10, 13, 20, 22; common enemy, relation to, 25; cultural assimilation, relation to, 26; Jewish identity
and, 16; Jewish politics, relation to, 28;
in Jewish polity, 23, 29; normativity,
relation to, 27; objective, 24; supersessionism and, 47, 61; traditions, relation
to, 21

Avineri, Shlomo, 64–65

Bagehot, Walter, 131

Balfour Declaration, 16–17

Barak, Aharon, 33–34

Baron, Salo, 81

"Basic Law: Israel the Nation-State of the
Jewish People," 33, 34–40, 154, 170n63,
184n5

Basic Laws, 32–33

bayit shelishi, 106–9

Beem, Christopher, 184n21

Begin, Menachem, 67

Ben-Gurion, David, 67, 106, 148, 156,
157–58

Ben-Zvi, Rachel Yanait, 112

Berdyczewski, M. Y., 53, 59

Bergman, Hugo, 130–31

ABOUT THE AUTHOR

YAACOV YADGAR is the Stanley Lewis Professor of Israel Studies at the University of Oxford. His research revolves around issues of Jewish identity, religion, politics, and secularism. He focuses on placing Israel in theoretical and epistemological frameworks that bear obvious relevance beyond the specific case history. His scholarship is multidisciplinary, encompassing Jewish, political, cultural, religious, and media studies. He concentrates on Israeli sociopolitics (especially Israeli Judaism) and on the epistemological, historical, and political dimensions of Israeli identity. His previous books include *Israel's Jewish Identity Crisis: State and Politics in the Middle East* (Cambridge University Press, 2020), *Sovereign Jews: Israel, Zionism, and Judaism* (SUNY Press, 2017), and *Secularism and Religion in Jewish Israeli Politics: Traditionists and Modernity* (Routledge, 2011).

www.ingramcontent.com/pod-product-compliance
Lightning Source LLC
Chambersburg PA
CBHW021845090426
42811CB00033B/2146/J